THE GRATITUDE GAME

The Gratitude Game

21 Days to a Healthier, Wealthier, More Beautiful You

Natalie Pace

Copyright © 2014 by Natalie Pace.
Published by Waterfront Digital Press
For information and inquiries, address Waterfront Digital Press, 2055 Oxford Ave., Cardiff, CA 92007, or call (760) 632–9190.
Book cover designed by Bryan Zee. ZMusicCorp.com.
Author photo of Natalie Pace by Marie Commiskey. AvalonPhotography.com.
Audio book produced by Paula Wolack.
Set in 12 point Times New Roman
Cataloging-in-Publication data for this book is available from the Library of Congress.
ISBN 978-1-941768-09-9
Natalie Pace's books are available at special discounts for bulk purchases in the U.S. by corporations, institutions, and other organizations. For more information, please call (310) 430-2397, or e-mail info@NataliePace.com with the subject Natalie Pace Bulk Book Order.

For Davis Lau, who will always be my happy place
(and who played for the picture on the cover of this book)

TABLE OF CONTENTS

Week 1: Cleanse
Getting Rid of Old Thoughts and Actions

Week 2: Exercise
Practice and embody the divine laws of prosperity and abundance

Week 3: Party
Invite friends to the party! Partner up for exponential results!

Additional resources on the home page at NataliePace.com:
Investor Educational Retreats
Ezine and monthly teleconferences subscription

Check out *The Gratitude Game* audio book for a bonus feature of
Natalie Pace's song "Peace."

FOREWORD

By Kay Koplovitz, board director of Time Inc., Kate Spade (and more), chairman of Springboard Enterprises, founder of USA Networks and the first female CEO of a television network.

Natalie Pace has been offering the straightforward advice that your mother never told you – *The ABCs of Money* that we all should have received in high school – since I met her back in 2002. Just a few years before that, she'd found herself in a tough position as a single mom. She couldn't make ends meet, and she knew that the conventional financial advice she was receiving would only bankrupt her. So, she began reading economic theories and she taught herself investing. With great results under her belt, others took notice, and before she knew it, she was sharing her strategies with world economists and business leaders.

Among Natalie's cadre of supporters include Nobel Prize winning economist Dr. Gary Becker (who passed away earlier this year) and TD AMERITRADE chairman Joe Moglia. Why did they rally round her? As Dr. Gary Becker noted when he recommended her first book, "Many people, including educated men and women, often get into trouble when they neglect to follow simple and fundamental rules of the type provided by [Natalie]."

Natalie's budgeting and investing strategies are easy to understand, easy to implement and effective. They also make daily life less stressful and far more fun. You sleep better at night knowing that your money is protected, and that you are not overspending to make ends meet. You can celebrate knowing that your retirement plans are compounding their gains, that your assets are protected, and that there will not be any toxic surprises when you open your bills. You gain peace of mind when your financial world is in order.

Many people find themselves in financial trouble simply because they never really understand the consequences of their financial decisions. It's something parents never shared with them – or perhaps they never learned themselves. I know that my parents taught me good habits. As kids, we had savings pass books at our local bank into which we would deposit our allowances or any other money we earned. I used to love to look at the mounting total and know that I could use the balance for things I wanted. I also learned about the value of compounded interest, a value that has stayed with me throughout life. Not all people have this early childhood advantage.

Fortunately, Natalie Pace makes *understanding* the use and misuse of money as simple as ABC. The 21-day program of *The Gratitude Game* affords you the time and the step-by-step instruction and real-world examples to *implement* healthy fiscal habits into your daily life.

The Gratitude Game is filled with practical and achievable advice for:

1. People who have gotten themselves into a bit of a debt problem and can see no way out.
2. Teens who are wondering how to prepare for life as an adult, and whether or not college is the right answer.
3. Young professionals who are burdened with the balancing act of trying to rise up the career ladder, while setting up their budgets, 401K, IRA and health savings accounts.
4. Parents who are sandwiched between the expenses of kids and providing for aging parents.
5. Empty-nesters and retirees who need to protect their assets, will their estates, reduce expenses and limit their tax burden.

Again, the book isn't just a reading book. It is a *doing* book.

Call it common sense if you will. Each day, Natalie Pace outlines concrete step-by-step solutions on how to start compounding your gains so you can, as she says, "stop making everyone else rich and start scoring gains for the home team." The first step is to pay yourself first. Always. Credit counseling services, and other *free* debt relief sources, will never give you this sound advice. And it runs counter to what one might think, since most people believe they should pay off their debt *before* they start saving and investing. *The Gratitude Game* is your handbook to shift out of Debt Consciousness and into financial freedom and prosperity.

With almost $12 trillion in consumer debt, many Americans need to know how to dig out of an underwater mortgage, how to stop the downward spiral of credit cards compounding debt, and how to avoid trouble. It's easy to fill in the gaps of an unsustainable lifestyle with the quick, high-interest capital offered by credit cards.

Like any bad habit, shifting out of overspending and debt, into prosperity and abundance, requires a daily commitment – until the new healthier fiscal habits become the *new normal* for you. *The Gratitude Game* is a 21-day program designed to, in Natalie's words, "make prosperity and abundance your daily habit." Each day, she offers a mantra, an action plan and a new way of thinking, so that at the end of 21 days, you have an entirely new and effective way of operating. While some of these mantras will sound familiar, Natalie's unique approach rings fresh and true and takes good sense out of theory and puts it into practice. *The Gratitude Game's* step-by-step exercises offer smart and simple solutions to your most pressing problems, making it easier to greet each day with a can-do positive attitude and attract the partners that all of us need to achieve great things.

The Gratitude Game also brings together two worlds that are often distinctly separate – money and your spiritual self. Only a few years ago, it was common for money managers to brush off the desires of clients who wanted to have a social conscious about their investments with the phrase, "Let me make money for you, and then you *do good* with those profits." Natalie Pace believes strongly, and her track record supports her stand, that we can invest in products that are good for our world and profit – that we can enrich and get rich at the same time.

The Gratitude Game debunks the myth that money is the root of all evil. (Greed is).

The essence of entrepreneurialism is that success consists in adding value by creating the products and services that make our lives better. This focus on creating value will transport you quickly up the ladder of financial success. This book is about you, your financial security and how you can achieve it to live the life you want to live. *The Gratitude Game* invites you to tap into your passions and talents, and discover what you are uniquely positioned to offer our world.

Natalie's advice does not require you to get an accounting degree to understand or implement. She carefully relates it all to everyday Main Street situations. This is why I recommend *The Gratitude Game* to every person, regardless of age, who wishes to live a financially secure and purposeful life. Her advice is easy to read, easy to grasp and easy to implement. After that, we have more time for the things we love: family, friends and shared experiences with the "let's have fun" budget Natalie helps us all to construct.

Introduction: The Origin of Money is Gratitude

The origin of money is gratitude, not Wall Street, not the Federal Reserve and not the Illuminati. We lose track of this because "money" has become the dominant way that we exchange our gifts and talents in today's world. Because we seek security, comfort, status and protection for ourselves and for our loved ones – and because the world is challenging – fear, worry, doubt and even anger can be our dominant emotions with regard to our income and outflow, even if we are advanced in meditation and spirituality or quite rich in assets and material goods.

Shifting out of fear and into gratitude is fundamental to all of the things we truly desire – whether it is happiness, a better planet, a sexier body, more loving relationships and even to live a rich life. Fear immobilizes you, prevents you from seeing possibilities that lie right under your own nose, and releases cortisol, the "stress" hormone. I know rich people who are histrionic about how much everything costs, who are overworked and stressed out every minute, and who never enjoy their money, even when wearing expensive clothes, sitting in a corner office and eating in fancy restaurants. Of course, I also know multi-millionaires who are grateful for the material rewards of their labor, who feel their finances offer them freedom, who feel loved and in balance, and use their money to bring a lot of good into the world. The former worry they will lose their money and status; the latter are grateful for their blessings and are aware of the responsibility that comes hand in hand with prosperity.

There is nothing wrong with having *less* money, unless you feel "broke." There is nothing "right" about being rich, unless you feel free. Many people who live the richest lives are not those with the highest net worth. Nelson Mandela was a lot more valuable to the world than Muammar Gaddafi (and had a significantly more desirable end). And it was the love of the people who made J.K. Rowling as wealthy as The Queen of England; Rowling started out on public assistance. We are grateful for Nelson Mandela and for J.K. Rowling, and that was why they won their way into our hearts, and why we so willingly made them "rich."

As another way to explain gratitude as the origin of money, I want to take you back in time to when "money" first exchanged hands. Back to the cave.

The Origin of Money

Imagine a family in the Stone Age, living in a cave. On a frigid night, the parents are crying in one corner while their seven-year-old daughter lies dying in the other. They have tried everything – cold compresses, hot broth, prayers, herbs, dances in the name of the Gods, libations – and still the fevers rage. Finally, the mother races out into the neighboring tribe and drags the medicine woman, through the snow, back to her home. The medicine woman clears the cave with smoked sage. She lances and drains an infected wound, and administers her special poultices and remedies that, over the course of a few days, save the child's life.

Overwhelmed with gratitude, the father slays a deer. The mother serves a feast for the medicine woman. The father breaks out his mead. The brother scratches a painting of the medicine woman healing his sister on the wall of the cave with a stick and beet juice.

Every morning for the next six months the mother delivers a loaf of bread to the medicine woman – out of gratitude. It was a close call. She might have lost her daughter forever, were it not for the healing gifts the medicine woman brought to her. And she is *over the moon* grateful. The medicine woman is thrilled as well. Daily bread means she doesn't have to cook, which leaves her more time to heal, to gather her special herbs and to brew her remedies.

When you think about it, you don't want to risk your life jamming a hot wire into the electrical grid to warm your home or cook a meal; instead, you write the check to the utility company and are grateful for the light, the ovens and the warmth. (Live a day without it, and you'll definitely be dying to have it back. So, stay with me here for a moment. I know it's hard.) You don't clean the home of your cleaning person or babysit the kids of your babysitter. You give them, instead, a magic token of gratitude – money – which we all agree can be exchanged for other goods.

Similarly, when Tesla builds a gorgeous, 100% electric luxury sedan, you are grateful that they made electric cars sexier than a golf cart, with enough battery range to get you to work. You don't want to have to research the technology, mine the lithium, create the leaner/meaner lithium ion battery and then build it yourself. Out of gratitude and desire, you purchase the Tesla S sedan over the gas-guzzler, and invest in the company to boot (if it's trading at a good price and not carrying too much debt, etc.).

Money as Magic Tokens of Gratitude

When we fear that we don't have enough (as so many of us do in today's world), then we pay our bills with sadness, with concern, with worry, with anger… It is impossible to feel grateful, even if we force ourselves to count the blessings of what we are receiving as we pay our bills. That is why "spirituality" and meditation are not enough. The mindset is a good start, but the skillset and wisdom-based action are necessary to change things. Praying to get out of a mud puddle won't work if you continue to sit in the silt. This is particularly true if there isn't enough money to provide for basic essentials. I know I felt that way, many years ago, as a struggling single mother who had no hope of making ends meet. When you feel like you are being eaten alive by bills, there is little chance you can be grateful for the services they provide.

However, there are solutions. They are just not well publicized. And that is why I wrote this book.

In order to make prosperity and abundance your daily habit, you must adopt solutions to exit the "buried alive in bills" life. A more exciting and sustainable existence awaits you. Once you find your sense of purpose, pay yourself first no matter what, double your fun budget and get your basic needs down to 50% of your income, you will start thriving, and that's when the soil is fertile for gratitude. Stop the leaks, and the vase can fill to overflowing with water. And yes, this will require bold choices where they count most – increasing your income and decreasing the amount that you are spending on survival and basic needs. We can't do it in one day. We can start on the path during these 21 days. Do anything for 21 days and it becomes the new normal.

That is why the next spiritual evolution involves financial literacy – sound money habits that allow you to integrate your moral code into your daily life, which is, like it or not, bought and sold with "money." It is not just a matter of hitting the jackpot, or cutting out ice cream and café lattes, or praying and visualizing prosperity better. The entire system you were tossed into at nineteen is set up to make everyone else rich – from the tax man, to the insurance and car salesmen, to the debt collector and everywhere in between – until you learn how to keep that hard-earned money for yourself and be mindful about what you buy and invest in. We co-create our world, and when you are unconscious about that reality, your "money" funds the very problems and issues in the world that you are most opposed to. As we learn how to master our own lives, then we can take conscious ownership of our planet as well.

The cure to your money angst is wisdom and right action, which is exactly what you'll be doing for the next 21 days, as you play *The Gratitude Game.*

If you can't be grateful, it's not because the products and services you are buying aren't outstanding. It is because your budget is out of whack.

The beauty of *The Gratitude Game* is that as you become a person that others are more grateful for, they will begin showering more tokens of their thanks (money) on you. Who knows? You may be the next J.K. Rowling or Nelson Mandela; there is absolutely something that you are here on this planet to do better than anyone else. And when you find that, you will be richly rewarded – not just in material possessions, but also in living the life of your dreams.

Remember:

I am a co-creator of my home, my neighborhood, my city, my state, my nation and our world. Every cent I own and every moment I spend is always an investment. I'm committed to being an angel in the lives of my family, my beloved, my neighbors and those around the world. I'm also committed to being a renegade, to follow what I know is right, deep in my heart, instead of having blind faith in the status quo and what *others* tell me to do.

Week 1: Cleanse
Getting Rid of Old
Thoughts and Actions

Day 1: Love
Today's Mantra: Love

Getting rid of old thoughts and actions

This 21-day Walk to Wealth™ plan is designed to make prosperity and abundance your daily habit. Each day is grounded in a daily mantra, a new way of thinking and an action plan. You'll increase your mindset, your skillset and your tool box. You will use that knowledge and those widgets and wisdom to reshape your entire life.

You cannot just *visualize* what you desire. The biggest word in the Law of Attr*action* is *action*. However, we need to be pointed in the right direction before we leap toward our destination. We need our action to be based in effective, time-proven strategies in order for the desired outcome to manifest. Acting blindly, running around in circles, or having blind faith in a guru who really doesn't have good strategies and solutions (think of snake oil salesmen trying to cure pneumonia or a celebrity trying to lead a sweat lodge) is an expensive, and ineffective, exercise in futility. Sometimes the "cure" is the disease. Sadly, over the last 14 years, I've seen far too many people attend millionaire schools that bankrupted them or warrior weekends that, in the worst cases, were deadly. The simple truth is that there are a lot of gurus on stage who are salesmen and showmen, not shaman.

When you know your destination and employ a reliable map, there is a high likelihood that you will get where you desire to go. The key factor in all of this is *you*. Don't hand the keys to someone else to drive your life. Take the wheel yourself. That doesn't mean that you don't ever hire a car or hail down a cab. It means that when you do, they don't get to take you wherever their fancy desires. They take you exactly where you wish to go.

Shifting to Wisdom from Blind Faith and Victimhood

Redrafting your money plan for the next 21 days offers an interesting three-week dynamic. Week One will feel like cleansing. During Week Two, you will start to embody the new way of thinking and get more comfortable with these time-proven precepts. You will become adept with this new way of contemplating, maneuvering and being. Week Three is when we invite friends to the party. When we partner up with others who are living in the flow of prosperity and abundance, we exponentially increase our capacity to create more opportunities, businesses and projects. The Golden Gate Bridge wasn't built by one woman, and it didn't happen overnight.

This doesn't mean that you get rid of all of the people in your life who don't think and act according to *The Gratitude Game*. It means that *you* drink from the well of healthier water and get your renewal from nutritious sources. When you get your sustenance and inspiration from pristine, flowing, plentiful springs, then you are better able to water and renew arid land – including those friends and family members who are feeling *broke*, beaten up or bankrupt. You might be a blessing in their life, and that is valuable, even if their energy weighs you down. Don't expect renewal from them. Renew yourself in order to give from an overflow.

We live a mortal existence in a world full of challenges. There are times when you will find yourself slogging through the mud. At other times, without knowing how the magic happened, you'll be dancing in the rain. Someone will cross your path. The fairies sprinkle a little dust. And behold everything sparkles and sings.

In this rather fragile, and blessed, mortal existence, it's important to remember, in both good times and bad, that everything is better with partners. When you have others to aid you, you can co-create a venture much bigger than you could possibly achieve on your own. When the load is heavier than you can carry, you will benefit from someone lending you a hand – whether it is a stranger or a close friend. You want the most capable physicians for healing; the most visionary engineers for developing the next wave of renewable energy; the best coders for your website and problem-solving wayshowers for the sojourn of our children into an unknown tomorrow.

Everyone in the world has a divine calling, but not everyone is stepping up to the task or to her full potential. It pays to love people as they are, and to not expect them to perform above their skill set. Sometimes, *you* are the blessing and the calling in *their* life, inspiring them to step up and start shining a little more brightly, something they will not be capable of in the nascent steps of their spiritual development, or if they are consumed by negativity. Some people increase your load, while others lighten it. Sometimes you are someone else's North Star.

Being selective about where you get your renewal from is not elitism. When you surround yourself with others who are veterans in their spiritual journey, a lot of good can be created in this world – from the volunteer fire department in your hometown, to Petra, to L'Opera in Verona.

Week One: The Cleansing Week

I like to think of Week One as a physical cleansing. Getting rid of the old crap is uncomfortable.

It is stinky, painful and unpleasant. It feels *wrong*. It's important to remember that what is *comfortable* is not necessarily good for you. It is only comfortable because that's what you are familiar with. Anyone with an eating disorder can feel starving after eating three or four times what their body actually needs to sustain itself – simply because it is a habit – one that they can only break with a steadfast commitment to a healthier, more sustainable *way of life*, and to feeling starving, sad and unfulfilled while their mind and physique adjust to the new normal.

If you are completely satisfied with your life and these 21 days are easy for you, then chances are that you are already doing a lot of the spiritual principles outlined in *The Gratitude Game,* and you just don't have that many bad habits to break. Good for you! Use the mantras to deepen your practice.

For the rest of us, remember that when you are breaking bad habits, what is *uncomfortable* is actually what is *good* for you. In the case of eating disorders, eating reasonable portions of healthy fuel that is packed with nutrition might feel like starving, while your body cleanses itself of the unhealthy craving for fat, sugar and other caloric but nutrition-deficient junk. As you begin to embody the things that are uncomfortable, you will find that you are shifting your life, that your body is becoming more beautiful and your thoughts are filled with new possibilities. Exciting opportunities for more love and adventure present themselves. You feel in control. You worry less. You plan and execute more.

Changing habits creates a state of confusion, particularly for the lizard brain of your body (the fight or flight amygdala). One way to calm the backtalk and fear is to imagine that your brain is a closet that is cluttered with old clothes that are outdated, frayed and make you look and feel terrible. They don't fit anymore. We're going to throw them out.

It's dirty. It's dusty. You're going to be saying, "But I don't want to let go of that. I feel comfortable in it. I don't care if it has holes in it." Throw it away anyway.

During Week Two, we'll continue filling this closet of infinite potential with new designs for your sanctuary home – from what you wear, to what you sleep on, eat on and sit on in your new home. You don't need the old junk. It doesn't fit in. You'll be so proud and happy to show off this new you when you host a housewarming party in the last week. You don't want to be embarrassed by keeping the mothballs in the room. There will come a day, even if it is only a glimpse by Week Three, when you truly feel like popping the champagne and toasting to your next grand adventure in life.

This change is fueled by you. Your results are going to be in direct proportion to your commitment, your diligence, your action and your intention. If you make excuses why you don't have to do the daily mantra or the daily task, you will stagnate your own growth. Athletes don't improve their game by sitting on the couch. They watch highlights, train, eat right, sleep, rest, recover, practice with the team, practice alone, correct their weaknesses and hone their skills. Kobe Bryant's work ethic is legendary.

One Chapter Each Morning

Each morning when you wake, please grab your book, or your earbuds or headphones, if you are doing this series by audio. Go on a walk while you read or listen to this book. It will take 30 minutes or less on most days, with 40 or 50 minutes on the first day of each week when I introduce the week. The reason walking is key is that while you're learning these new things you need your blood to be flowing. The blood flow is creating new synapse pathways in your brain. We are cutting down the overgrowth and cobwebs of areas of your brain that have not yet been chartered, and while we do that, the blood flow is like a river of freshness watering new seeds.

Since you need to be repeating the daily mantra throughout the day, it's important to read and listen to each chapter first thing in the morning. For most of us, that is going to mean setting the alarm an hour earlier than normal.

Day One: Love

So, let's step into Day One. **Today's mantra is Love.**

Think of love in every thought. Let love be obsessive. Write the word down on an index card. Put it on your mirror, on your computer, on your vision board – anywhere that you will be glancing repeatedly throughout the day.

Having love as a mantra sounds much easier than it really is. Particularly if you are currently stressed out, depressed, fed up, discouraged, angry, numb or feeling helpless.

Many people already love unconditionally in their spiritual practice, but fall out of love when they leave church and hit our rather challenging daily grind, where so many of us feel underappreciated, overworked and underpaid. Do you smile and think kind thoughts about your fellow man as easily on Monday as you do on

Sunday? Can you remember anytime over the last week when you said something rude or disrespectful to someone? Do you feel justified to have done so?

The highest good is to be loving. Always. The next is to create a Peace Zone, and figure out how to be loving, or at least pleasant and kind. The Peace Zone concept is something I learned from the Dalai Lama. I really wish I had known what a fantastic alternative the Peace Zone is, instead of timeout, when my son was young. You gotta love evolution! And the divine gift and wisdom of the Dalai Lama. Each generation finds some gift to offer their children that the ancestors could never have dreamed of.

A lot of spiritual folks have a hard time *loving* their money. They like the words prosperity and abundance, but *money* feels more like filthy lucre, bills and greed. A lot of us have been trained that money is evil, or that if we have money it is because we are taking from someone else. You might feel like you don't have enough money or food or shelter, in which case, rather than love, you feel longing, fear, angst or even anger and injustice.

Many still believe, falsely, that *money* is the root of all evil. The biblical quote is "The *love* of money is the root of all evil." In other words, **greed**, not money, is the root of all evil. This oft-misquoted phrase is another thing that we must unlearn. In fact, Mother Nature is a great example of overflowing abundance and the flow of prosperity, and has been throughout humanity. Bees and butterflies drink nectar and pollinate more plants in the process. Fruit is the bait the plants hand out to facilitate their own ends.

Some very spiritual people are actually creating a lot of problems in the world, directly as a result of their money issues. They keep their spiritual practice separate from their daily bread, thinking, "I'm just doing my job here and providing for my family," or "I'm going to earn a living any way that I can, and then I'm going to do good with the money that I earn." Old-school money managers used this phrase as a mantra, telling clients to let them handle the heavy lifting on investing and do whatever they need to do to earn a good return on investments, and to just *do good* with the returns.

If your father died of lung cancer, why would you want to fund tobacco companies and profit from their sales? How would you *do good* with the money you make? Buy a finer headstone for your dad? Purchase some chemotherapy for the customers that made you rich?

Our finest spiritual leaders teach us that a higher consciousness is very different from this. **What you do daily is *who you are.*** There is no exception to this, no matter how much you try to rationalize your active participation in things that you know are not good for the world. If you were selling mortgages and homes to people who couldn't afford them in 2005, justifying it with your *personal truth* that you were doing so to feed your own family, you were still doing great harm to others, to the economy and to the world at large. Doing what you know is wrong to benefit your family is acting out of *fear.* Refusing to earn a living that is harmful to others is acting out of *love.* You see now why even spiritual people, with a strong and daily practice of *love*, might be challenged with this deeper and broader definition that I'm forcing on you.

You might have told yourself that you had to do what you did or that you have to continue building bombs at work, but that isn't true. It is just convenient. And comfortable. And everyone I know, including myself, is faced with these exact choices in our career and in our investments. So, you see how the rather overused, airy-fairy definition of the word – *love* – is much more difficult to embody than most of us admit.

You cannot truly love until you eliminate fear.

If you picket wars and profit from defense contractors, you are not in *love*. If your father died of lung cancer and you invest in tobacco companies, you are sleeping with the enemy. This is not love either. If you are a greenie and you haven't dug into the holdings of your mutual funds to clean up your own portfolio, you own, promote and profit from petroleum and other dirty, last-century energy.

I talk to many of our most revered spiritual leaders – the famous ones – and far too many are still resonating in the energy of fear around their money. Of course, on stage they act like experts on prosperity and abundance, even when they don't really understand how money moves around in our world. Privately, when I confront them on their own investments – and I do – they hide behind the idea that they just don't know which companies they own in their pensions, their 401Ks, their Individual Retirement Accounts and their insurance policies. Or they might say that they can't make changes – that their policy doesn't allow them to. Or they claim that someone else is in charge of those things on their behalf. I'm standing two feet away with solutions, resonating in the same spiritual space and with a divine commitment, and with the wisdom and power to align their money with their spiritual practice, which can offer profits far greater than what they are experiencing. But they turn their back, leap onto the stage and punch the air with their fists, proselytizing about a change that will never come – because it's all words, and their actions are promoting and profiting from the very things they preach against.

These excuses are barriers to the full and complete integration of love in our lives, and this self-imposed ignorance costs us so much. Blind faith, with the promise of better returns, is the sonnet that cronyism economics seduces us with. A picket sign is a joke compared to all of the billions of dollars that Greenies unknowingly feed into the oil, chemical, pharmaceutical, GMO and defense industries. Fear reigns. Love rules only for a few short hours on Sunday, or at a conference for the weekend.

Once we integrate love seamlessly throughout our life, into our homes, our careers and our investments, then we naturally become happier. The world benefits from this mindfulness as well. Main Street owns Wall Street. Our collective dollars create the products and services we enjoy in our world. The power of this is enormous. The first step is taking ownership of our lives. The second is taking ownership of our world.

Don't worry. Day One will not require a complete and forensic dissection of your career and investments. But I do want you thinking about these things, as you continue repeating the word and the thought of *love*.

Let me give you two quotes that illustrate how you can integrate love into your daily life and career.

One is by Confucius. He wrote, "Choose a job you love and you will never have to work a day in your life."

This makes complete sense. However, you might still be feeling, "That's easy to say, but who can ever do that in today's grind, when you are lucky to just have a job?"

Getting from where you are to where you want to be will require a plan, wisdom, guidance and action. In high unemployment times, whether you are fresh out of college and only getting offered internships, or over 50 and getting forced into early retirement, it might feel impossible to do what you love. Instead, you might feel like you are clawing and scratching to get or to keep any job and income at all. If this is the case, fear is, again, driving your thoughts and feelings, rather than love.

Let me give you some data that will be helpful in rethinking the next chapter of your career. The first piece of data is this: education is the highest correlating factor with income. If you would like to get a different job, chances are you need to educate yourself to get it. If you don't have enough money to take the necessary classes, then you might need to look into a junior college (where classes are more affordable) or a student loan. Student loans are the kind of debt that can be a good investment – unlike credit card debt.

If you want to become a surgeon, you will be going to college, then medical school and then onto your in-hospital training. This will be a commitment that spans over a decade of your life. You can't just visualize this through the Law of Attraction and suddenly start operating at the City of Hope. You'll have to learn a lot about anatomy, a lot about the body, about antigens, about cures that have been developed and honed over the past hundred thousand years. You'll have to practice on cadavers. You will hone your expertise.

However, after all of that training, your income will be high for the rest of your working life. I have a family member who is an M.D. with $250,000 in loan debt. However, her income is over $125,000 annually. So, this is a debt that she can pay off, and a career that she would never have without that investment.

Just as importantly, people with masters and PhDs, are employed; whereas someone without a high school education is seven times more likely to be out of work. There was only 2.5% unemployment during the Great Recession for professionals with advanced degrees. Even during the Great Recession there were over three million unfilled jobs – mostly in computer science and engineering. If you only had a high school education, the unemployment rate was more than 14%.

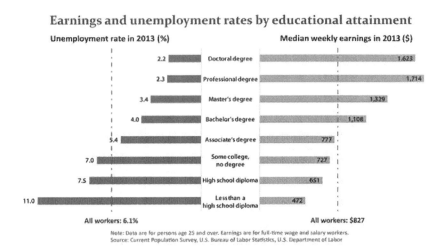

Earnings and unemployment rates by educational attainment

Unemployment rate in 2013 (%)   Median weekly earnings in 2013 ($)

Unemployment rate		Median weekly earnings
2.2	Doctoral degree	1,623
2.3	Professional degree	1,714
3.4	Master's degree	1,329
4.0	Bachelor's degree	1,108
5.4	Associate's degree	777
7.0	Some college, no degree	727
7.5	High school diploma	651
11.0	Less than a high school diploma	472

All workers: 6.1%   All workers: $827

Note: Data are for persons age 25 and over. Earnings are for full-time wage and salary workers.
Source: Current Population Survey, U.S. Bureau of Labor Statistics, U.S. Department of Labor

Here's the second quote that I promised to give you. This one is from Oprah Winfrey. Oprah was the keynote speaker at the California Governor and First Lady's Conference for Women, when Maria Shriver was the First Lady of California. Oprah told the audience there, "There is a calling for your life. I go to work. It doesn't feel like work. It feels like *breathing*. That's when you know you are home."

Oprah didn't just fall into the dream job and that was it. She consciously created her dream job. Early in her career, she was competing with all of the other shock jocks on daytime television. At one point, she describes interviewing the head honcho of the Ku

Klux Klan. It was a big coup that she had gotten this interview, and quite a big sensation given her ethnicity and the controversial subject matter. Oprah describes being so disgusted after the interview that she made a conscious choice then and there to create a show about empowerment and self-improvement – all of the things that she has become the queen of. She invented that career path for herself, in a moment of brave confrontation with what the industry said she had to do to keep her show. And in so doing, she became more successful than any of her competitors. The universe came rushing in to support her higher calling and her commitment. Of course, she had to get her production team and network on board and rewrite her vision for the show. The entire team had to make a strong, new, bold commitment. There had to be days when this new path seemed destined to fail, and yet, even in the darkest times, it never felt as dirty as sensationalism TV.

Creating more love in your life and career will demand a sober look under the bright light of truth of exactly what you are doing and creating. If you want out, then better strategies, blueprints and hard choices will be necessary. You'll need a team of people who are determined to help you succeed.

You might want to change from within – to get into a position of authority. Perhaps a raise and promotion are necessary, and taking night classes to get the degree you need to achieve this plan is the next step. You may have to work a day job while you launch your dream business. T.S. Eliot was a banker who loved to write poetry.

Love Can't Be Forced

It is important to remember that love is an outcome. You can't force yourself to love. You have to create the circumstances that allow you to experience love for the feeling to spark on its own. If you are not experiencing the sensation of love, then there are circumstances in your life that need to be addressed in order to get there. If you are not feeling love toward your sacred companion, there are actual steps you can take to get to that place regardless of what your companion is doing to make you so mad. It's not about changing them. It's about changing *you*. If you hate your job, then it is time to soul-search and discover what you really want to be and do, to work toward that outcome and get a new career path. It might be a process that takes a while – up to a decade for some careers.

Jesus Christ was a master of love and peace. All kinds of people approached him, and his desire to enlighten and heal was ever constant, no matter what their circumstances were, or how much they had *sinned*. With the exception of the moneylenders, who were sinning in his father's house. Tossing out thieves or protecting yourself from an attack does not strangle the flow of love. *Love* demands that you stand up for what you believe in. It might require anger and resolve to stop being complicit in a career and industry that you know is harming your neighbor or our planet. Love can be constant and flow without interruption, even if there is a limit and a boundary to what others can do in your sanctuary. Anger might be the fuel you need to lift yourself out of your comfort zone and into your higher calling.

Chronic Anger, Sadness or Frustration

If you have questions such as "Why can't I experience love?" go ahead and write them down, but quickly, like you are pulling a thorn out of your finger and discarding it. You don't want to ignore these opportunities for self-reflection, so journal the issue, without hyperfocusing on them. Don't take up too much time on the problems. Don't overthink or attempt to solve the problem. Rather than obsessing on finding solutions today, simply return to the mantra: love. Yes, just saying the word *love* and using it to push aside all of the doubt, confusion, resentment, anger, fear and questions, is part of the journey forward.

Rather than think, "I can't love because ___," think about something that you *can love* – even if it has to be a dream job *in the future*, or a dream scenario with a loved one that you are currently at odds with, or a distant past that takes time to recall. Live in a love dream, instead of the challenging reality, today. Once you dream up a better life, then you can design the blueprint to create it. Whistle. Sing. Count your blessings. Skip.

Choosing Love over Fear

Wherever there is dissonance, wherever there is disease, wherever there is anger, wherever there is doubt or fear, and you want to replace those emotions with love, there is a way to actively create the circumstances for love to show up. The process includes *solutions*. We cannot solve all of the problems in your life in one day. We can begin developing the Day One solution, which is learning to feel, express and create more love in our life – mostly by focusing on that mantra and not allowing negativity into our thoughts. Start dreaming of that job you'd love. Start envisioning what a loving companionship looks like.

Do not think of love as some mystery, or obsession, or lust, or simply just as a stupid task. Embody the essence of love. Separate yourself from the idea of *receiving* and focus on *giving love*. Let love be an outward expression toward everything and everyone you come across today – even strangers.

Today's Task

This morning think "God bless you" or "I love you" as you pass people on the street. Say this to the trees for giving us oxygen, to the streets that we drive upon, to the cat chasing the dog, to the bike you are riding to work on. My uncle describes what life was like during the Depression, of driving over a dirt road for hours on end, bumping along in the back of a truck, to have a date with my Aunt Rita. He was probably drunk at the time, which didn't help, but the journey sounded excruciating. I have a new appreciation for asphalt.

As much as the word *love*, I mean for you to embody the sensation, the emotion, the vibrant, active choice of noticing people and things around you, and sparking a selfless spurt of good wishes toward the object of your gaze without any expectation at all that something good might come back to you as a result of that. As His

Holiness, the 14th Dalai Lama tells us, "Remember that the best relationship is one in which your love for each other exceeds your need for each other."

Watch What Happens

I don't recommend saying "I love you" or "God bless you" loud enough for the person walking by to hear you. That's a little creepy. And it feels like you are looking for them to return something to you. Say it loud enough for you to know that you are saying it. Take notice of how others react when you extend a good wish toward them. My guess is that you're going to get a flood of smiles and good wishes in return, and that you'll find yourself feeling a little flush from the experience, if you do this wholeheartedly for a full hour, or longer.

Life is a mirror. I noticed this in spades one day when I was feeling a bit grouchy. Love has become my default feeling, and wishing "God Bless" and love on strangers is something I do without thinking most of the time. I'm not smiling like some loon or creep who is trying to make eye contact to get something from you (like those pamphlet people). I'm exuding the joy that I feel internally, which is the benefit of living the life of my dreams. I am very, very happy in my life and my career choice, and that is visible. As a result, normally when I walk down the street, I'm greeted with smiles and waves and greetings – from every stranger who walks by. I receive gifts from strangers almost daily. (Receiving a gift graciously is part of the flow of abundance and prosperity – something we'll discuss more in the chapters to come.)

That wasn't the case on this one crappy day that I was having, however. I hardly acknowledged people that I passed on the street and they barely noticed me in return. It was like I was invisible.

I had a problem that was gnawing on me. I felt unloved. I was down. No one was reaching out and helping. Not one smile. And I couldn't understand it. I thought, "Don't they see that I need them to help me! Even a smile might help to make me feel better." Then I remembered the Dalai Lama quote. Instead of *needing* love, I would try to *give* love.

What was missing wasn't them. It was me. (That is always the case. When you want something, give it first.)

I ignited my smile, which took some doing, and instantly, not even a nanosecond later, I found every stranger glowing with the visible, tacit message of good wishes as they passed by. One person said, "Good morning!" Another (a woman) told me how beautiful I was. After a few encounters like this, I felt so much better.

The truth is that it is almost impossible to pass a smile without returning the favor. You have to be very committed to your dour mood to be grumpy when someone is blessing you.

Don't Fake It

During your 60-minute walk of smiling and blessing strangers (and things), don't force a fake smile (unless that is all you can muster up, and if so, then at least give yourself the exercise of lifting the sides of your mouth). Real smiles are born from experiences that naturally make you feel that way. Do your best to find your Happy Place before you embark on your task. Oftentimes, the simple exercise of blessing everyone and everything you meet with the phrase "I love you" stirs something special in you.

Learning New Skills

As I mentioned at the beginning of this chapter, it's hard to extend love if you feel crushed beneath life's circumstances. Learning how to thrive is key to finding your way to love, prosperity and abundance.

The Thrive Budget™ is a simple premise: 50% to survive and 50% to thrive. When you limit your basic needs expenditures to 50%, you have 50% left to invest, to be charitable, to educate yourself and to double your fun budget. Every person – without any exception – who has created a permanent, positive shift in her life, out of struggling to survive and into thriving, did so by reducing their basic needs first, so that they could invest in the life of their dreams. We will be discussing how to do this in greater detail as we carry on this week. For now, I'm going to give you the formula, so that you can start the visioning process.

The Thrive Budget: 50% to Survive and 50% to Thrive

1. Deposit the first 10% of your income into a 401K, IRA, Health Savings Account, or other retirement plan.
2. Give 10% to the charity of your choice.
3. 10% should be going to education. (Saving up for your child's college. Educating yourself. Paying off student loan debt. Even tango lessons and exercise classes count.)
4. Double your fun budget (20% of your income). Fun increases your health, which is the foundation of all you do.
5. Limit your basic needs bills to 50% of your income. Basic needs include taxes, your home, your transportation, food, clothes, insurance, utilities, water…

For anyone who feels buried alive in bills, the Thrive Budget will seem impossible. But, if a divorced and desperate single mother (me, decades ago) can live her way into a dream life using this formula, so can you.

Additional Resources

We will be discussing the Thrive Budget at length throughout *The Gratitude Game*. You can learn more about the Thrive Budget in the section of the same name in *The ABCs of Money*. The Billionaire Game™ chapter, Chapter 8 of *Put Your Money Where Your Heart Is* (aka *You Vs. Wall Street* in paperback) also offers important insights into the Thrive Budget.

DAY 2: BREATHE
TODAY'S MANTRA: BREATHE

Chances are that when you read that word, you are already taking deeper breaths, and that is definitely part of the idea.

Take a deep, deep breath nice and slowly. After you fill your lungs, then I want you to take another shot of air that fills up all the way down to your root chakra, beneath your diaphragm. Hold it there for ten seconds and then release. Let the exhale be painstakingly slow.

As you breathe in again, let your chest fill up, your lungs expand, and then take that extra shot into your diaphragm and force it deep and all the way down into your root chakra again. Hold your breath, and then release with patience and intention. Make sure that you are doing that kind of breathing frequently throughout the day. Oxygenate your cells.

Breathing as a Companion to Prayer/Meditation

As you are breathing in, visualize that you are breathing in divine wisdom. Use whatever words make sense to you, whether it is God, heaven, divine intelligence, or the great mystery of life. Regardless of what you *think or believe, life itself* on this beautiful blue third rock from the sun is something to be in awe of. Breathe in the wisdom that created the stars and galaxies, slowly, deliberately. Suck in more air/wisdom/inspiration/imagination into the root chakra.

I like to imagine that there is an upside down pyramid on the top of my head – at the crown chakra. Then I take the foundation off of the pyramid, so that the pyramid becomes a funnel. If you are more comfortable with the word prayer, then sit still, or kneel, and just imagine that you are a vessel waiting to be filled with the word of God. If you are comfortable with meditation, then empty your thoughts and allow yourself to be filled with divine inspiration. If you believe in nothing, then just sit still and stop thinking. Empty your brain of all clutter – including the silly human desire to *know* the reason for everything. Just *be*. Breathe in slowly and deliberately, while at the same time, imagining the source of breath enriching you top down – from the crown of your head, through your lungs, heart, blood vessels, organs and cells. Renew your life force and vivify your sacrum.

As you exhale, release stress. Release old thought patterns that no longer work for you. Toss out bad experiences that you've had with money. Let go of judgments about what you have done in the past. Discard resentment towards others. Exhale all of this old garbage that you have been carrying around for far too long – particularly around money – and allow it to flow down the stream of your breath, as though a river is carrying this waste out of your cells and flesh and into the Earth, where it can be recycled. Worms, plants and trees are good at taking our exhaust and giving us back life force. It might be far more difficult for you to let go of these familiar, but toxic, frenemies, even for just a few moments in a mediation/prayer. *Vaya con dios.* (Go with God.)

Let this mindful breathing be something that happens randomly throughout your entire day. Think of these daily mantras as a symphony. Continue singing the mantra *love* that you practiced on day one. Breathing is going to be the melody today.

Yesterday, I outlined the Thrive Budget, which includes a donation of 10% of your income to charity. Charity is important for many reasons, not just because it makes our world a better place, but also because it cultivates *you*. It aids you in rediscovering your soul and passions, and puts you in contact with people who have similar interests and desires. The people you meet through your charity work are *your people* and will make good partners for you in all kinds of endeavors outside of the organization that you might meet them at. Charity is the best networking.

We spoke a little yesterday about how Oprah describes work as *breathing*, now that she is doing what she feels is her soul's calling. Charity is often the bridge to finding that dream calling. Almost every job I've gotten, promotion I've enjoyed, business I've launched and capital funding I've received has come directly as a result of my service projects. Certainly I'm living out my dream career because I committed to adding a splash of green to Wall Street and transforming lives on Main Street back in 2002. This is my charitable contribution to humanity. My business hasn't paid me a real salary in over a decade. (My investments have, however.)

So, as you breathe deeply in this prayer/meditation, singing the song of love and inviting in divine inspiration, start thinking about things that you care about improving in our world. What or who needs help? If money and time weren't an object, what would you do right here and now to make our world a better place? It might take a little digging or soul discovery, but you should come up with something.

Try thinking of people in need who are very close to you. When my son was in elementary school, it was important to me to establish a playground with a grassy field where the kids could play kickball and soccer, to install a Wi-Fi computer lab, and to secure funding for a music and arts curriculum. When he went to college, I began mentoring schoolgirls from Kenya. I continue to promote financial literacy worldwide.

Some years, I've taken family members or friends on some sort of excursion that might enrich their lives, or just be fun for them. A day at Disneyland (or the beach, or hiking) as a Big Sister can offer a fun way to guide and direct someone who needs your wisdom at a pivotal moment in her life. The focus on these trips is first and foremost just having fun. However, there will be down time during the fun, when you can talk about the importance of college, and how to find the best scholarships, grants and loans to get there. And, if you know anything about human psychology, then you know that your mentee is going to be more receptive to your wisdom and help if she trusts you. Her heart will be more open if she's having a good time.

Giving to others reinforces very good money skills. It reminds you that you have more than enough to give, and it tells the universe that you are living in the overflow. You might think it's just another bill that you can't afford; but in actuality, if the charity you are donating to qualifies, it is tax deductible. That means you are taking from Uncle Sam to give to a cause you think can really use the dough. Targeted relief offers a better shot at lasting, positive change in the world than just writing a check to the IRS and hoping for the best.

In addition to writing a check, commit to donating at least one hour of your time this week on or before Day Five. You don't have to actually donate your time today, but you should identify who or which organization you are going to help, and call them up to commit to the exact day and time.

Breathing: Performance Enhancement

Breathing is beneficial to the restructuring and revisioning of our life, our careers and passion, and to reshaping our physical world. Oxygenation increases personal performance in everything from weight training, to exercise, to beauty, to sleep and even in a more healthy relationship with food. Try pounding down the calories when you are mindful about breathing deeply! In fact, if you want to lose weight, breathing deeply is a powerful tool because it helps you calm down and chew your food slowly. When you take your time with food, you give your body the opportunity to tell you when it is full.

Lance Armstrong was using red blood cell therapy to increase the oxygenation of his muscles, which carried him onto victory. Even without blood doping, you can increase the oxygen flow, and, thus, your own health and physical and mental awareness, simply by breathing more deeply. That's part of the reason why you should be walking every day as you read (and listen) to this book. Blood flow ensures that the information floods new areas of your brain, and enlists your cells and your muscles in the unconscious, muscle memory of this reality. New areas of your body will be stimulated and activated – aided by oxygenation.

When I first started doing indoor cycling classes, which is a high-performance aerobics class, the challenges that they ask you to do are some of the most daunting physical tests that I've ever experienced. The interesting thing, however, is that you can only succeed by relaxing, not by pushing harder. In fact, in almost every endeavor that you might wish to excel at – whether it is scuba diving, tango or even writing – relaxation is the key to the sweet spot. You'll notice how easy virtuosos make it look – from Derek Jeter's effortless homerun swing, to Mariah Carey's awesome five-octave vocal range. And the only way to relax when someone is challenging you to go faster, or do more reps, or add extra weight and resistance, or sing an octave higher, is to breathe more deeply, mindfully and slowly and get extra fuel (oxygen) to those muscles. The same is true for severe emotional stress. The simple act of breathing more deeply and mindfully relaxes you – no matter what has you all worked up.

Before indoor cycling training, my average blood pressure was normal – 120/80. After years of spinning and enhancing my performance through breathing, my resting blood pressure dropped to 90/50. My heart became far more efficient. High-stress situations no longer boil my blood. It takes far more to get a rise out of me today than it did before I started exercising and breathing.

Love and breathing help quite a lot by keeping you calm, cool and collected. Particularly when they become *who you are.* However, wisdom, experience, knowledge and a better plan also reduce stress and create the foundation of a far better life. And that is why each day of this book is not just about the daily mantras, but also includes education and action.

Turning Hate to Love through Breathing

When you are experiencing anger or hatred, you may not yet know yet how to get to love. However, you can begin by breathing deeper and praying/meditating. There is a saying that the battle you win is the one you don't show up for. Do you really have to deal with this at this moment? Can you get out of the line of fire and get calm?

Yes, you'll still have to deal with the problem, particularly if it is acute and must be addressed. However, just as athletes perform better with oxygenation, every problem will be better dealt with from a position of power, wisdom and strength, which is achieved through breathing, calmness and clarity.

You are only on Day Two. So don't expect yourself to be the Master of Love, Breathing and Solutions yet. If you feel helpless or that others are hurting you or ruining your life, you already have two new tools to think other thoughts – even if you can only take your mind off of your problems for a few minutes at a time. Force yourself to love (at least think of a Happy Place) and to breathe, and have faith that 19 additional tools lie before you in the days to come.

If you start feeling anger, resentment or hatred today, breathe deeply and return to love. Force yourself to think of things and people you love, instead of the conflict or distress. Go back out on that love walk. Plant the seed (*love*) and start watering it.

Suspend the need to have a better answer right now. Write down the questions and frustrations that you have. Journaling will be very helpful during these 21 days. It can be a voice memo, or a written memo. It can be a drawing if you are a visual person. It can be a dance if you are kinesthetic, or a song, if you are an audio learner. … Get your questions out, but don't dwell upon them. Today, you're supposed to be religiously devoted to breathing, not problem solving. The time will come, as you gain more wisdom and tools in the days ahead, to take action.

How will two airy-fairy words power the kind of life transformation that I'm promising you? You might feel like you are not doing enough, that I'm not explaining things well, and that the Thrive Budget is impossible. These thoughts and doubts are normal; they are part of the process. Remember: what is *normal* and *comfortable* landed you where you were two days ago. If you want change, then you have to commit to being abnormal for a while.

Hate and Love Are Connected

Hate and love are on the same continuum – at polar opposite ends. Breathing and death are on the same continuum – at polar opposite ends. Getting to the destination you desire involves walking in the right direction. You can't board a jet to enlightenment, and thank God for that. Otherwise, when you jumped off the plane, you'd proceed to polluting paradise with the hell that you thought you had left behind.

The sad truth about all negative things that we experience is that they are our best teachers. Plato wrote, "Necessity is the mother of invention." Atisha, a great Buddhist teacher, often said, "Our enemies are our greatest teachers." When you are comfortable – fat and happy – there is really no motivation to change anything. I would never have selected them; however, the hardest moments in my life have inspired the most profound learning.

Wake Up! The American Consumer Owes Almost $12 Trillion. Almost 70% of Americans Are Overweight and 1/3 Are Obese.

Unhealthy fiscal habits have been the unconscious "reality" of most Americans for so long that most people think that is just the way *life is*. Should consumers really be carrying almost $12 trillion in debt? Is that healthy? Unhealthy physical habits have made 1/3 of Americans obese. *The way things are* is wrong, and this *reality* must be debunked and discarded, in order for a better life plan to be adopted. Statistically speaking, two out of every three people in your life need to start this program now.

Debunking myths that are so pervasive they have become a national ethos is not easy. Our cultural body needs a psychological and intellectual tune-up. Thank you for reading this book and becoming part of the solution.

The more I relax and breathe deeply, the stronger, faster and better I become.

When I don't exercise, I'm not as happy. When we are not oxygenating our cells, and our brain, the healthy body knows this and reacts by saying, "Hey, I'm having trouble breathing here. What happened to the workout today?" It's pretty hard to be depressed when you have endorphins flooding your system.

Health is Wealth

Having your physical body tuned up makes everything in your life hum along better. If you can't get out of bed, there is no prosperity and abundance. Health is essential for you to earn a great living, have an adventure-filled life and provide a comfortable home for your family.

Meditation

I want to take you on a guided mediation.

Get yourself comfortable and quiet in a dimly lit room. I prefer savasana (lying like a corpse), but you can choose whether you wish to sit or lie down. Close your eyes. Focus on your breathing. Take a deep, conscious breath in, with that extra shot into your root chakra. Expand your heart, lungs and throat, and imagine that all areas are completely open to heaven and white light. Pray for wisdom and guidance from a source that is much more loving and intelligent than you are, with broader awareness and vision, that is more divine, more masterful, more capable, more magnificent, with an astonishing ability to create the planets and life as we know it. Breathe in inspiration from a loving God, a loving intelligence.

As you breathe in, you should feel a tingling sensation. As you release and exhale, start to feel relieved and clean. Let go of our mortal small-mindedness, including all of the fears, doubts, worries, limitations, and angst that strangle and silence our divine nature. Let the flotsam and jetsam of your life travel on the river of your exhale out of your body and mind.

Go back to the breath, and really take your eyes out of focus and let your tongue melt into your throat, so that you take relaxation even deeper. Start noticing the sounds around you. What do you hear? If it is pleasant, then keep it. If not, what sound would you like to hear? Imagine that you are walking up a pathway to your dream house, with that sound in your ears.

What do you see? Is it warm or cold here? Who greets you at the door as you walk up the steps? Take in the exterior of the house, including the plants, trees, flowers and landscaping. Then open the front door and walk inside. What do you smell? What is the first thing that you touch?

Take a tour of your home. How many bedrooms and bathrooms are there? How many stories? Is there a garage? Walk to the rear of the house and look over your backyard. Are kids playing or dogs barking? Is there a giant meadow or a peach orchard? Can you walk outside and put your toes in the sand?

Now the doorbell is ringing. Guests are arriving. They are your Board of Advisors.

These advisors can be living. They can be fantasy. They can be dead. Pick icons who represent various areas of your life that you want mastery over. Some might represent:

- Beauty
- Wisdom
- Money
- Career
- Family
- Social Justice
- Peace
- Power
- Humanity
- Compassion
- Happiness
- Humor
- Health
- Athleticism
- Adventure
- Entrepreneurialism
- Imagination
- Talent

For me, my beauty and compassion icon would be Guanyin. Jesus Christ would be the Peacemaker. Humanity would be represented by Martin Luther King. Power would be Queen Elizabeth I. Wisdom is definitely Sophia. Adventure would be Amelia Earhart. Talent might be Rene Fleming. Humor could be The Dude from *The Big Lebowski.* Choose your advisors based upon them being the best example of what you want to be. And have a sense of humor about it. Include fictitious – even cartoon – characters, if you wish, alongside real icons.

Imagine that this dream come true board of advisors is here to support and guide you. So, every time you breathe in today, you are breathing in their wisdom, their humanity and their goodness – all throughout your body.

Each one of your guests has been given a glass of champagne and they are ready to toast you. Their toast is a special message to you that will help you on your journey to become more like them. Listen carefully as each one toasts you. Thank them for the message, and tell them that you will write down their message, take it to heart and work to embody it. Make a pact to remember what they say and live it.

After your last guest gives you a toast, you can take one last look around your dream house. Feel it. Smell it. Listen to it. Look at the people who live in your sanctuary home. Gaze at the artwork and the furniture.

Then start wiggling your toes and fingers. When you are ready, open your eyes.

Write down the messages that you have received in your journal.

You can do this meditation at any time, and you can add more advisors to your board whenever you desire. You can seat them at a round table, like King Arthur and the Knights of the Round Table, or have everyone sitting cross-legged in the sand. It's your call. Include both men and women – the Divine Masculine and the Divine Feminine – in the mix.

You are starting the powerful shift out of a person who is tossed about by life, without knowing how to take control of the ship, into being a conscious creator. You are learning to love more. You are seeking solutions from beyond your current way of thinking.

Breathing helps.

Daily Tasks
Charitable Giving of One Hour

Arrange to donate an hour of your time to charity on or before Day Five. Set up the activity and appointment today.

Aerobic Activity

Do an aerobic activity for 30-60 minutes. Whether you need to do it in a pool to make it easier on your joints, or enjoy racing up and down 300 stairs, where, why and how is up to you. (60 minutes is better.) If you are not yet very athletic, then try a brisk walk for at least 30 minutes. If you are athletic, go beyond your normal routine. I want you to challenge yourself, so that breathing more deeply and thoughtfully will be the only way you can hit your peak performance. Focus on breathing and relaxing, and watch how that makes it easier when the going gets tough.

Yoga

Experience yoga today for at least 20-30 minutes after your aerobic activity. Feel free to go longer if you wish. If you don't have a yoga class that you can attend, or a yoga DVD to watch, there are a lot of yoga positions that are available for free online. So, don't use an excuse. Find a way.

Meditation

Do a five-minute (or longer) savasana after your yoga workout. This is also called the final relaxation. Start by dimming the lights, lying flat on your back (like a corpse) and breathing deeply, just as we did at the earlier in this chapter. The goal of this meditation is complete relaxation. Your palms are facing upward. Your body is still and comfortable. Your breathing is deep and steady. Your thoughts are clear with no distractions. Let your tongue melt into the back of your throat. Feel the skin between your brows soften. Your eyes should also feel like they are sinking into the sockets. As you release the tensions in your face, you'll find yourself going deeper and deeper into the final relaxation.

New Experiences

Write down a list of new physical experiences that you want to have. (All physical experiences count, from jumping out of planes to Kama Sutra.) Put them in order of what you most desire. Commit to doing the one on the top of the list sometime over this 21-day period.

If it's something ambitious, like climb Mt. Everest, then you will never be able to achieve that feat in this time frame. You have to train quite rigorously for that. However, your commitment would then be that you start the necessary training now. Put the date on the calendar when you wish to go, and make the necessary preparation – travel plans and physical training – to achieve that goal.

Learning New Skills

For many of us, today's work will involve learning new skills. If you are a yogi master, then the aerobic challenge might be something new. If you are a veteran athlete, then yoga and meditation might be unfamiliar.

Additional Resources

Learn more about breathing and other principles outlined in this chapter by reading the *Tao Te Ching* by Lao Tzu and by attending yoga, kirtan and meditation classes.

Day 3: Gratitude
Today's Mantra: Gratitude

Today's thought is gratitude; however, it's important to keep the prior days' mantras in mind as well. Embody love. Breathe deeply, and notice the health and *joie du vivre* that those simple, but powerful, actions can bring.

The Origin of Money is Gratitude

Let go of *thinking* for a moment, and just recall, without judgment, what I said in the introduction of *The Gratitude Game*. The origin of money is gratitude. This is very, very difficult to understand. Even for spiritual people. So, take a moment now to visualize that cave, that mother, father and brother, that dying 7-year-old girl. Have you ever experienced a moment like this in your life, when you would have done anything to save someone or something dear to you? Did the miracle arrive? Are you still grateful? If so, why not put this book down and send a note or a gift to that gift giver who delivered the results you so desperately wanted?

Before money, there was gratitude. You could barter your time, your expertise or your talents. When someone did something for you, you did something for her in return. They shared meat from the kill; you shared fruit from your farm. My grandfather, who lived well into his 90s, shopped at the local mercantile until the day he died because they offered him credit during The Great Depression. His gratitude spanned more than half a century.

Today, the *expectation* of money has taken gratitude out of the game. Are you grateful for your job? Have you ever stopped to give thanks for it? Or do you just expect, in a bit of a cold-hearted way, that check to arrive because you've done your penance at the old nine-to-five (or these days, more like nine-to-nine for professionals).

Nobody *had* to discover electricity, or figure out solar power generation, or how to juice up the power lines and make your toaster pop! With the press of a finger. If you are in tune with the truth of this, and are grateful for all of that, you can offer back something valuable of your own. Money is the easiest, most convenient bartering tool, rather than delivering bread to someone daily, or cleaning their house for them, or shimmying up a power pole. But dollars and cents aren't the only currency of value in the world.

Magic Tokens of Gratitude

Money is a magic token of gratitude in its highest sense. The reason you don't feel that way yet isn't because that isn't the core essence. It is because your life is in such a state that you cannot feel good about things that you really should be counting as a blessing.

What are you worried about? Instead of looking forward to each day, do you wake up annoyed, or afraid, or loathing something? Those worries, doubts, fears, annoyances, bills, burdens and issues can and will be dealt with over the course of this 21-day Walk to Wealth that we are taking. There is a way out of debt consciousness, out of struggling to survive, and into thrive, wealth, abundance, prosperity consciousness. And it is not by ignoring the problem. It is by boldly facing your problems and employing time-proven solutions.

Other "magic tokens of gratitude" are time and talent. If someone has done something amazing for you, and you are not in position to *pay* her for it, then think of how time or talent might be a gift. Many people barter time and talent all of the time. Charitable giving is one way – something you'll experience on Day Five when you donate at least an hour of your time. Mentoring is another. When you are "giving" it is helpful to think of this as "in the overflow." So, do not over-give so much that you are draining your own well dry. And remember that a gift given with the expectation of something in return is not a gift at all. That is a loan. So, when you do give, give freely and with maximum outflow, knowing that charity, like love, is a ripple in the pond. It expands in concentric circles far beyond your touch, and even beyond your sight, every time.

The Zen of Discomfort

Maybe it's hard for you to feel grateful for anything right now. That's really okay. Gratitude, like love and happiness, are not things you can force. For many of us, these are all elusive states. You cannot chase them down and strangle them into existence. You can't say, "I'm grateful," and mean it, in the same way that you can say, "I'm going to breathe deeper," and then take in a lung full of air. Gratitude, love and happiness are sensations that we feel organically *after* something happens. They are *effects* of an external stimulus. In order to feel the thrill, we have to create the circumstances that spark the emotion. Fertilize the soil of your soul, and from there gratitude blooms.

The fertile soil of gratitude begins with simply counting your blessings.

So, today, even though you are not there yet with the feeling, I will give you some tools to being *the* practice that can eventually lead to an honest feeling. You must step in the direction of where you wish to go. The way to gratitude, which you don't feel yet, is a process. As Lao Tzu says, "The journey of a thousand miles begins with a single footstep."

Today and tonight, at least twice today, stop and count your blessings for at least five minutes. Don't stop until five minutes is done. Set a timer or the watch on your phone.

Can you name 25 things that are blessings in your life? Say out loud, "I am so thankful that ____." Elucidate each gift out loud. You can thank God. You can call and thank someone who made that miracle show up in your life. You can celebrate health.

When you start counting your blessings, you will find that you have a lot of conveniences that make life easier and more enjoyable. You have a lot of gifts that people give you. When I was a young mom, I liked to watch *Hook* starring Robin Williams with my son. He has to find his happy place in order to start thriving again.

Gratitude is that simple. It's finding your happy place. As you are walking along today, think of those things that make you beam. Remember how you felt – all of the senses. Write it down. Journal it. And then think of another, and another. And then try to figure out which one is the biggest blessing in your life. It could be what you are seeing while you are walking. Oftentimes, we are so in our head that we don't even notice what's around us. We don't look at where we are.

Could you wake up a little earlier and maybe go a little bit farther to a place that is so beautiful that you can say, "I'm really glad to be walking here."

Think about your children. Your career (if you love it). That first car that you bought. There has to be at least one moment in your life when you were dancing on the ceiling. Make these memories come alive. Do a Happy Place vision board – at least in your own brain. Remind yourself, and have visual cues that take you to that Happy Place. Not that future happy place that most people do for their vision boards, which is a variation on the theme, "I'll be happy when… (I find true love, I win the lottery)." Celebrate the miraculous moments you've *already enjoyed*, but have neglected to honor for a while. And, as you think of them, say "Thank you." Out loud.

As you say "Thank you" for those memorable moments in your life, you might naturally feel grateful for whatever led to that beautiful experience. Use the words "Thank you" as a discipline today. Say it so often that you feel like a mash-up.

"Thank you, bed. I'm so grateful that you are such a fluffy bed. I had a great night's sleep."

"Thank you, son. Look at how fast you got dressed. Now we're going to be early for school. Thank you."

"Thank you, my sacred companion. You have no idea how great it is to have you in my life. You inspire me, and waking up to you each morning is a dream come true." Think of something that your sacred companion does that makes you respect her.

Thank the people at work. Thank the trees for providing oxygen so we can all breathe. There's so much in our lives that allow us to exist that we walk right by without noticing – even our breath. Today, more than you have in a while, feel that interconnectedness with the air, the soil, the sky. Be very, very aware of and in awe of the divine nature of this creation.

The Currency of the Smile

Once you start practicing gratitude religiously, you will find that the "Currency of the Smile" works on your behalf.

My life, particularly when I was a young child, was very hard. At the same time, it has also been quite charmed. One was fate; the other was both a conscious and an unconscious choice. I was born into poverty as a copper miner's daughter. But I didn't know it because I loved so many things. I loved bean burritos. So, when my father would go on strike and we had to eat beans for months on end, I really liked it! I still like beans a lot. It's a crazy thing to love so much, but I'm grateful for beans. Every kind imaginable just thrills me – from hummus to refried.

As another example, as a child, I was a bit of a Tom Boy. I liked riding horses and running around barefoot. So, I didn't notice that we didn't have enough money to buy shoes in the summer. I thought that I was *allowed* to go barefoot! I grew up associating wearing shoes with going back to school (uggghhh) and going barefoot with summer time, swimming and horseback riding (hurray!). The whole thing was twisted up in my mind as a privilege. When all of the kids are doing it, you don't think it's strange, like you would feel walking barefoot down the street in Hoity-Toity Town.

Because these simple pleasures made me so happy, I've always had the Currency of the Smile working on my behalf. Yes, I work hard and I do have a genetic bent toward academic achievement. So that helps a lot, too. I attended my dream college – which was the University of Southern California – by earning scholarships and grants. That process is largely academic, but the papers you write count, too, and my smile seeps through the pen. If you, or someone you are mentoring, are writing a college essay paper, don't forget to get personal about what makes you unique.

I've had the privilege of learning from peers I admire greatly – from Dr. Gary Becker, to Kay Koplovitz, to Ambassador Melanne Verveer. I admire them so much. I'm grateful for them. While my commitment to financial literacy is what brought each of these icons into my life, I'm pretty sure that my infectious optimism didn't hurt.

Here's another example about the Currency of the Smile – and truly one of the best illustrations. Mario is a waiter at one of my favorite, affordable Mexican restaurants. (Beans!) He's always laughing, cracking jokes, trying to do the right thing and, yes, smiling. When I say, "Trying to do the right thing," I mean in actively being a good person – to the other waiters, to his bosses, to his wife, to the guys he rides bikes with. Not in a fake way. He's the real deal. He's a waiter, and his disposition is very service oriented. Having said that, he's not a choirboy. (He can down margaritas like a sailor.) But his wife refers to him as Jesus occasionally for that side of him that is always trying to help and heal people.

We were talking one morning, as we often do, and he said, "Hey, I moved last weekend. All of my friends showed up! We loaded up the van. We moved and we were done in a couple of hours, and then I treated everybody to lunch. "

He was so proud of himself – that all of his friends had come through for him. He couldn't gloat too much, however, because just the weekend before his boss, one of the many owners of the restaurant, had to hire movers. No one offered to help his boss move at all, though he had dropped multiple obvious hints to the affect.

Mario said, "That's because he never gives anything to anybody. He's so stingy that no one wants to help him."

As Mario was telling me this story, another regular at the front of the restaurant yells out, "Hey Mario, do you want Lakers tickets? I can't go." They were season tickets, which, at that time, could have been resold for over a thousand dollars.

Mario walked up to get his gift, and as he's walking back to me to finish his story, another patron hands him a bag of avocadoes from his tree.

Now, Mario is dancing back, hands full, saying, "Look at that! Avocadoes and Lakers tickets. All I need now is a margarita!"

If you are adding up the value of those gifts, Mario scored over a thousand dollars in tips that day – all simply as a result of the Currency of the Smile. If you add in the savings of not hiring movers, there's another five hundred or more.

None of this came about because people "owed" him. One person had more avocadoes than he needed, another tickets to the game he couldn't use and didn't want to resell. (Some people really care about who is sitting in *their* seat at the games.)

On the other side of the equation, Mario is always there when your coffee is ready to be warmed up. He knows your order. He's such a joy to be around. And if you honestly needed him to, he might help you move.

That's what I want you to be. Start tapping into the magic of this world. Be effervescent about something. When you really add value to people's lives, they will give you more for your services and products. Like the medicine woman, if you save someone's life, and have taken eleven plus years of study to perfect that skill, you will be paid more than if you just know how to mow lawns. This is not because one person is *better than* another in the eyes of the divine. It is because we live in a mortal, tough world, and quite often, we need all the help we can get to stay alive, much less to thrive.

Final Thought

The more that you can spark the sensation of "gratitude" when you are buying products and services and paying bills, the happier you will be. When you think of clean energy, electric cars and hybrids, imagine how much time and money go into developing these breakthrough products. When we write that check to Toyota or Tesla, we're giving them the fuel they need to keep developing more fuel-efficient cars. Conversely, if you own a gas-guzzler, when you fill up at the gas pump, you are affirming that you hope the auto manufacturer will keep making them and that the oil companies will keep drilling in the Gulf of Mexico. So, make sure that when you buy products and services now and going forward, that you do so more mindfully.

It's not another job. It's simply holistic living. Which makes things much more simple and gratifying. And it doesn't cost more. In fact, if you were conserving energy, powering your own home (if you live in a sunny state) and driving an electric car, you'd find a lot more money to spend on those dream come true vacations. For most people, the savings could be up to $7,500 every year.

You might now start to get a sense that there are solutions to your most pressing problems, and that, as your vision gets clearer, you will see them. You can do this. Count your blessings. Post the word *gratitude* prominently – perhaps on your computer, so that you see it constantly today. And each time that you see the word, count another blessing in your life. All day long.

Action Plan:
1. Count your blessings. Take five minutes twice today to name, out loud, all of the things that you are grateful for. Time yourself. Don't cheat.
2. Write down all of the things that you are truly grateful for in your journal. List as many visceral qualities about the experience that you can. As you remember the experience, say "Thank you."
3. Pay some bills. As you write the check, give thanks out loud for the product or service that you have purchased with your magic tokens of gratitude (money). If you cannot find something to celebrate about the check you are writing, perhaps you should rethink purchasing that particular item. For instance, it's hard to be grateful for writing a check to pay down credit card debt that is compounding – particularly when you can't even remember what you bought. That can be fixed, too. So, rather than pretend to be "happy" about your debt, when you clearly are not, put that bill in the "Problems to be Solved" pile (after you pay it, of course).
4. Play the Fire Ritual™.

The Fire Ritual

The Fire Ritual is designed to prompt you to dream up solutions to your worries, doubts, fears and regrets – particularly as it relates to money. This is very different from the Law of Attraction because rather than focusing on affirmations and positive thinking, I want you to get down and dirty with reality – with those problems that plague you and keep you from sleeping at night. This is so that you can formulate, create and *live* a richer life.

Instructions

Take a piece of 8x10 paper and fold it in half. You may need a few extra pieces of paper, so go ahead and set them out now.

List all of the things that you:

- Are worried about
- Haven't accomplished that you wish you had
- Regret
- Fear
- Wake up in a cold sweat over
- Hate
- Resent
- People who walking on your dreams or standing in your way

This is a whining and complaining list.

Write on only one-half of the paper (which is folded in half). If you get to the bottom and have more things to write, just get a clean sheet and continue writing to your heart's content. Do not write on the backside or the other half of the paper.

While you might have been trained to have a good *mindset* about things, if you are not dealing with the real problems and issues – those things that honestly drag you down – then essentially it's like trying to put sugar on moldy bread. You have these concerns, issues and problems. They are real, and they require real solutions if you want anything to be different going forward.

Over seven and a half million people lost their homes in the Great Recession. Some people lost their job. Incomes have stagnated for almost 30 years. Many people are drowning in credit card debt. Some people still have their home, but are draining their nest egg to keep it. You might have a great job and income, but are carrying hundreds of thousands of dollars in student loan debt – and that is preventing you from purchasing your first house. There have been a lot of things to worry about in the New Millennium. You can't just dream them away with visualizations and positive affirmations. You'll never get anywhere if you don't take action.

However, you must have a good plan *before* you take action. (Acting without a plan, or acting on blind faith, can be worse than doing nothing.) You are more likely to come up with a solution if you first identify exactly what the problem is. So, whining and complaining is a prerequisite.

Here's an example. Let's say that you decide you want to earn a great income right out of high school. That's your wish. But you worry that you're going to end up flipping burgers at a fast food joint for minimum wage.

You know (from chapter one) that the best way to earn a great income in today's world is to go to college. That's a solid solution and a good game plan. People with a college degree make four times as much as people with a high school diploma. In fact, by focusing almost all of their resources on education, Asian Americans have become the top earning ethnic group in the U.S.

Some people try to justify not going to college by saying that they can't afford it, or that they don't want to take on the student loan debt. Community colleges might be the solution.

I'm not saying that every single person in America has to graduate from college. Steve Jobs was one of the world's most famous college dropouts. However, even artists can benefit from college courses. And most of us need both the education and the piece of paper to be able to provide for ourselves.

No matter what the challenge is, there are solutions to your problems, dreams and desires. Once you open up the door of possibilities, you can start the process of envisioning the solution. Don't expect to immediately figure out the *exact* right plan of action. You just need to jostle your problem-solving brain into activity, and start walking on the path away from complaining, fear and doubt and toward imagining and creating. Have a North Star and start walking, knowing that you can take more than one path and course-correct along the way.

It should take a minimum of ten minutes to list all of the issues that need solving in your life. Use as many pieces of paper as you need to. Just be sure to fold the paper in half first and only write on one-half of the page.

The more specific that you can be, the better. You might say, "I'm stuck in a dead-end job, and I don't have enough money to feed my family."

Or, "I went to college and I can't find a job that pays more than $10 an hour, which isn't enough to even pay my student loans."

Another one might be, "I'm in my 30s and I want to have children, and I haven't found my sacred companion yet."

Think of all of the things that you need to be a complete, whole and happy person. Typically that is going to include a lot of basic needs requirements, such as food, transportation and shelter. You might have concerns about friends and family or your love life. Be sure that you are covering all of the bases – from survival, to money, to companionship, to health, to career. Once you get those things covered, you might be more concerned with protecting your assets, giving back and willing your estate.

There is no judgment here on how small, or materialistic, or spiritual your concerns are. No one should be looking over your shoulder and judging you. Eliminate self-criticism, too. You benefit by being honest with yourself about what you truly desire and what you need to fix. Allow this to be a complete release. Take a bold look at your rage and your fear. Even if you are so spiritually enlightened that you only experience those emotions in a watered down way, there is something to improve. There is always something that you would like more than what you have – whether it is enlightened or greedy. If the problem itself is so acute that it is hard to face, I encourage you to have the courage to write it down. Paradise lies on the other side.

The Next Step

Simply take the paper and unfold it. You'll discover that one side of the paper lists your problems, while the other side is completely blank.

Create the solutions on the blank side of the paper, according to the guidelines below.

Solutions

The solution to your problem is the exact opposite of what you fear. If you wrote, "I'm stuck in a dead-end job and can't feed my family," then the solution to your problem is quite literally, "I'm so grateful that I have a job that pays well, and that my family and I have three hots and a cot!" (Just kidding. This is a reference to jail.)

Before you start writing the solutions, there is another very important piece of the puzzle, however. You need to **take action to make it real**. It is action and a good plan that are required for you to create a new reality for yourself.

The solution you might act upon could be, "I'm going to get a job that I love in my area of specialty, because I'm going to go on interviews every single day of the week until I land the job of my dreams."

Here's another example – this time in your personal life. "I'm afraid that I'll never find my sacred soul mate." The mirror opposite is: "I'm so happy that this year I've found my sacred soul mate" *because* "this year I am going to make sure that I'm a sacred soul mate myself, and I'm going to place myself in circumstances where my beauty, my inner light and my unique qualities shine through." The action you might take could vary from tango lessons, to church socials, to joining a group that is training to climb Mt. Whitney. You want to choose a community where your gifts and talents flourish, and where others who will appreciate that beauty in you are present.

What's beautiful about you creating your own solutions is that you can personalize them to be uniquely *you*. You really do know what is best, and as you exercise your problem solving muscle, it will become more and more the *way life is* for you.

It is easy to worry about what is wrong instead of creating what is right because that is what we are surrounded with. Our senses are bombarded, mostly through the "daily news," with worry, doubt, fear and rumors, and the underlying message that we have no voice, and you have no hand in beautifying our world. We can make the choice to turn off the television. Put down the paper. Pick up literature. Surround ourselves with Conscious Creatives here and throughout history. Bathe ourselves in inspiration, innovative ideas and divine imagination. And when we do, creating what is right becomes what is easy. Worrying becomes simply a waste of time.

Why be so specific about the details? Because you can't board a plane to "the life of my dreams." You can get on a plane to Hawaii. You can get on a plane to many different destinations on Earth. If you're at the airport, you're going to have to choose a destination, and life is definitely an airport. You are always headed somewhere – unless you are walking in circles... Your life cannot change until you move out of whatever rut you are stuck in or whatever entanglement you are embroiled in.

Also, there is no destination *away from* this or that thing. That is why it is so important to reframe all of the things that you *don't want to happen* into things that you *do want to happen* (and are working toward). Saying, "I don't want to go to Antarctica," doesn't get you any closer to the vacation you do wish to go on. In fact, if you say, "I don't want to go to Antarctica," to your travel agent and somehow s/he misses the *don't* part, you'll end up in Antarctica. This is part of the reason why so often we actually manifest what we fear – the very thing that we don't want to happen.

When the only thing you can envision is what you fear, how can any other reality manifest? If it did, would you even see it? If you haven't learned how to create, or recognize, what you desire, there is no way it can show up. Let me use an example. So many of our highest paid athletes and lottery winners end up broke. Mike Tyson and Marion Jones are two high profile examples, but according to Mint.com, 78% of NFL players file for bankruptcy within five years of retirement. Why? They don't learn how to manage their money properly. These athletes have shown dedication beyond comprehension while sculpting themselves into the world's premiere players. If they spent even an iota of that time and passion on budgeting and investing, and overseeing their money, then the bankruptcy statistics would look very different.

Often the reason we fear something is because we know it's coming. If you smoke four packs of cigarettes a day, you might fear getting cancer or emphysema. The solution is quite simple. Stop smoking. Start exercising and eating right.

If you checked off a bunch of boxes in your 401K at work without knowing what you were doing, and you fear you'll go broke, the solution is simple. Get educated on what your options are, and employ a strategy that is protected from downturns, and profits in bull markets – rather than guessing. Don't fear the inevitable. Create a better reality.

Let me give you another example of how to write a solution that is health related. Let's say that this year, you had five colds and each one took you down for a week. You missed so much work that you couldn't take a vacation. You desire to be healthier. The solution is, "I'm so happy that I'm so healthy *because* I boosted my immune system with Essential Fatty Acids, vitamins and minerals all throughout the flu season. I took zero sick days this year and instead spent three weeks in India. This was on my bucket list!"

Now, you might still be censoring yourself and thinking, "That's crazy. I can't write that. I can't afford the time or the money to go to India!"

As you see. So it is. It's very easy to say you can't and then not even try to do it.

But what if you *could* start envisioning India? When you write something this outlandish down, you actually start the crystallization process. The Wright Brothers had the outlandish notion that we could fly. Galileo was convinced that the Earth revolved around the Sun. He undoubtedly checked and rechecked his calculations and his telescopes time and again before he became certain of it – particularly since thinking this was apostasy and sure to get him in trouble.

Seeing into the future is much easier when you are creating it.

So, you envision India and you end up in Indiana. Don't expect your first attempt at flying to be a breeze. As Thomas Edison used to say, "Genius is one-percent inspiration and ninety-nine percent perspiration." He very famously tried and failed hundreds of times before inventing the light bulb. Rather than admitting defeat, Edison said, "I didn't fail 1,000 times. The light bulb was an invention with 1,000 steps."

The Fire Ritual is your chance to reinvent your life. Your results will be in direct proportion to the energy and the wisdom – the perspiration and the course correction – that you put into them. Invest no time or money and nothing will change. Invest all your time and money, and the sky is the limit on what you might achieve.

I'm always amazed at this in my own life. Since 2000, my mission has been to transform lives on Main Street. After I was named the #1 stock picker in 2005, I could have moved straight into managing a hedge fund. I made the choice at that time that I would stick with Main Street – that I would feel spiritually bankrupt if I woke up every day with the primary task of making rich people richer.

That choice has given me access to experiences that I would have never stumbled upon and could never have afforded – even if I were earning multi-millions annually. You can't *buy* the endorsement of a Nobel-Prize winning economist, or have guided, behind the scenes tours of the homes of royals. When you really commit to something, you're going to be surprised at the magic that shows up.

When I see the results of empowering people with financial literacy and financial wisdom, that is something that really makes me happy. That's another thing that money can't buy.

When I do the Fire Ritual now, even when I write down something outlandish, I always expect what I've written, or something better, to show up. And it always does. Because I wrote it down. I envisioned it. And I take steps to make it real. I keep working and honing my creation, and I take notice of synchronicity and the wisdom of others.

It is normal to censor yourself when it comes to the solutions that you think you can create. Think of this as a silly game, where madness is actually better than sanity. Allow yourself to aim higher than you think you can shoot. Don't draw the curtains too low and block your view of the moon. The first step you take toward your dream can be a baby step. But don't make the dream itself something that you can achieve so easily. As you get more familiar with this game, it will begin to *astound* you how efficacious this system is. Have a child's mind. Dream up solutions that are impossible. Then go back to being the forensic scientist as you seek to manifest the impossible. Because you have widened your scope in the creation process, you have a lot more room to experiment and maneuver in, and a lot more possibilities for a desirable outcome.

Pause Now and Write Down the Solutions and Action Plan for Your Problems

Try to enjoy this process. When we play this game at my retreat, we do it in a gorgeous setting. Often we are overlooking the Pacific Ocean, at sunset, while drinking a glass of champagne (or coconut milk). We're playing the game together, sharing examples, asking for help to solve problems that we cannot see beyond. There is a lot of laughter, and wide-eyed amazement at the beauty of the sunset.

You want to start associating fun, relaxation and beauty with money. So, take the time to set up a special space to solve your problems. It might be sitting under a tree in the park. A candlelit yoga studio. With hot tea or a cold beer.

If, while you're in this relaxed, somewhat enticing, setting, a wild idea flies in, write it down. Don't censor yourself.

Keep the Solutions; Burn the Problems

After you finish brainstorming your action plan, you'll discover that your problems are on one side of the paper and your solutions are on the other side. Wet your finger a little and run it along the crease in the middle of the paper. Then fold the paper on that line again while it is moist. You can now easily tear the paper along this seam, separating the problems and the solutions.

Tear up your problems. Put that in a pile.

Fold the solutions into four. I put my solutions in my pillowcase. There I'm dreaming on the possibilities without obsessing over them or sticking too close to the script. Every time I wash my sheets, I have the opportunity to reread what I've written.

You will know when it is time to do a new Fire Ritual. Maybe six months or a year from now, you'll realize that you have solved last year's problems and have a new set of challenges for the coming year.

Yes, this is a great game to play on New Year's Day.

As you play this game going forward, you'll discover that your problems start feeling less and less overwhelming. That is because your mind has shifted from worry to confidence, from fear to empowerment, and from feeling powerless to knowing that you can create a different reality for yourself. Your life becomes easier. You'll trust that you can solve even really big, global problems. It may take more wisdom than you have currently, more partners, more money – but these can all be envisioned, planned and created. Others are already thinking of these problems and solutions, too – looking for partners, wisdom and financing.

The Fire Ritual

It's important to do this safely. If you don't know fire safety, then flushing your problems has the same affect. At the beach, we dig a hole in the sand, shield the fire from any wind and cover up the ashes with sand before we leave – to ensure no wild, airborne embers might escape. If you have a fireplace, it might be easy and safe to just throw your problems in there and sip your champagne as you watch them burn.

The world is asking us for solutions all the time. The only way solutions come to pass is for a problem to arise. Once you become a master of solutions, you are no longer resentful of problems. They are just an invitation to participate in the evolution of our planet.

We are the most alert, and the most imaginative, when we are tossed out of our comfort zone.

Day 4: Forgiveness
Today's Mantra: Forgiveness

If you've ever experienced forgiveness, you know that getting to this reality requires a lot of hard work. That is why I'm starting this chapter by explaining why negative experiences are such an important part of self-actualization (and wealth).

The Blessing of Anger

Who doesn't want it all? A better world and a more delicious body, home, partner, career and champagne? What most of us don't realize is that dream come true living starts with honoring, but not wallowing in, your righteous anger…

Anger is a fantastic fuel. It is the dis-ease and fire you need to create lasting, positive changes in your life. You think, "This sucks! I hate this!" and that sparks your thrust out of what is wrong for you into that which is more right for you. As Nobel Peace Prize winner Betty Williams writes, "The thing that started the peace movement in Ireland was anger – my anger. It wasn't anger. It was fury. And I've never been able to lose that. But to transform all that. It's a lot of hard work."

Betty Williams' rage fueled a crucially important peace movement that has been active for the last three decades and continuing. *What a blessing.*

When anger is ignored, however, the hatred and malice becomes internalized, and all of that fire and dis-ease burn up your body temple, instead of fueling your creation of a better life and world.

Anger is a stop sign to show you that you're headed in the wrong direction. Betty Williams was apoplectic about nonstop war and terrorism in Ireland, after watching three innocent children die in a car collision with IRA fugitive Danny Lennon. The country was embroiled in a maelstrom of nonstop violence. The Irish Republican Army and the British Authorities were determined to continue extracting an eye for an eye – even if it was blinding and killing innocent children. People stood by – outraged, grief-stricken and helpless. Betty Williams became the spark that ignited her community into action.

Betty Williams and Mairead Corrigan (the aunt of the slain children) began the peace movement in Ireland a relatively simple way. They organized a peace march to the graves of the children. Citizens, who had previously been numb to the daily headlines or without a plan to curb the violence, now had a radical, simple, yet powerful way to come together, thanks to Betty and Mairead. The first march attracted 10,000 people, but was disrupted by the Irish Republican Army. The following week, Williams and Corrigan organized a second march that attracted 35,000. Williams and Corrigan are certainly examples of what remarkable results ordinary people can achieve through their righteous anger.

It's daunting to think of doing something as important as creating a peace movement, but this focus on using anger as fuel to create more peace, prosperity and love in your own life can be powerful, too.

When I first began hosting retreats, I debuted the event at an expensive, beachfront hotel. As can happen with the first time you do anything, I was over budget. Not only that, but all of the money had been siphoned out of my business account (more on that later), and I still had a few details to finalize. I was in a panic on how to pull it all off, and more than a little steamed.

I had pre-negotiated a price for the meeting room for three full days at a price that the business could (barely) afford. On one of the evenings, we were to host a bestselling author and his wife, who was a singer/songwriter. The idea was to create a fun evening, with this author lighting everyone on fire with his inspirational message, and the singer/songwriter leading us in celebration, song and dance. Since the microphones and PA system were included in the rental, our singer only needed a piano. As I was pacing up and down the hall outside the meeting room at the hotel, trying to picture the evening in my mind and all of the extras I'd need to pull it off, I spotted a grand piano. Hurray! I raced down to the lobby to see the catering person about getting the piano wheeled into my banquet room.

Now, Adam (not his real name), who creates the budget for events with under 100 people, was giving me a lot of problems. The price of the event was to be XYZ because each of the participants was in charge of paying for their own room and food. Hotels like to get guaranteed, upfront payment on food, rather than rely upon the guests to eat on their own, so Adam was a little miffed with me. He decided that I should have included food in the order, and without authorization or notification, charged almost twenty thousand dollars on my credit card, which was more than double the cost of the event. He never gave me an acceptable reason for doing that, but pawned a lame excuse off on his general manager – that he *assumed* I needed to feed my guests (which was the opposite of what had been contracted and discussed).

So, when I met this manager in the lobby to discuss the piano rental, we were both sneering behind forced smiles. I didn't trust the weasel, for obvious reasons. He wasn't going to last very long in his job, because when you treat your clients terribly they don't come back. For now, however, my event was only days away, and I had a lot of fine-tuning to do…

A-Hole, I mean Adam, clutched his clipboard in front of his chest, like armor, and pretended that it might drop if he shook my extended hand.

"Yes, Ms. Pace," he seethed. "How may I help you today?"

Adam was in a tizzy about all of the things that his other clients needed and wanted to rush through my inquiry, but finally relented – after I suggested that his boss might have more time to help me – to come up to my meeting room for a final walk-through of the event. When we sauntered past the piano, I stopped him. I didn't want to give him too many details about anything because every time I opened my mouth he tried to charge me another $10,000.

"Can we have this in the room?" I asked. "It's just sitting out here not being used."

"This?" he chuckled superciliously, as if the piano were as priceless as Liberace's gold-plated Steinway. "Well. It's out of tune and we have to hire a union tuner. So that's about a thousand dollars. And then we have to get union movers to move it, which is *really* going to cost you."

"Are you kidding me?" I blurted out. "You keep an untuned piano and charge your guests for tuning it? And you're going to charge me thousands of dollars to roll it less than sixty feet into the meeting room?"

"Union rules," he said. "They have to do it."

"You and I could roll it in there right now," I responded. I pushed it a little for emphasis, which caused Adam to percolate.

"I'll draw up the budget and have it delivered to you this afternoon," he sputtered. "But now I have meetings with other clients." With that, he spun on his heel and left only the scent of his designer cologne hanging in the air.

Ohhh! I steamed! If I didn't have guests arriving in two days, I would have changed the venue right then and there. First the freaking $20,000 and now A-hole (and a slew of other curse words) wants to *rent* me an untuned piano for more than I could buy one!

What to do? What to do?

I had already promised to pay the speakers. I had promised the guests that they would have this amazing experience on the second night. What a disaster! Should I just cancel everything and refund the money? Nope. Even if I wanted to, I couldn't because I was still trying to get $20,000 back into my account. Kill Adam? Take his clipboard, erase three zeros off of the bottom line and whack it into his skull for interest? Complain (again) to the general manager about the creep?

Nothing swirling in that fit of hatred and bile – centered on Adam and what a jerk he was – had any hope of being the right answer. But this was a beachfront hotel. And being a local patron, I knew where all the most stunning, secluded spots were. I took the elevator to the eighth floor, stood beneath a vaulted, glass ceiling with sunbeams glistening down on me and stared out at the pier below.

When I have trouble thinking beyond my own lizard brain (which was still obsessed with how to extract revenge on Adam), I turn to prayer.

"Please, dear gods. Help me!" I pleaded, sinking to my knees.

Okay. Not exactly Zen, but better than bile and stomping. I arranged myself into a Yogi position, with my fingers on my knees and continued, "Help me to see what I cannot see. Help me to think what I haven't thought of. I know there is a solution out there. And I know that miracles happen every single day."

Every time I say that last line of my begging prayer, it sparks my memory to other miracles I've experienced. The miracle of getting out of Morenci, Arizona – where so many of my friends were trapped their entire lives in a cycle of poverty. The miracle of surviving my mother's death when I was seven and thought the world had ended. The miracle of buying my first baby blue convertible. The miracle of getting scholarships and grants to attend the University of Southern California – the college of my dreams. The miracle of having such a wild and wonderful young son. Oh yeah! And those books of his that I forgot to return to the library. Oh my. I hope the fine isn't too steep. Crap!

With that, I raced home, rummaged through the scattered chaos of video games, stinky clothes and undone homework in my son's room to find the overdue books. I flew back to the library, only to find that it had moved. (After two years of renovations, the remodeled library had just reopened.)

Thankfully, it was only a street away. As I screeched up to the entrance, I noticed a new auditorium – The Martin Luther King Jr. Auditorium. Hmm, I thought. What about hosting our New Year's Eve Celebration in the Martin Luther King Jr. Auditorium? That had a great ring to it.

I paid my fine, which was under $2.00 (thankfully), and then asked where I could learn more about the auditorium. "Upstairs," the librarian instructed.

Upstairs, there was a thin, kind young man, with blue paint on his nails. Brian was eager to answer my questions, but he also had a set of guidelines for the auditorium that had been established by The Board. He pushed the rules toward me, while he continued explaining the features of the facility.

"Well, the auditorium seats about 130. It's brand new. New sound system. The interior was designed by a sound engineer to have excellent acoustics," Brian said.

"Does it have a piano?" I asked timidly.

"Yes. It has two pianos. A Steinway and a Bösendorfer. You can pick which one you prefer."

"Are they both in tune?"

"Yes. We tune them once a month. They were just tuned yesterday, in fact."

"And do you have to have union people roll it in and out?"

"No, of course not! The pianos are on wheels. You or I could do it. But we just have our security team set it up for you."

The library's security guard gave me a tour of the auditorium, during which my jaw dropped and never once settled back in its rightful place. Imagine a new, crisp, modern theatre with a stage, compared to a room with faded carpet, low ceilings, folding chairs, Arctic temperatures, muffled acoustics and that dreaded out of tune piano. The sound system included microphones and mike stands – everything I needed to have a magical night.

Brian and I contracted the logistics over the course of the next 15 minutes. I paid $90 and agreed to make the evening's event open for free to the public (one of The Board's rules). I was all set to go for the special performance, which would now be hosted by my group (with VIP seating for them)!

The night of the event, the auditorium was packed with my guests, my friends, Santa Monica locals and others who had just wandered in by chance to join our celebration. The bestselling author, the singer/songwriter and I had an almost seamless flow between keynote addresses, song, celebration, dance, meditation and even an impromptu Q&A session with audience members. The auditorium was pleasing on every aesthetic level – great sound, flattering lighting, perfect acoustics. Far more delightful than the cramped, out-of-tune, over-priced experience that Adam was offering.

But it never would have happened that way without Adam being so rude and adversarial, without my anger, without me pleading/praying for a miracle, and without spinning in the complete opposite direction to find helpful Brian and the perfect Plan B. All that was available to me at a price I could easily afford – once I focused on solutions, instead of dwelling on problems.

Creating the life of your dreams, here in the real world, ultimately means: respect the wisdom of your anger. When you hate the problem, create the cure. Find what you would love to experience in the place of what makes you so irate, and stomp with as much self-righteous anger or desperation toward that solution, as you would in flattening the enemy.

Hating the problem and not acting means that you get to stew in your own juices – literally. Studies show that heart attacks, strokes and premature deaths are linked to high levels of anger.

Betty Williams and Mairead Corrigan created peace. Joseph Strauss envisioned the Golden Gate Bridge, but it took twelve years from when the first blueprint was submitted until construction began in 1933. Michelangelo spent four years painting the Sistine Chapel; he also designed the dome of St. Peter's Basilica in 1546. The cupola and dome weren't completed until after his death, almost twenty years later, in 1564.

Toni Morrison wrote extraordinary novels, and was (finally) awarded a Pulitzer Prize in 1988 at the age of 57. She was over 60 when she won a Nobel Prize for the body of her work. Perhaps the most awe-inspiring example of enduring patience amidst extreme oppression and of transforming from an angry militant to a peace-promoting president is former South African President Nelson

Rolihlahla Mandela, who was imprisoned from 1962 until 1990, and then emerged to rule South Africa from 1994 to 1999.

What great thing are you here to create and/or co-create with someone else? Whether it's a peace movement for your country, or simply one for your family, it's important. Don't let anger stop you from creating it. Let anger be the fuel to spin you around and point you in the direction of what is right. And then stay focused and fired up enough to see it through.

How in the world do you do this? Sometimes, in truth, your *oppressors* are riling your anger to throw you off of your game. If they can get you swirling in the juices of your anger, instead of swimming in creativity, then you can be shut down and manipulated, instead of rising and shining. Williams and Corrigan responded to the accusations and shouts of the IRA by organizing a bigger, stronger and more resolute march for peace the following week. Their peace cries were louder and more sustained than the rat-a-tat-tats of the machine guns and bombs of the IRA. The same with the civil rights movement here in the U.S., and Gandhi's India.

Daily Tasks
So now, back to our mantra: Forgiveness

Focus for just a few moments on the people who you believe owe you something. It might be an apology, or money, or something someone has taken from you. In the case of some people, it might have to do with life and death issues –the toughest circumstance to ever forgive someone for.

Write down their names. Write down what they owe you or what possession of yours they destroyed. Look at each person's name. As you look at the name, say a prayer for that person. Ask that they be blessed. Resist the urge to say anything negative at all, or to pray for revenge. Force yourself to say the words, even if they sting your tongue coming out.

Now ask what you need going forward so that you never have to experience the pain or loss that you experienced with this person.

Take each person whom you've written on the list one at a time, thinking of what you might do to avoid ever being in a position where someone can take something like that from you again. Write down an idea next to their name. It doesn't have to be the perfect solution – just something that is pointed in the right direction.

In this exercise (or prayer/meditation), you are asking for wisdom and guidance so that you are less likely to place yourself in the line of fire of what you don't want. As adults – in most but not all cases – no one can do anything to us that we do not give them permission to do. Very often, the loan that wasn't paid back was loaned to someone who didn't have a prayer to be able to pay it back. If we wanted to give the person money, we should have called it charity and never expected a payback. Or we should have never loaned the money at all.

If you think the *broker* lost all of your money, you are simply passing the buck. You gave her permission to do whatever she wanted to do – without building in checks and balances and regular reports. Rich people don't have blind faith in others to make them rich. If they hire outside counsel, they expect them to perform, and monitor the performance to make sure that they do.

If you blame the realtor or the mortgage broker for selling you a house you couldn't afford, who is really responsible for that? You wrote the down payment and signed your name on the deed. You are the one who chose to spend too much of your income, or to take a chance to buy and flip it for a quick buck.

After you have written down a new action plan for yourself, select the person whom you are having the most difficulty forgiving. Take twenty-one dollars. If you know something that person would like, then purchase a gift with your twenty-one dollars and mail it to him or her anonymously. (I once purchased cigars for an adversary because I knew he loved them more than almost everything else.) Say a blessing for them as you mail the gift.

Then tear up the piece of paper with all of the people who need forgiving and burn it. Don't waste any more time today thinking about anger or revenge or people who owe you things. Don't worry about remembering all of the ways that you are going to think and act differently. The exercise teaches you to stop thinking like a victim and start actively creating your life. The situations that you will step into going forward will be different. As you take responsibility for your life, then you will rise to the challenge, and give yourself the time, space, resources, wisdom and information that you need to make a rational choice, have an admirable plan and ensure a successful outcome.

Don't expect yourself to *feel* forgiveness right away. However, every time that you go back to resentment, anger or hatred that is directed at someone else, simply force yourself to refocus your energy on something that is more worthy of your time – creating the solutions so that what you regret will not happen again. Focus your time and attention on discovering the gifts, talents and passions that you have, and how you are going to share them with the world. And use the $21 gift (or some other ritualistic token) to show forgiveness to that person, even if you can't feel forgiveness yet.

As Carrie Fisher reminds us, "Revenge is like drinking poison and expecting the other person to die." When you forgive someone, what you come to understand is that the gift is to you, not them. You have been drinking bile/poison, carrying around baggage, and forgetting to celebrate and magnify your own beauty and talents. That's the way to become the old, evil, hunchbacked crone in a Shakespeare tragedy.

If you want to fly, you have to lighten your load. Forgiveness is one way to jettison baggage you just don't need.

Anger becomes dis-ease becomes disease (if not dealt with); whereas love becomes beauty becomes endorphins becomes health.

Blame becomes "you owe me" becomes "people abuse me" becomes bitterness becomes dis-ease becomes disease, whereas gratitude becomes "thank you" becomes "together we can create the Golden Gate Bridge and Machu Picchu and the Taj Mahal and Trevi Fountain."

Today: I'm counting my blessings, including the blessing of anger.

Learning New Skills

So many of us have anger around money – what someone has done to us to take money, or a loan that was never repaid, or a bad hot tip or an investment that nearly bankrupted us. The solution is to take charge of our money.

Write down exactly how you are going to make sure you don't loan money to people who can't afford to pay it back (or consider it charity, instead of a loan if you do). Write down what *you need to do* to ensure that you adopt a solid financial strategy that ensures a rich life for you now and security going forward. How are you going to ensure that your assets are protected? How are you going to stop making everyone else rich – from the taxman, to the debt collector, to the insurance salesman and more – and start compounding gains at a 10% annualized return? What do you need to get there? More education? Different team members? A new CPA or CFP? A new brokerage?

Identify what you need and take action to make it real. As Benjamin Franklin wisely noted, "An investment in knowledge always pays the best interest."

Remember that the water of wisdom you drink is only as good as the well from which it is drawn. There are a lot of fly-by-night organizations with no track record (or a miserable past) offering you software and get-rich-quick schemes that are expensive to the investor and have no guaranteed rate of return. Grade your guru *before* you listen to anything they say – and before trusting that their Harvard MBA, or television show, or even their Nobel Prize have actually resulted in measurable gains. I can think of someone famous with each qualification, who has a miserable track record – costing investors far more than they have ever made them. Some have bankrupted quite a lot of folks – often repeatedly.

Revisit Your Happy Place

When you are imprisoned in resentment, you've forgotten how to laugh. It's not that the situation is funny. It isn't. It's just that laughter helps the healing and is part of what you need to *practice* in order to forgive.

Writing down the Adam experience helped me to see him as the comedy he truly was! Everything got corrected... The money was all resolved, almost immediately, once I got the general manager involved. The concert was far better than it would have been without Adam's downright comical insolence. There was no need to dwell on bitterness for Adam. He was fired because he did a lousy job – not because I was vengeful. And yes, knowing that he would not be able to treat others the way that he had treated me... That did feel good.

Mourning is very different from resentment. If you are mourning the loss of someone or something, then reflecting on the loss and experiencing the pain is an important part of the process of recovery. Once the grief stagnates into vengeance or bitterness, that is when it is time to examine whether our anger is righteous and we should take appropriate action. Or if we have made a mountain out of a molehill, and need to chill out, lighten up and laugh a little. Or if our bitterness is actually misplaced. When we have given our power to someone else and they have used that power poorly, then our focus should be on strengthening ourselves – not fixing, or correcting, or chastising the "offending" party.

Additional Resources

What is your favorite comedy? It can be a film, or a book, or a person. Don't just write about it. Experience it!

The ABCs of Money offers Easy-as-a-Pie-Chart Nest Egg Strategies™ for real estate, stocks, bonds, gold, hard assets and more. It is quite literally *The ABCs of Money* that we all should have received in high school. *Put Your Money Where Your Heart Is* outlines the systems I developed to earn (and retain) the ranking of No. 1 stock picker. Both can and should be part of your money toolkit and wisdom.

Day 5: Faith
Today's Mantra: Faith

This book is designed to make prosperity and abundance your daily habit. For most of us, day five is still uncomfortable, and we are far from feeling that we are living a rich life. You'll need to have *faith* that you are headed in the right direction, and that the path that I am illuminating in this book works, in order to have the resilience and dedication necessary to master these mantras. When I was learning to play classical piano, at the age of eight, I had to have faith that the scales and simple songs that my teacher was teaching me would mean that one day I could whip through a Mozart sonata. In the beginning, my plunking on the keys was far from musical.

Faith is different than blind faith. Faith means that you do your due diligence to find someone who is qualified to shine the light in the direction you want to travel. Blind faith is what you are employing when you are too busy to double-check a person's claims and track record, and instead rely upon someone else's recommendation. This could be a very vicious, costly cycle, particularly if that was how the person fell into their lap, too. According to FINRA. org, 70% of fraud victims in their study made an investment based primarily on advice from a relative or friend.

When it comes to money, you may not feel that you are qualified to grade the achievements of the "expert" in front of you. Or the money manager might carefully manipulate the results to look better than they really are, which is not very difficult to do. Or, as in the cases like Bernie Madoff, there may be real fraud involved.

So, how do you have confidence in your ability to evaluate whether or not the person in front of you is qualified?

How do you feel when I tell you that I started out as a copper miner's daughter, and, out of necessity, I learned about and developed a new approach to money that is enthusiastically recommended by a Nobel Prize winning economist? That I lived my way into the answers and strategies that I write about in my books? Does that feel true? If it doesn't, then the solution is easy. Do more fact checking. However, there are a few things that should help you to know that I'm being honest with you.

1. I'm teaching you to fish, instead of giving you a fish. When someone is telling you what you want to hear, or playing on your fears, then s/he is going to sell you a big, expensive fish at the end of the day. Sometimes that fish will be fresh and tasty, but not always.

2. *The Gratitude Game* is designed to empower you to do more for yourself. When someone says, "Let me do it for you," prepare to be oppressed (and to write a big check). When someone says, "Let me teach you how," prepare to fly. When they try to flatter, confuse you or demean you, have your guard up.

3. I make money easy to understand and to do. When someone makes things complicated, or uses language that you can't understand, that is to make you feel beneath them, so that you'll view her as the expert, even if everything is little more than a sophisticated sales tactic. Most of the people we think are experts are salesmen. The experienced money experts are rarely dealing one-on-one with Main Street investors.

4. I offer transparency. It's very easy to review my track record, and to access back issues to my ezine. Fraudsters talk fast, push you to make swift decisions before the opportunity disappears and rarely provide any supporting documents for their outlandish claims.

There are a lot of ruses and scams out there. Intuition is the marriage of wisdom and recall. It is complicated pattern recognition. If you have some experience, a number of files in your brain fly open to make a judgment of what kind of person is in front of you and what they want from you.

You cannot pick healthy fruit from a rotten root. Nor will the fruit be any good if the soil is leached. You can tell a lot about the person just by how they make you feel.

Do you feel empowered or ridiculed? Is the expert flattering you to sideswipe your questions? There are many people who claim to be experts, gurus and prophets, and they are really just interested in profits – their own, not yours. Any of the Seven Deadly Sins can motivate an unscrupulous person to convince you that they have the secret to something that you desire and need. She may be a very convincing salesman who plays on your emotions, or makes you feel inferior or dumb, or promises you the moon and the stars (or heaven) to gain control of you. Make sure that her track record, for more than eight years, is worthy of your faith. Pay attention if you don't trust her, if she's had trouble with a regulatory authority in the past, or if she looks or acts too flashy and fast.

So, today, focus keenly on faith – wisdom-based faith. Continue the underlying themes of forgiveness and gratitude. Breathe and love more deeply. Smile. The more you do these things, the more they will become second nature.

We have already talked about the elusive nature of forgiveness and gratitude. During the Fire Ritual, you discovered that when you feel negative emotions, the answer lies in the opposite direction.

When you are feeling hatred, do things that you love. Just stop thinking about that which you hate, and start doing something that you love. Remember that the bile in your mouth is harming you more than the person you are stewing over.

If you are catching a cold all of the time, the cure is to hyper-focus on health – to build up your immune system. We are all constantly exposed to viruses and bacteria. The question is whether or not your body is strong enough to reject the bugs.

If you are feeling fear, you have to find faith, and that is going to require wisdom. When you try to have faith in something that you fear, without educating yourself and feeling confident that you've chosen wisely, you are employing blind faith, which can be costly and sometimes even deadly.

A Good Plan Can Save Your Life

When you are in a life and death situation, your only chance at surviving is to employ a plan that is based upon best practices – and have faith in it. Fear will kill you. Your only chance at providing a great future for yourself and your family is to employ a great money plan. Blind faith and fear could cost you dearly.

I recently watched the film *Blackfish* about the orca whales in captivity that have killed humans. Yes, sadly, this type of death has occurred at least four times and has *almost* happened countless other times. One trainer was rescued by the quick, trained response of her spotter, without whom it is doubtful that she would have survived.

Another trainer, Ken Peters, saved himself by being prepared in advance and by staying calm under enormous pressure while he executed his life-saving plan. He was in great shape. He was an experienced scuba diver. When the orca whale yanked him by his ankle, rocketing down 30 feet to the bottom of the pool and held him there for over a minute – twice – instead of panicking and thrashing (which would have sparked more aggression in the whale), each time the whale resurfaced for air, he calmly patted and comforted her, while breathing steadily and deeply to recover himself. As a result, Ken Peters, thankfully, escaped death.

Investors who have been through the Dot Com Recession and the Great Recession may feel like their 401K is swimming with the sharks on Wall Street. However, in truth, there are a lot of great, well-run companies that are making products that we love. At the time of writing this book, Whole Foods Markets was still making gains on traditional food markets by offering local, organic food. Ross Stores was making fashion more affordable. Yes, there are a few killer whales in the mix, but you don't have to get in the water with them. That's the beauty of buying a fund, where you take ownership in a large number of companies, instead of individual stocks. It protects you from a crisis in any one individual company.

If you are drowning in credit card debt, or barely staying afloat financially, then chances are your budget is out of whack. It's easy to overspend in America. Once you get out on your own, you land a job (if you're lucky), find a place to live, buy a car to get to work, are forced to secure insurance and by the time you've paid for all of that, you realize that your life costs more than you are making. It takes courage and mindfulness to have a Thrive Budget plan for:

- Where you will live,
- How you will get to work,
- Your health, and
- Your future.

Once you limit your basic needs expenditures to fifty percent of your income, then you'll be able to compound gains, protect and build up assets, be more charitable and have more fun, while also reducing debt. You might think this is impossible, particularly since the cost of living – housing, gasoline and transportation – has risen dramatically, while incomes are only slightly higher than they were a couple of decades ago. But all kinds of things are possible. In his book *Giving*, Bill Clinton featured a laundress who saved up a quarter of a million dollars for charity by taking public transportation to work every day.

With creative thinking, most of us can spend less on housing, gasoline, cars, insurance, health insurance and health care. And all of us should be increasing our assets by contributing 10% of our income religiously to our tax-protected retirement plans (including health savings plans), and educating ourselves on how to compound gains at 10% annualized (which is the average return of stocks and bonds over a 30-year period).

Your ticket to freedom consists of not being chained to a home mortgage that is eating you out of house and home, or a car payment that prevents you from having the dough to actually go anywhere. If you are healthy and spending an arm and a leg on health insurance, then it's time to consider a higher deductible plan and a health savings account (which operates like another retirement account, where you can invest and compound the money for additional gains). The money will be there if you need it for a medical emergency, and in the meantime, instead of making the insurance company rich, you'll have thousands of dollars extra in your budget every year – and thousands in tax credits, too.

All of this helps you to thrive, but it also helps you to survive. As you increase your assets, you'll enjoy a better credit score, which means that the interest you pay will be lower. When your budget is in order, you won't have to take on debt to make ends meet. Cutting out café lattes or focusing solely on paying down debt doesn't work. That's debt consciousness. It doesn't get you any closer to prosperity and abundance than dancing on hot coals would put you to sleep.

For both budgeting and investing, faith and a good plan are more effective than blind faith in someone else to do these things for you. Most of the experts out there are getting paid on commission to sell us *more* than we need and can afford – from the car salesman, to the insurance salesman, to the real estate, stock and mortgage brokers. And none of them are teaming up to make sure that it all adds up for you right. In fact, if they do their job right, and earn more commission for themselves in the bargain, then you'll be overdrafted.

Don't be too hard on yourself if you had blind faith in the past. Most Americans were never properly educated on financial literacy. Only a generation ago, the company, or the government, promised to take care of us into retirement – to pay us a pension and cover all of our medical expenses. Many of the companies that made those legacy promises didn't keep them. Most companies in the airline and auto manufacturing industries have reduced their pension and other post-employment benefit liabilities by going through bankruptcy or buying out the pensions and OPEBs of their employees in one lump sum. Going forward, employees must manage their own 401Ks, and many of us have to fund our own health care.

We spend almost three trillion every year on medical costs. Why? One of the biggest contributing factors is that 1/3 of Americans are obese. That equates to $9,419 *per person* every year! Who can afford that? It is clear that a focus on health is the cure. If you are a healthy person who relies on natural cures, then a health savings account could be putting thousands in your pocket every year, instead of making the health insurance company richer. Here's another example where having blind faith in the status quo is costing you money that you could be using to take vacations. Have faith that learning all of the ways you can spend less, invest more, compound gains and stop making everybody else rich *work*.

As you start getting smart about money, and discussing it in a more intelligent way with your friends and colleagues, more qualified guides will show up to help you find your way. You will no longer be a target for scam artists. When you start doing the right thing, life becomes easier, even if it feels scary and unpredictable in the beginning.

Follow Your Heart and Listen to Your Gut Instincts

I am proof that an imperfect person, who spent a lot of her life scared to death, can use these mantras to become comfortable and adept at walking toward the right answer.

Magic shows up when your heart is pure, when you act in integrity, when you reject the easy way out and when you ask for help to do the right thing – even when it seems impossible to achieve. When we are honest with ourselves, most of the time when we employ blind faith, it is because we are looking for the easy way out, and actually acting *against* the alarms that we hear sounding in our gut.

I don't know of any better example of when I had to follow my heart, my inner knowing and have complete faith that everything would work out – even though it looked like a complete disaster – than when I was eighteen. After only two months at college, I found myself in the nurse's office facing a health issue that would force me to quit school.

When I was a child and through my teen years, I had lived through a lot of very challenging life events. Before I was five, my parents separated and my mother was diagnosed with terminal cancer. She died when I was seven. My sisters and brother lived in different foster homes than I did. By the time I was 18, I had lived in a different family environment and setting, with different foster parents and siblings, almost nonstop – changing on average every eighteen months.

As the baby of the family, the only time I'd been around children was once, at the age of twelve, when I tried to babysit for extra money. The mother warned me that her baby was "colicky," which was not a very apt characterization of her 6-month-old demon. This baby wailed and thrashed nonstop for the two solid hours and forty-five minutes that his mother was gone. (The mother showed up fifteen harrowing minutes late.)

There was nothing – not a bottle, not cuddling, not rocking, not changing his diaper, not singing – that could stop the screaming. When I put him down, he smashed his own skull against the side of his crib. When I tried to feed him, or change him, or rock, sing and cradle him, he arched his back, kicked and boxed at me, as if daring me to drop him.

The child was hell-bent on hating me and bursting my ear-drums. (Looking back I'm still astonished at the tenacity of that child's screaming.) Everyone has a breaking point, particularly when you have no skills or tools to help you stop something that has hotwired your dormant lizard brain. Instead of rocking the child and comforting him, you want to shake some sense into him. Nursery rhymes become screeds of "Stop it! Stop it!" Only a lizard brain would think that screaming and shaking a child would convince a baby to stop crying. I had enough sense to know this, but I did not have the wisdom, the training or the mentors to figure out a better strategy. The parents of that particular year wouldn't have been of any help.

The immediate goal was to get through the next two and a half hours *safely*. If I couldn't comfort the baby and make him happy enough to stop crying, then at least I had to protect him.

I laid him back in his crib. This seemed to be the safest choice, and had been the instruction the mother had given me to do, if I found myself in the position when nothing was working. I walked into the living room, collapsed onto the footstool, put my head in my hands and covered my ears. The thrashing and screeching continued, though slightly muted behind the closed door. I turned the television on high volume – a sitcom. The laugh tracks didn't drown out the screams either. Every few minutes, I peeked through the door to make sure he hadn't jammed his head through the rails of the crib and to see if maybe he'd had a change of heart. Each time I did, he screamed even louder. He wanted his mother, and that was it.

When the mother finally returned, I was pretty sure that I should give up the idea of ever having children. I was simply not fit to be a mother. I was a Scorpion through and through – rotten to the core – just like one of my foster parents had been kind enough to inform me. Hurt me even just a little bit, and I *kill* you. Scream for too long, and I'll shake you to death. (This particular guardian was always quite happy to tell me that I would never amount to anything, which I'd begun to believe.)

The mother didn't seem the least bit phased when I told her that her baby had wailed nonstop the entire time she was gone. She actually seemed a little pleased that he had missed her that much. She told me that is what colicky babies do, and that I'd get used to it. She asked me if I'd babysit again the following Wednesday night so that she could go bowling again. I said, "Sure," politely, and then had my stepmother call and cancel the following day.

I never took another babysitting job again. Ever.

Imagine my terror when only six years later, at the age of eighteen, I found myself pregnant. Not only was I petrified of how I might ruin a child, if I somehow managed to keep it alive, I was pretty sure that my 21-year-old husband had no hope of doing much better.

I was very young when I met my husband – only 16. I was an emancipated minor, living with my older sister and her four-year-old son. I went to high school for four hours each morning and then worked eight hours each night to support myself (receiving high school credit for working). I considered myself mature and grown-up, though in truth I was just overworked, with a heart that had been crushed when my mother died, and a series of shocks thereafter. I was working so hard that, thankfully, there wasn't a spare moment to think about anything, until *he* walked into the restaurant where I worked.

Loving my husband was like diving into the Caribbean Sea – warm and beautiful and healing, and as close to heaven as I'd ever been. I'd never experienced anything like him ever before. I opened up my heart completely. Getting married to the man of my dreams seemed like the right thing to do, as my family was religious and would be more approving of us living together if there was a ring involved. The love was authentic and pure. But the real world pounced upon us almost immediately, with a harsh lesson on how love and commitment, without a foundation of respect, resources and boundaries, are not enough.

He was a kind-hearted young man with good intentions, who was constantly high (on pot) and ran around with local, small-time drug dealers, who were always convincing him to "invest" my money in their latest get-rich-quick scheme. Unfortunately, I'd already seen those dreams get snorted up their noses on more than one occasion. I'd lost a car, my insurance policy (because of my husband's driving record), and a small inheritance from my deceased mother's estate with nothing more than a few giggles and shrugs from my husband and his band of fools to show for it. Once my promise to love, honor and cherish my husband starting stripping me of all of my worldly possessions, the marriage began losing its appeal. I enrolled in college and decided to leave my husband as soon as I could get my finances together. Within two months, I found myself in the nurse's office, vomiting up my guts, with a diagnosis that I was having a baby.

And here is where the faith kicked in. I had no job, no car, no medical insurance, no income and no home (unless I stayed with my husband). I was going to have to quit college in order to work to support myself through my pregnancy. Everyone warned me that no one would hire a pregnant teen. In other words, I was in an impossible situation and was doomed to fail. However, the love that I had for the unborn child that I was carrying fueled my determination to make it work. Being around someone who smoked cigarettes and pot nonstop, where I would have a constant knot in my stomach wondering what more his loser friends could take from me, was a bad idea. I wanted to raise a healthy baby in the womb, and that required good food, clean air, joy and happy thoughts.

I floundered for a few weeks, living with friends, and then finally landed a job at a cleaning service. The first job I went on was to clean the home of an oil heiress in the expensive section of town. She hired me on the spot as live-in help for her middle-school girl, even though I was pretty lousy at cleaning (though doing my best to learn quickly). Instantly, I had healthy meals and a pool to swim in. There was even a grand piano in the sitting room, which I could play for an hour each day when the house was empty. The family loved hearing me play classical music after dinner and thought that it was quite novel that their "help" was a bit Renaissance. (I had studied classical piano as a child; the following year I would be accepted back into college as a classical performance major.) What a blessing – not just for me, but for my baby, who would be nourished from a *very* healthy and happy birth mother. It was the first time I'd ever felt warm and safe at home, anywhere.

The adoption process was another leap of faith. There was a couple lined up to adopt the baby. My divorce attorney had found them through a friend. They seemed overjoyed at the thought of becoming parents to my child. I had no real way of determining what good parents looked or sounded or felt like, so I was relying on prayer and divine intervention in the matter. However, in my gut, I really didn't believe that this couple was going to stay together and provide a loving home. I had nothing to base this on and had no clue of how to find someone better. So, I prayed like a nun, constantly and fervently, that my baby would be placed in a loving home, where the parents knew how to be kind and supportive and had the means to send my child to college.

Everything was going great. My prenatal visits were being paid for by the adoptive family. The baby was healthy. There was only one point of contention. I'd read a number of books on giving birth, and every book reinforced one very key finding. There are valuable antibodies in a mother's breast milk that are transferred to the baby in the first three days after the birth.

About a week before my due date, I told the attorney who was handling the adoption that I wanted to take the baby home for three days to nurse her, and that after those three days, I would happily give her over to the adoptive parents. The couple refused those terms, telling me that if I did not surrender my child at the moment of birth, they would not pay for the medical bills and they would not adopt the baby. The attorney threatened to send me his bills, too, if I screwed up the adoption by insisting on taking the baby home. Further, they would force me to reimburse the family for the prenatal visits they had already paid for.

Here again, I was being forced to choose between matters of money and comfort (what fear would choose), and what I believed was the right answer – my baby's health (what faith would choose). I didn't know how things would work out, how I would pay for the prenatal visits or where I would ultimately deliver the baby. I only knew that I wasn't going to give her away at the moment of birth. I knew that denying a newborn something you know can promote lifelong health was the wrong answer. I couldn't bear the thought of never holding my baby, or of never letting my ex-husband hold her. (He and I were too young to be parents, but I loved him.) While I was deliberating, and leaning toward breastfeeding for those vital three days, the couple found another baby and adopted that baby instead of mine. I don't know how that family turned out (and I wish them all the love and peace in the world), but in my heart I have faith that that was a blessing for my daughter.

My ex-husband and I spent three lovely days with our newborn, in one of the most luxurious homes in the area. (Thank you so much, Sara). I breast-fed my daughter. I sang to my daughter, as she lay sleeping across my lap. She was so easy that I almost thought I could school myself quickly on the fine art of parenting and raise her. But I wanted so much more for her than an unemployed teen mother could offer (particularly one with no skill set for mothering). And I saw no possible way – even with all of the miracles I had just witnessed over the past few months – that I could provide a healthy, loving home and family and a springboard to a better tomorrow for her.

On the fourth day, we took our daughter to the adoption agency, with a few personal affects and notes to the adoptive parents on how much we loved our daughter and to please make sure that she knew that. We just wanted her to have a better home than either of us could provide.

Today, my daughter is the mother of her own children with three adopted siblings. She lived in a foreign country for a while during elementary school. She has a college degree. Her husband is very creative and loving. She has received everything that I wanted for her. *What a blessing.*

My role was very small. Her life wasn't perfect. But I am confident that it was much better than what her life would have been like with me.

Faith was the pathway to everything during that important time. I had to make the highest choice – even when it seemed impossible to realize – and have faith that leaning into the right answer was going to call in the miracles that were so desperately needed.

How many times are we making decisions that we know are wrong, and asking God to correct things for us? How often do we hang onto the *comfortable* choice, rather than employing the right answer? Having "faith" that everything will work out in the end, even though you *know* that what you are *doing* is fundamentally *wrong* is like hoping that the bus you just boarded for Boise will actually fly you to the Caribbean.

I had to make the right choices for someone who had no voice in the matter. Every time that I stepped forward into the fog, cold and shivering, it was a leap of faith. Just a few steps ahead, on the other side of the storm, there was a world beyond my wildest dreams. Miracles have a hard time squeezing themselves down the chimney into your living room. But when you venture out, with eyes, ears and heart wide open, with a mission greater than your own comfort, magic happens.

That is why it's a good idea to think of your "money" and your investments as your *estate* – something that you create and preserve for your children, and something that you can give back to humanity. Having that kind of commitment will be a great foundation for you to get the wisdom you will need to be the steward of your own future and legacy. There is a higher good and a responsibility that comes along with wealth that you will never understand if you are just concerned with status symbols and accumulating things.

Daily Task & Action Plan:

1. **Complete your charitable giving task today.** Remember that part of your "job" is to live in the overflow and to have the mindset that you have more than enough to give. If you have selected someone you love or a charity that is close to your heart, this shouldn't be too difficult. You'll find yourself immersed in helping, and probably smiling as you do. No thinking will be required. You might just be the miracle that shows up to someone's prayer.

2. **Journal.** If you haven't already started a new journal as part of this process, then do this now. Think about the five mantras that we've already discussed and about your charitable act. Write down today's date. Then write anything you desire for at least 30 minutes. Was there anything that being charitable gave to you that you least expected? Write it down.

Learning New Skills

Brainstorm. Start the creative process of brainstorming on how you are going to cut back on basic needs, so that you are spending 50% to survive and having 10% for your retirement plans, 10% for charity, 10% for education (whether it is paying off student loan debt of your own or contributing to your child's college fund) and 20% for fun.

Additional Resources

The Law of Success. By Paramahansa Yogananda

Day 6: Wisdom
Today's Mantra: Wisdom

Some people work hard, while others work smart. What's the difference? Wisdom.

When I first started playing the piano, I spent a lot of time plunking the scales and flimflamming every time my baby finger slipped off of a key because it wasn't strong enough to strike the ivory and produce a tone. I worked long and hard, but the result – for years – wasn't anything anyone wanted to listen to. Not even me. It was excruciating!

The same thing happened when I first starting dancing tango. Like all dancers in the early stages, I stepped on a lot of toes. In order to get up to speed, I took lessons from some great dancers, both male and female, who worked with me to point my toes right, and showed me the difference between a *molinete* and a *gancho.*

One has to practice piano endlessly before it sounds good. Tango poses are perfected to the nth degree before they flow seemingly effortlessly. Time spent has nothing to do with the quality of the outcome. Wisdom does. I've seen dancers and pianists who never get any good, despite years of practice, because they don't make an effort to learn good technique, under the guidance of a mentor. They just wing it.

How do you attain wisdom? Wisdom is knowledge and skills applied, learned and adapted, over time. If you try to do something without first learning the best practices associated with whatever you are attempting to do, then you are destined to work longer hours, to have a more difficult journey and to achieve inferior results. There are a few outlier visionaries who can see into the celestial wisdom and understand the complex coding that eludes most mortals – but they spend countless hours peering into the great unknown before the truth is revealed.

So, why is it that we expect ourselves to strike it rich in stocks, real estate or gold on our first attempt? Is it because the person on the other side of the table is luring us into believing this? Are they Thomas Edison or just a commission-based salesman? Hmmm. Did you ever hear the tale of the fox and the crow – how the fox convinced the crow to sing because her voice was so beautiful, when all the fox really wanted was the cheese that the crow had in her mouth? As long as the person on the other side of the table stands to win if you invest or buy, it pays to have this fable playing on the silver screen of your mind. That doesn't mean that every broker is a fox. But it's best not to assume the best about the genius, or the education, or the ethics of anyone in this world, and particularly those who are trying to sell you something. After running into financial hard times, Kareem Abdul Jabbar, the legendary basketball star, admitted, "I chose my financial manager, who I later discovered had no financial training, because others were using him."

When it comes to money, why do we trust someone without seeing how well she dances? You wouldn't want to learn tango from someone with two left feet, or from someone who wasn't willing to step on the dance floor and show you a few moves. Yet so many people are letting people manage their money – assuming they are masters – when they can't dance on Wall Street!

How do you check out the dance moves of your potential money manager? It's not that hard to see really, if you ask for a demonstration of their abilities over the past eight years, alongside a chart of what the Dow Jones Industrial Average Index and the NASDAQ Composite Index have done. It should be clear enough whether they are riding on the Wall Street rollercoaster, performing at double the speed (as NASDAQ has been doing on the Dow since 2009), or riding under the radar and charging their clients for losing their money.

So, when you think about today's mantra, wisdom, think about Edison, about Plato, about Rosalind Franklin (who first photographed the DNA helix), about Sandra Day O'Connor (the first female U.S. Supreme Court Justice) and any other person who embodies the discipline of wisdom. Remember your personal board of advisors from Day One. Great comedians, musicians and actors devote a lot of time to their craft as well.

Committing to the 21-day program of this book is – at its core – a commitment to replacing naivety, fear, silliness and bad advice with wisdom, best practices and confidence. Over the past five days, you've already started to learn a lot. I hope you're still smiling at strangers and gaining insight into how that small, simple act is fueling you with more positive energy.

By breathing more consciously, you should be realizing just how valuable stress-reduction strategies and health are.

Have you started to feel the sensations of gratitude and forgiveness? Once you take charge of your life and the outcomes of your choices, then you can release the judgments that you have of others, and of yourself. Whatever happened in the past, you were making choices with the tools and information that you had at hand. You are getting better at both going forward, using time-proven tools that simply work better. Release. Even if you can't "forgive" yet, focus on learning and doing better going forward. Let learning seed your thoughts, rather than regret. In this new parkland of your mind, where you are growing fruitful plants and trees that oxygenate and offer shade, the past is the manure that can provide nutrition for the soil. It is hazardous to consume but does have an important role to play.

You were a part of the dance of whatever brought you to this moment – through certain moments that you love and others that you are embarrassed about. You're learning to choose better partners and to dance better yourself so that you won't fall victim in the future. If the person who harmed you is continuing to harm others, then you should report him/her to the authorities. That is an action. It doesn't require hours and hours of mind banter. As Salman Rushdie once said, "When thought becomes excessively painful, action is the finest remedy."

Embracing Wisdom Means Shutting Out the Noise

There is a constant barrage of blather and propaganda, mixed in with usable information and data, everywhere you go – in the "news," in ads, in the films and television shows that we watch, and then parroted in the public. Wisdom thinks, "Is this helpful and useful? Am I being entertained, educated or fooled? Should I be drinking my wisdom from a cleaner well?" There is a running joke that the way to make a million by watching the popular financial news channels is to start with one hundred million.

Make today a media-free day. Read a classic book from a wise author, whether it is Shakespeare, Homer, *The Bible, The Tae Te Ching, The Autobiography of a Yogi,* Toni Morrison, a spiritual leader or even *Man on a Wire.*

Sometimes the noise is your own mind's sewage. Wisdom is not known for barreling through the wall of your own ignorance. It is a quiet visitor who must be beckoned in. That's why meditation is so important.

Sometimes when we are trying to get out of a hole, we don't realize that we are digging in deeper. If your car is stuck in the mud and you gas it to try and get out, you only dig a deeper hole. If you put a rock or a piece of wood beneath the tire in the direction that you want to go, then you get the traction you need to exit. Action without wisdom is perilous; wisdom without action is glacial.

Money is key to our comfort and our future. And yet every day I meet someone who says, "I have someone who does that for me." That is fine if you know what you own, and what your annual rate of return is, and have confidence in the long-term viability of the financial plan. However, that is rarely the case. People are so busy trying to make ends meet, trying to get a raise and a promotion, and trying to place their kids in the best neighborhoods, schools and soccer teams, that they overlook the easiest ticket to all of that – which is to have a solid financial foundation. Wisdom means making sure that your financial team is held accountable and doing a good job.

If *you* don't incorporate a smart budget and investment strategy, then you are just making the taxman, the debt collector, the insurance (and car) salesman and countless brokers rich. When you do incorporate best money practices, then your tax-protected retirement accounts could be worth more than you earn within seven years and make more than you do within 25 years. Your education fund will be worth far more than your kids will need to attend college. This is based upon depositing 10% of your income and earning an average annualized gain of 10%, which is what stocks and bonds have earned over the last 30 years. This is not rocket science. And, by the way, I dislike the name *retirement accounts* because they provide enormous benefit to you and your family *right here and now* – from tax credits, to untaxed passive income, to better credit scores and more capital – for emergencies and investments.

Now that Americans have to provide for their own future, wisdom is imperative. Getting the wisdom and the systems now, so that is the foundation of life is so very empowering. The earlier you start, the higher you will fly. Sadly, far too many people wait to deal with this stuff until it is forced upon them. When you are overwhelmed with tragedy or loss – divorce, death, natural disaster, depression, job loss, early retirement – it is difficult, and costly, to make sound money decisions. When you set everything up in advance, you can avoid a lot of unnecessary lawsuits, bickering, penalties, probate and taxes.

Yes, money is a very private topic, and it is hard to know whom to trust. Famous athletes find themselves bankrupt; devotees of James Arthur Ray passed away. Make sure that your shaman is not a salesman – or worse, a shyster. So, we often draw wisdom from the wrong, unqualified, source. Make sure that the well you drink your wisdom from is not polluted.

Every one of us needs to be financially literate, and to know and understand the basics of:

- The average returns of real estate, stocks, bonds and gold
- Solid investing strategies based upon Modern Portfolio Theory
- Thriving in a Debt World where the cost of living has increased dramatically, while income growth has stalled

- Gift Tax, and how and when to start willing our estate
- Marriage and companion laws in our state
- Health Savings Accounts and high deductible health insurance
- Capital gains taxes, both short term and long term
- All of the tax-protected accounts that you might qualify for
- College funds for our kids

This might sound overwhelming. However, it is more important to learn these budgeting and investing basics than it is to calculate how fast a train can travel between Boise and Chicago. And it is imperative that you learn them from qualified, independent, uninterested sources. Are you getting your budgeting plan from the debt collector?

The easier that your strategy for your 401K and IRAs is, the better. When your plan is so complicated that you have to read through pages and pages of holdings, and you still don't have a clue what you own or how well it is performing, then your plan is working against you. How can you arrive at a destination if you can't even read the map and don't have a clue how much closer you are to arriving at it? This is a red flag that whoever is driving your car is not on the road to financial freedom.

When someone tries to complicate something to the point that you have to have blind faith in their capabilities, step out of the car. That means that they are not being held accountable, which is a ticket to drive as recklessly as they desire with your money. If they know you are expecting results and demand a good strategy to achieve those results or they will be hitting the road, they will have a great plan and provide you with regular reports... or else. If your accounts are increasing in value, your money managers will be willing and eager to show you the great gains and how well their system is working. They will answer your questions in plain, simple language that you can understand because they want you to know just how valuable they are. When there are a lot of words you don't understand, and pages and pages and pages of holdings, and dust and confusion flying in the air, the more likely there is something to hide.

Ways to Grade Your Money Manager
1. Check out the **BrokerCheck** on Finra.org.
2. **Google** the name of your financial professional with the phrases "SEC complaint" or "FINRA complaint" or "FTC law suit." I often get someone asking me about a claim made about this or that guru, and more often than not a simple, targeted search reveals just how dismal that person's track record is and how many lawsuits have been filed by disgruntled investors in the past. Over and again, the story repeats itself: the information was misleading, investors lost millions and the expert lined their own pockets with gold.
3. **References.** Even when someone is on a stage or on television, you need to know her track record before you listen to, believe or buy anything. I've personally known bestselling authors who take 50% or more of the sales of anything sold on their stage – without properly vetting the businesses. Their fans buy because they believe the opposite, that this beloved sage would only present reputable, time-proven and exclusive opportunities – which is, simply, not the case.
4. **There are 12 Questions** you should ask your money manager before hiring her in the chapter "Brokers Are Salesmen, Not Surgeons" from *Put Your Money Where Your Heart Is.* Also read "Grade Your Guru" from *The ABCs of Money.*

When I was writing *The ABCs of Money,* I ran across a bestselling, gloom and doom author who was always on the wrong side of the markets. Right before the Dot Com Recession, he had predicted that the Dow was going to hit 40,000 in the Roaring 2000s. Another theory, that the euro was going to replace the dollar as the world's global currency, was published in 2009, right before the PIIGS crisis in Europe. When Portugal, Italy, Ireland, Spain and Greece hit hard times, it became questionable whether the European Union could even stick together. Both recommendations would have cost you a fortune, and yet these authors are still out there selling books and newsletters, without anyone knowing any better or bothering to check just how poorly their past predictions have gone.

FYI: the dollar has lost global reserve currency status. However, it has been replaced by "unallocated reserves," not the euro. I reported about this in my ezine (in the March 2014 issue). Meanwhile, as I finished this book, the S&P500 was hitting another all-time high.

An expert will have outstanding *results* over the last decade, not just a lot of book sales or a television show.

Be careful confusing power or popularity with wisdom. Fools, crooks and megalomaniacs can rule for a time. Bernie Madoff was the president of NASDAQ. Enron won Fortune's Most Innovative Company six years in a row. The last time was only a few months before the company declared bankruptcy. The Nobel Prize winning economist who wrote the book on options had one of the biggest bailouts in U.S. history when his hedge fund went belly up.

Be careful confusing a bull market with wisdom. After the Great Recession, NASDAQ earned 38% annualized for five years in a row. Money managers were boasting of 20% gains, without anyone knowing that they were performing below the NASDAQ – at almost half the speed. If their clients lost half or more during the Great Recession, they weren't back to even yet.

Don't confuse advertising for wisdom. A brokerage might advertise that its options trading software has 88% accuracy, without ever telling you that only 2% of its options trading clients actually make money. Or a company might advertise increased sales without ever telling you that they owe over $100 billion dollars and are teetering on the edge of solvency, as General Motors did before its bankruptcy.

I'm sure at this point, you're just exhausted over the proposition of finding a reputable, wise and trustworthy financial mentor. However, I've just listed all of the complicated strategies that are *not wise*. Just like multiplication is easier once you learn addition, budgeting and investing are easier once you get *The ABCs of Money* that we all should have received in high school. Once you know what smart budgeting and investing look like, it will be far easier to identify your dream come true financial partners – including a great accountant and the brokers you deal with to purchase your home, stocks, bonds and other assets. With search engines, doing your due diligence on your financial partners can be lightning fast, particularly when you know what you are looking for.

Rather than trusting a name, or a title, or having blind faith for any reason at all, trust only results. You want everyone on your team to have a PhD in *results.*

Take ownership of your money house. That doesn't mean that you have to hammer every nail as it is being built. But if you don't know how many square feet, how many bedrooms and bathrooms, and you just turn it over to the contractor to build whatever she wants, then you're going to end up with a lot more than you can afford. The bills might even bankrupt you, just as bad investment strategies have bankrupted so many Americans over the last two recessions.

Anyone who says, "Trust me," instead of providing reports and explaining the performance in plain language, is suspect. People that have something to hide, hide. People who don't, don't.

When you have blind faith in a guru who loses your money, then you're going to feel like they owe you something. And you've just added another person to the list of people that you are angry with and can't forgive. But you are ignoring your role in the equation. That wouldn't have occurred if you hadn't hired her and given her permission to act. When you take charge and hold people accountable, then you have better results. In one of your regular checkups, if the strategy isn't working, you have ample time to protect yourself and improve the plan. When you incorporate wisdom-based faith, you have fewer people to forgive because you are working with a team of professionals. You have wisdom on your side. It also makes it easier to be grateful because your results are going to be better.

Before you learn *The ABCs of Money,* you might think that budgeting, taxes and investing are complicated and snooze-worthy. After, you realize how simple and empowering financial wisdom is. Being in charge is simple, fun and easy when you follow good strategies.

And it saves a lot of time, aggravation and disagreements. Wisdom means better results with less time and money. Have you ever noticed just how many fights you get into are over money, or how much sleep you lose? Wisdom replaces the heated debate with time-proven systems, and lets you rest well at night.

Keep forgiving those who harmed you in the past and counting your blessings today and going forward. Freeing yourself up from the burdens of the past is going to give you a lot more energy for future endeavors that could pay you handsomely! This rewards you monetarily, but also spiritually, physically and more. You'll enjoy life so much more. Everything will be more fun – in addition to having more money for fun! As Lao Tzu wrote centuries ago, "When I let go of what I am, I become what I might be."

Creators are not stewing in resentment and hatred. They are swimming in pools of possibility, in the direction of opportunity, rewards and fulfillment.

Daily Task & Action Plan:
1. Turn off the television, the news, films, all forms of media for one day. Turn on time-proven wisdom in classic books.
2. Grade your gurus.
3. Draw a pie chart of your investments. Understand what you own and why. Check into the wisdom of the strategy.
4. Write down 30 insights that you have gained over the last six days – five for each mantra.

Learning New Skills

For Easy-as-a-Pie-Chart budgeting and investing strategies, read my book *The ABCs of Money*. Learn the time-proven strategies that I used to earn and retain my results as a number one stock picker in the book *Put Your Money Where Your Heart Is*.

Additional Resources

FINRA.org, SEC.gov, IRS.gov, FTC.gov. These government and regulatory agencies offer a treasure trove of information on investing, on bank and insurance products, on financial professionals, on tax strategies and more. They also have good search tools on the sites, making it easy to locate exactly what you are looking for.

Day 7: Create
Today's Mantra: Create

As you walk today and in the days ahead, think about traversing unfamiliar territory. When you are learning new things, it is beneficial to have different visual and auditory stimulation – out of your normal routine – as much as possible. In an ideal world, you would be doing this 21-day reprogramming in a foreign land, where you are inspired around every turn with another wondrous site and everyone speaks a language you don't understand. The miraculous thing about this kind of immersion into new prosperity possibilities is that your brain is enticed into thinking thoughts that would never surface in the submersion of the familiar.

If you are rolling your eyes at this idea, then you are illustrating exactly what I'm talking about. You are too stuck in *what is* to imagine what *might be.* In the first case, you don't create anything at all. You just stay stuck where you are. When you can start seeing new possibilities, then you can start creating them. Columbus sailed off the end of the world to discover America. The world in his time was flat – not round. Have you ever gazed up at the moon and the stars, and wondered how to make your flat world more round and divinely inspired? How would you live if you had all of the money in the world?

When you visualize something, and when you have a plan to create it, and that plan is based in wisdom, and you are diligent about acting to implement that plan, then you can create what you desire. Paramahansa Yogananda writes, "Faith in God can produce any miracle except one – passing an examination without study." Daily life is one big exam that most of us are trying to pass by just guessing at the right answers. If, despite your prayers and mindful meditation, you are still consumed in fear, worry and doubt when it comes to money and your future – it is because you haven't yet figured out how to *create* what you want. (You are, unfortunately, creating what you don't want.) Be careful about trying to figure things out without study into best practices, and with only visualization and affirmations because, without a solid plan, it will be tempting to default back into worrying about what you *don't* want to happen. Even if you are chanting affirmations regularly – the fear is what manifests because it is all that you can really *see*.

Your world is made up of "what you see" and what you cannot "see." If all you see is fear, then you will create what you fear – even though you would rather create the opposite of that. If what you see is opportunity, then you will seize opportunities and create that which you envision. So, when you fear something, think of the opposite and focus on creating what you desire, rather than dwelling on what you fear.

When you are frozen in fear, you can never take a step forward. That is the purpose of this 21-day walk to wealth program. You are replacing all of the negatives in your life with the solutions. When you see a problem, don't stew in the problem. Envision a better reality. When you fear something, chances are because you know that you are headed in that direction. Don't drive off the cliff. Correct the course of your action.

If you think of it in terms of sports, it is much easier to get this... Kobe Bryant is hyper-field goal focused. If you see a photo of him going up for a shot, all he "sees" is the basket – not the five guys trying to take him out.

As you study and practice, then your results can become masterful. As Kobe is going up for a basket, his eye is on the basket. He knows that there will be three or four opponents every step of the way, trying to prevent him from scoring. His job is to fend them off, without ever taking his mind off the goal.

Once you get focused on what you really want to create, and you are sure you have a good strategy for creating it, you will be able to have your focus on the ball and on the goal. Rather than being waylaid by the obstacles, you'll charge past the barriers and achieve your success. There will be plenty of real obstacles, including those phantoms of your mind – worry, fear and doubt. The creator anticipates roadblocks and course-corrects, rather than stopping and declaring defeat.

Think of create, create, create all throughout the day today, with the visual of Kobe, or another successful athlete, inspiring you to remember the study, the practice, the routine, the discipline, the physique, the stamina, the resolve, the mindset and the skillset of a winner. Kobe's commitment to his craft is legendary. If becoming the Kobe Bryant of investing sounds too exhausting to you, relax. Nest egg investing is more like building a house. There is work in the beginning to get it done right. If you do that work right, then you have a great home where you will live comfortably for the rest of your life.

Once your money house is set up right, all you need to do is to rebalance once or twice a year. That's like a walk-through. If you see a leak in the plumbing or a hole in your roof, it's better to address it soon, rather than waiting for the damage to spread. If the trees outside are filled with fruit, then harvest!

Think for a moment about the greatest things that have been created on the planet. The founders of the United States of America created a meritocracy at a time when monarchies – birthright – were the norm. Think of our civil rights leaders and the Suffragette Movement who secured equal rights to people of all color and gender. Our ancestors fought long and hard to give us financial freedom. It actually takes less time, heartache and money for us to exercise our rights to financial freedom than most of us are currently spending. Most nest eggs have been riding the Wall Street rollercoaster, promoting nausea, hazards and losses – bank bailouts, real estate bubbles and pervasive cynicism. If you let these emotions control your decision-making, you'll be on the losing side of the equation. Creators are visionaries who problem-solve until they manifest their dreams. They don't let stomach acid drive their daily routine.

We are creating things with every choice we make, whether we are mindful of this or not, even when we think that we are victims without a voice who are not making any choices at all. As adults, we are creators of our life (and our community and our world) – even if the life we enjoy (or not) has come about haphazardly because we *weren't thinking* about how all of the pieces work together to empower or enslave us.

In fact, the less you think about your financial life plan, the more likely that you are making everyone else rich at your own expense. By now, you've heard that Warren Buffett pays a lower tax rate than his secretary. You can dramatically reduce your taxes – easily – here and now. Your debt, too. We are bombarded in the media to buy buy buy, without any message on how to budget budget budget so that we don't fall into an imprisoning cycle of compounding debt, which makes credit card companies and banks rich.

Many of us would just be happy if we could take a great vacation once a year and get to the end of the month without running out of money. And that is entirely doable, though probably not with the current plan. Even super rich people have to get smart about their money. Otherwise, they'll end up giving *Uncle Sam 40% of their income and their estate upon death.*

That's not what usually happens, because rich people care about their money and spend time learning how to protect and grow their wealth. Warren Buffett and Mitt Romney both pay closer to 15% in income taxes. Royals have their estate plan in place from the moment their children are born, and transfer the wealth to their heirs steadily and annually, under the gift tax rate, so that the ownership is complete before they die. Families who keep their wealth over the centuries do so with a strategic plan. It is not happenstance, or an afterthought. In England, despite a 50% income tax rate, there are families who have willed their estates to their heirs for centuries.

If billionaires can pay 15% in taxes, so can you. You can create a life that is much easier and far more rewarding to you personally. These are the things that money *can buy.*

I'm going to give you an example of someone who created a different life for himself – against pretty steep odds.

Joe Moglia, the executive chairman of TD AMERITRADE, talks about growing up in gangs as a kid, and helping his father sell vegetables and fruit to make ends meet. In an interview with me from March of 2014 (which is published in the NataliePace.com ezine, volume 11, issue 3), Joe revealed that two of his high school buddies died. Joe survived because, instead of being out carousing with them, taking drugs and robbing liquor stores, he played high school football.

Joe went on to become a successful defensive coordinator at Dartmouth College. This job was very fulfilling to him. However, after a divorce, and with four kids to raise and two households to support, the football career wasn't paying enough to make ends meet – even though Joe was sleeping in a frigid storage loft above his office. So, he made a tough choice to regroup and find a different career. He entered the Institutional MBA Program at Merrill Lynch – along with 25 others who already had MBAs.

Joe discovered that he had quite a mindset and natural skill set for finance. He went on to become the CEO of TD AMERITRADE, where he took the company from a market value of $700 million to $10 billion. At age 65, Joe remains the executive chairman of TD AMERITRADE (as of July of 2014), but you won't believe what he's doing now. He's head coach of the Coastal Carolina Chanticleers football team. In 2012, he won Conference Coach of the Year, and in both 2012 and 2013, Joe was a finalist for National Coach of the Year.

Why did he go back to coaching after creating enough wealth that he could provide for his family and also do anything that he wants? According to Joe, "Having an impact on an 18- to 22-year-old boy's life, helping the boy become a man, it's tough to find another field of endeavor that gives you greater satisfaction than that."

Education and football were Joe's keys to surviving and thriving. He has reinvented himself many times, and now guides his players to higher personal achievements through his Be a Man Program.

This has nothing to do with gender, according to Joe. "We coach our players to stand on their own two feet and accept accountability for their actions," Joe says. In other words, Joe teaches his players how to *create* a winning life for themselves and a winning team for their community.

There are many ways that you can create a different situation than the one that you are in. Don't worry about knowing all of the right answers yet. One of the first steps is to stop acting like a victim, thinking that everyone else – the bank, the employer, the government – are all screwing you. There are a lot of ways that all Americans can get into trouble if they let others drive their life. So I'm not saying that bankers, CEOs and politicians are saints. The solution is to take the wheel and drive where you want to go.

You might be being taken advantage of. I'm not saying to ignore that. I'm actually telling you that if that's the case, then step up (man up), confront the situation, brainstorm on the best solution and fix things. (My book *The ABCs of Money* has a lot of ink devoted to learning how to extricate yourself from debt, from an underwater mortgage, and from overspending on everything from cars to gasoline and electricity.) If our forefathers could toss tea into the Boston Harbor to make a stand for freedom, imagine what you are capable of doing to right the wrongs in your life and in our world. Find a way to *create* what it is that you really desire. When you think, "Someone owes me this," flip that thinking into, "This is something that I want to create for myself," and "This is something I'm going to do to make my world – our world – a better place."

When you see a problem, envision and enact the solution.

Every time that you feel like you are getting the raw end of the deal from someone, go back to the mantra "create." BAM! Be a Man. As Joe Moglia says, "Stand on your own two feet and take responsibility for your actions."

If this makes you angry, acknowledge that. Write briefly in your journal about these emotions. (Time this, and limit your screed to five minutes. Today's mantra is create. Not complain.)

Creating Holistic Fiscal/Physical Health

When we think of creating good health, anyone who eats right, exercises, drinks moderately and never smokes is already on the path. True holistic health goes beyond this, however, and includes – not just *stress reduction,* but also – a less stressful life *at its core.*

Most stress reduction professionals, including the Center for Disease Control, focus on how to calm yourself down when you get too amped up. Hanging out with friends, consulting with a doctor, staying active, meditation, yoga – these are all important ways to make yourself feel better. However, they don't address the root cause of why you got so worked up in the first place. When the irritant remains in place, these time-proven tools are like putting salve on a poison ivy rash. If, every day, you walk past the poison ivy and get brushed again, you are applying a topical solution that might make you feel better for a while, but you are not addressing the real problem.

You might achieve satori in your meditation, but the constant rash could make you feel more like the Tasmanian Devil the rest of the time.

A more holistic approach to health removes the poison. For most of us, the biggest source of stress is "money." Once you are at *peace* with your "money," then all of these palliative stress-reduction strategies and healthy habits can indeed create a more fun, robust life.

Getting rid of money stress might seem impossible. When I was in trouble financially, if I heard another guru telling me to cut out café lattes, I might have gone Wile E. Coyote on them. You can't fix your money problems by cutting out café lattes, ice-cream, roller-blading, or whatever it is that you do for a little fun in your life. (If you want to reduce stress, you need to have more fun – not less!) What does need to occur is a simple three-step strategy.

The Solution to Chronic Money Problems
1. **Increase income.**
2. **Decrease expenses.**
3. **Adopt a Thrive Budget (instead of your current Buried Alive in Bills plan).**

This strategy is easier than it sounds. However, it requires bold, creative choices.

There are many ways to increase income. I'm going to highlight three important ways. There are many ways to decrease your expenses. I'm going to feature three important solutions. Adopting a Thrive Budget will be pretty easy once you do the first two steps.

Increase Income

When you think about increasing income, the first thing many people think of is getting a second job. The truth is that the *investments* you make today (of time and money) to increase your income over the *long-term* are the best ticket out of today's stress. Many times these investments don't add to your bills. They are taking money out of the pockets of the taxman, the debt collector, the insurance company, etc., and putting them into your own tax-protected retirement accounts, where the gains can compound.

1. Passive Income: We've talked about the importance of depositing 10% of your income into a tax-protected retirement account in every way that you possibly can – into your 401K, IRA, health savings account, college funds, etc., *even if you are in debt.* This is not another bill. You pay far less to the taxman and insurance company when you do this, and it is the surest path to financial freedom. Compounding gains means that you could have a million dollars by 55 if you start at 20 and deposit just $4000 a year. There are many other benefits to passive income that you'll learn as you get money wise. People who say, "I'll invest once I pay off my debt," rarely do, and they miss out on the multi-million dollar benefit of compounding gains. Check out the chart below for a visual on this.

2. Earned Income: The jobs of tomorrow are very different from the jobs of yesterday. Is it time for you to do a whole new analysis of your life, as Joe Moglia did? Will your current job pay you to increase your education? Do you qualify for grants and/or scholarships? Do you need to deepen your acuity in computers, financial literacy or STEM?

	IRA Monthly Deposit	10% Gains	Total
Year 1	$4,000	$400	$4,400
Year 5	$4,000	$2,442	$26,862
Year 10	$4,000	$6,375	$70,124
Year 15	$4,000	$12,709	$139,798
Year 20	$4,000	$22,910	$252,010
Year 25	$4,000	$39,339	$432,728
Year 30	$4,000	$65,798	$723,776
Year 35	$4,000	$132,015	$1,316.148
Year 40	$4,000	$195,140	$2,146.532
TOTAL	$160,000	$1,986,532	$2,146,532

Source: Natalie Pace

3. Passive Income: Could your biggest money burden be your ticket to financial freedom? If you are an empty nester, should you rent the McMansion and downsize to an Airstream? If you are a Millennial, should you rent a room or co-purchase a duplex instead of remaining a renter and making the landlord rich? If you're thinking of becoming a landlord, do your research first. It is important to calculate, realistically, what your true rate of return will be. Do the math on all of the expenses of your home, including new expenditures, like legal and income taxes on the rental income. Know the local laws of the land with regard to renting and renter's rights.

Ways to Reduce Your Bills

If you don't have money for R&R, it's your big-ticket items that are the problem. Here are three of the biggest bills in the budget, along with creative tips on how to reduce them.

1. Housing Costs.
2. Energy and Transportation Costs.
3. Health Insurance Costs.

Details on how to reduce the 3 Big Ticket Spending Costs

1. Housing Costs. In *The Odd Couple*, a vintage Neil Simon play, film and TV show, two divorced dads live together to make ends meet. I teamed up with another single mom when I needed to reduce my housing costs. A retired professional rents out her McMansion to a family and golfs every day from her new condo. She has lots of time and money for travel now! Downsizing, renting, or house sharing can be your ticket to more money and financial freedom.

2. Energy and Transportation Costs. The Hudson Valley Home that I toured a few years ago only had the heat go on *twice* during a frigid winter, using Passive House strategies. I saved money as a young mother by riding a bike, instead of driving a car everywhere. If you live in a sunny state, solar panels can take your electric bill to zero. (The payback time in a sunny state has dropped to four to seven years.) If you purchase an electric car or ride a bike, you can eliminate your gasoline bill – which amounts to thousands of dollars every year for most Americans. Saving on electricity and gasoline is worth over $7,500 annually to the average American. Learn more about whether solar or passive home improvements are right for you at Energy.gov and PassiveHouse.us.

3. Health Insurance Costs. If you are healthy, and you are paying an arm and a leg for insurance, you need to know about health savings accounts. Get more information at IRS.gov. In many cases, you can literally cut your health insurance bill in half, have all the money you need for a deductible and coinsurance in the event of a medical emergency, take a tax write-off, invest the money for even greater gains and increase your retirement assets all in one shot. Saving half off of your health insurance is worth thousands of dollars every year to most of us. Tax credits could make this option even more attractive.

There is one thing that money can buy, and that's freedom from stress. *But only when you get smart about how you allocate your income and invest your time, talent and resources.* Until then, even billionaires can be walking by poison ivy every day.

Here's to your peace and prosperity, which are holistically tied in with your health. Health is wealth. For most of us, it is ours to create.

Daily Task & Action Plan:
1. **Play the Billionaire Game (outlined on the following page).**
2. **Envision a better life.** Draw a picture. Create a vision board. Do both. Include all of the areas of thriving – from investing, to charity, to fun, to education... and your dream come true job.
3. **Meditate** on your new life. Open up possibilities. Don't *think* too hard about this. Your brain created what you have. We want to access a deeper wisdom. Breathe deeply. Call in your advisory team. Ask each one of them to give you a message about what your new, much better life should look like – about specific ways that you can cut costs, increase your income (active and passive), and live a more enjoyable and rich existence. Journal about it.

Learning New Skills

It's time to reduce your taxes, conserve energy, pay less on electricity, rethink your transportation, improve your health, reduce your health care and health insurance costs, purchase your things more mindfully (and according to the Thrive Budget), invest for a 10% annualized gain that compounds, and, as a result, have more time and money for adventure, love, happiness, fun, charity and education. Before you create, you must learn. It is worth it to study up so that you can pass this life exam.

Additional Resources

Energy.gov. PassiveHouse.us. The many green conferences that occur every year. My Huffington Post blog, where I feature some of the most prominent green projects and executives on the planet. Whether you believe in sustainability or not, energy efficiency and smart transportation promote personal fiscal and physical health.

Play The Billionaire Game
Materials

You'll need a pen or pencil, a few pieces of paper and a journal.

Preparation

It's a good idea to read this chapter from *Put Your Money Where Your Heart Is* (aka *You Vs. Wall Street* in paperback) and to read the Thrive Budget section of *The ABCs of Money* before playing this game. It's also more powerful, educational and enlightening if you play this game with friends. You'll be surprised how easy it is for some people to play this game, whereas others get stuck in various sections. A friend might have suggestions and insights that you can't see on your own. When you share your answers, you start the process of committing to creating results in your life.

The Billionaire Game is designed to have you ask and answer the question, "How would I live if I had all of the money in the world?" The Billionaire Game is also a way to teach the Thrive Budget, which is at its core 50% to survive and 50% to thrive. The Thrive Budget works infinitely better than the Buried Alive in Bills and Struggling to Survive Budget that most people who are living in debt experience. The Thrive Budget is something that anyone is capable of doing, but only if you are willing to make bold choices that allow you to invest in and create a better tomorrow than you are experiencing today.

Playing the Billionaire Game will take you at least an hour, and maybe an hour and a half. I don't expect you to know everything about my Thrive Budget before you play, so the game will be a new experience, full of novel strategies (that work). It may also feel foreign and almost impossible to you.

Remember that this is just a game, and that the goal is *new thinking*, far more than right answers. In fact, all of the answers that you have are right, even if they may be residing in the wrong category. The more that you align your expectations of what will happen with what is likely to happen, then the more life can bring you gifts. Expecting your charity to make you a billionaire, or that having a house you can't afford (but is so big and beautiful!) will be fun, or that investing in risky startups will offer a stable, steady return is simply not the way life works.

Have all of your materials at hand.

Another purpose of this game is to search your soul for what you are here on the planet to do. We won't be able to answer this question fully in an hour; however, we will be able to point you in the direction of where you should be walking – if you commit to thinking outside the box of where you are right now and allow yourself to dream of new possibilities – *dream come true* possibilities.

Have a child's mind. Be curious, instead of judgmental and cynical. Reach for the stars, even if it is ridiculous, even if you think space travel is impossible. Write down ideas right at the spark of them. Do not censure yourself or overthink things. Do not have paralysis by over-analysis.

Don't judge the outlandish things that you come up with by saying, "Oh, that is ridiculous. I couldn't possibly do that." Reframe it to be: "Oh my! That's ambitious! How in the world can I achieve that? Wouldn't it be fun? What if I just did this little small thing? It may not be much, but it is pointed in the right direction!"

Let this be a visioning period without limitations – with the freedom we have when we are asleep and the subconscious gets to dream up whatever it desires.

When I play this game on the beach at my retreats, I do so specifically because:

- It's beautiful
- It's fun
- The possibilities extend, literally, beyond the horizon
- There are external sounds, smells, feelings and even people
- It's easy to smile there

So, wherever you are right now, think of pressing pause and going somewhere where you will experience those sensations. If you're committed to staying where you are and playing this game right here and now, and you are not experiencing these sensations, then you are missing a great deal of the point.

In our circle on the beach, participants share what they are dreaming and imagining. This is because when you share your dreams with others, you have a greater likelihood of taking that dream to the next step – into action. Someone might have a good idea, or be willing to help you, or just lend their heartfelt support that what you are dreaming up is actually a good idea.

When you play with me guiding you, I am able to do subtle course corrections. There are no wrong answers, but there are sometimes wrong categories. When you play with friends, they can help with this – particularly if they have been through this 21-day course already. The further up the road to prosperity that they are, the easier it will be to illuminate the path for you to follow.

If you are playing this game by yourself, that's okay. It's not optimal, but it is better than nothing.

Let's dive right in. As I already mentioned, the Thrive Budget is a simple premise that when you limit your basic needs to 50%, you have 50% to thrive. Most people are spending far more than 50% on their basic needs, especially today. If you were to add up the amount of money that you spend on your home, car, gasoline, utilities, insurance, taxes, clothes and food, would it be more than 50% of your income? If so, that's why you feel like you're drowning. You are.

Bill Gates is ranked as the 2nd richest person in the world, according to *Forbes*, with a net worth of $79.2 billion. If he makes a 10% return on his principle, then his annual income is $7.9 billion. Do you think that he spends $4 billion annually on basic needs? (Remember his taxes are likely in the 20% range, which is the long-term capital gains tax for high-net worth individuals.)

The truth is that most self-made billionaires have never spent half of their income on basic needs. They will sleep on couches and launch the business out of their garage, in order to invest in their dreams.

In his now famous 2005 Stanford Commencement Speech, Apple co-founder and CEO Steve Jobs described sleeping on the floor of his friend's dorm room and walking across campus to the Hari Krishna temple for free food. He focused on learning calligraphy, simply because he loved it. He dropped out of college because he believed that it was bankrupting his parents. Now Jobs was a bit different from most college dropouts in that he had a massive drive and commitment to build things that people loved, and was hyperfocused on doing just that with Steve Wozniak in his garage. Even though his path was nontraditional (and risky), Jobs envisioned and created a life for himself that was much different than what he was born into.

At the beginning of the 20th Century, there were three ethnic groups who were still very underserved in America – African Americans, Hispanics and Asians. By the beginning of the 21st century, Asians were the top income earners in America. The way that they did this was by focusing on many of the tenets of the Thrive Budget. They reduced their basic needs dramatically and invested in educating their children, even if it meant that they had to put two and three families in the same little home.

Your ability to rise up out of basic needs and launch the investments that will pay off for you is even more ripe with potential today than it was for Asian immigrants transforming from slave labor on the railroads a century ago, to the top earning ethnic culture in America today.

These are examples of very different people who all reduced their basic needs expenditures in order to invest their time, talent and money on their future.

Let's Play the Billionaire Game

Take a piece of paper, holding it portrait style, and fold it long ways into four. Fold it in half and then fold it again. It should look like a paper ruler. Now unfold the paper.

Create four columns with seven rows. The top row will be fairly thin, with the following three rows on the front side and three rows on the backside spaced fairly evenly. On the first row, write $10,000/month in the first column, then $100,000/month in the second, $1,000,000/month in the third and $100,000,000/month in the final (fourth) column. See a sample of this in *Put Your Money Where Your Heart Is* (aka *You Vs. Wall Street* in paperback).

Your second row is going to be for your Buy My Own Island Fund (aka your retirement account). The third row will be charity. The fourth row education. The fifth row will be fun – immediate fun that you have on a regular basis. The sixth is fun again – but more delayed gratification fun – something you need to save up for all year long, like a vacation or a hot tub. The seventh row is your basic needs.

Since most of us have been drowning in basic needs forever, we're not going to focus on basic needs at all during this game. You have spent a lifetime focused on basic needs, so, while we play the Billionaire Game, let's just focus on thriving – investing, charity, education and fun. Remember that only 50% of your income is supposed to go to basic needs – not 70%, not 90%. Basic needs cover everything you need to survive, from paying taxes, to having a roof over your head, to your transportation to work, the clothes you wear, insurance and food. Fix this at a later day and time. For now, let's dream, create and thrive.

The Thousandaire Game

In this *game*, this month, you are earning $10,000 a month, which is $120,000 annually. You are a *thousandaire*. Remember: this is just a game. It could be less than you make or more than you make. Just live here for a moment. If that were the case, then you would want to get your basic needs expenses to under $5,000 a month.

The first check you write is 10% to your Buy My Own Island Fund. I call it that because who wants to think about their retirement fund? Most people are just filing that statement without even looking at it (until it's too late). But when you have specific goals attached to your investments, and give your accounts names, then you do care about saving and investing properly to manifest those dreams.

Write whatever your goal is in the box, instead of just using my Buy My Own Island goal. It could be the Send My Kids to College Fund. Or My Trip Around the World Fund. Or the Buy My First House Fund. Get my PhD fund. Launch My Dream Business Fund. You get the point.

Leave a lot of room in that box because you have to fill in a lot of details in just a minute. In that same $10,000/month column, write $1,000 in the charity row, $1,000 for education, $1,000 in the first fun box and $12,000 in the box for fun that you save up all year for ($1,000 X 12 months = $12,000).

The goal here is to be as specific as possible. What would you invest $1,000 this month in, particularly knowing that you have another $1,000 next month to invest?

With regard to charity, be specific. Don't just donate to a church, and let them decide where the money goes. Search your heart and passion for the things in the world that you think need more money and help. This is how you discover more about yourself. Donate where you want to create the greatest good and positive change. Is it donating shoes to children in Africa who need them to walk to school? Is it donating a net to people living in malaria-prone regions, where a simple net can save a life? Or drilling wells in arid regions? Or mentoring underserved kids in the community?

Education is the highest correlating factor with income; financial literacy and passive income are the highest correlating factors with wealth. It makes sense that surgeons make more money than gardeners. However, surgeons who educate themselves around investing will make a lot more in passive income than those who have blind faith in experts to do it for them, and don't know anything about investing. Those are easy prey for scam artists; the victims of Bernie Madoff's scam were all very high net worth professionals who trusted him to give them a 12% annualized return, and were not looking into anything that he was doing to confirm how and if he was actually capable of achieving that.

Lifelong learners and people who take ownership and active roles in their life, career and investments are those who will enjoy far greater returns in income, in passive income and in happiness.

How will you spend $1,000 on fun this month? What will the $12,000 that you've saved up all year for be spent on?

The reason I focus on doubling your fun budget is that health is the foundation of wealth. You cannot earn a dime if you are not healthy. Another little known fact is that many people spend more on health care in the last six months of life than they earn in an entire lifetime. So, staying healthy is hugely important, as is protecting and willing your assets properly so that they don't get eaten up by health costs.

Endorphins are free health pills that you can take every day. You should be enjoying your life. There are so few priceless and rare moments that we have in this really rather brief life span.

Pause and Play

You are ready to pause from reading and actually spend your money now. Set a timer and spend only four minutes writing in exactly how you would:

1. Invest your money.
2. Donate to charity.
3. What do you want to learn? How to dance the tango? Skydiving? Guitar lessons? Investing workshops? Would you like to get your MBA or Ph.D.?
4. How you will double your fun budget?
5. Do not spend a minute thinking about basic needs. You are already a master of that. Dream a little.

Do not let anything stop you from playing this game. Suspend all of your worries, doubts, fears and smug pessimism that none of this is really possible any way. New solutions and possibilities are shut down if you don't allow yourself to dream a little.

If you finish before the timer goes off, go back and add more details to some of the categories. The more details you envision, the clearer the picture is, the easier it is to make it real.

It's not that hard to get investing, charity and education right at this level – as long as you are being clear and specific, and not just writing general words.

Feedback

As I said earlier, when we play the game at the beach, I always have someone share at each level of the game. Here's something that comes up frequently, particularly if someone knows that they are spending more than 50% on basic needs. Someone will say, "Well, my house is fun. Can I spend my 20% fun budget there?"

My reply is this, "Well, if it's fun, and you really do smile when you are there, then of course. No one has written a book on what fun is *for you.* That's something you determine. However, if you are whining about spending that $12,000 on your house because you can't take a vacation or eat out, then you really aren't having any fun. You can't force yourself to think something is fun when it isn't. It's a better idea to be honest here, and to figure out how to fix the overspending on basic needs situation after we finish the game."

At this point, that person takes another two minutes to spend $12,000 on something that would actually be fun for him/her. You see how the old programming can creep in and stop up the actual dreaming process.

You actually have to enjoy your house with a big authentic smile in order to allocate your fun budget there. It's a better argument to consider your house an investment and have a bit of that money allocated there. (Not all, you are very vulnerable when you are property rich and cash poor.) With spending and investing, the answer is not always just "yes" or "no." Oftentimes, we are just thinking of what we are doing in the wrong way – expecting an outcome that is impossible. You can't force fun. Don't lie to yourself.

The Millionaire Game

Let's give ourselves a raise now. Let's go up to the millionaire status. That means that you have $100,000 income each month. Remember: this is a million dollars a year in your *personal income.* This is not a business that has a million in sales, but ten employees and you end up giving yourself zero.

At this level, you will be spending:

1. $10,000 a month on investing
2. $10,000 a month on charity
3. $10,000 a month on education
4. $10,000 this month on fun
5. $120,000 this *year* on fun
6. $50,000 a month on basic needs. Write this number down, and then ignore this row.

Before we start playing on this level, we have to start imagining what life is like there. Think of Jennifer Hudson. She's the Academy Award-winning actress who started out as a 7th place finalist on *American Idol.* Her net worth and income is not public information. However, as a spokesperson for Weight Watchers, and with her acting career and hopefully a little return on her money, it's not a stretch to think she pulls in a million a year.

In order for her to keep making a million a year, she has a publicist. She has a personal trainer. She might have a chef and a diet plan. She may be educating herself on how to stay healthy and slim. She'll need to be earning more than 0% interest, so she should be learning about how to invest well. Most vocalists take vocal lessons to keep their voice healthy. She needs to make sure that she doesn't hurt herself when she works out or when she performs too many nights in a row.

You can't make a million dollars a year unless you are focused on thriving, on educating yourself and have a strong, wise, dedicated support team around you. So, as you are spending your money, you have to think of things in this way.

Pause and Play

This is the point when you put this book down and spend. Again, remember to set your timer for four minutes only and get very, very specific with details on exactly what you're going to invest in, what good you will bring to the world with your charitable contribution, how you will deepen your wisdom with education, and just how much fun you're going to have with all of that money!

Don't just say, "Oh, I would invest $5,000 in stocks and $5,000 in bonds." Or say, "I would invest $10,000 in real estate." What kind of real estate, what kind of bonds, what kind of stocks?

You can't board a plane for the destination of "vacation." You have to pick exactly where you are going. The same is true with everything. When you are general, it is just wishful thinking without a plan. In other words, you've already told yourself that it will never be real. When you have a blueprint, then you are ready to build.

As you sound your soul for the exact improvements that you want to see in the world, then you can start making some impact there. As you understand how you are going to build your wealth, you will get on the path to prosperity, and course correct when things are going south.

Feedback

Now that you've spent your money like a millionaire, take another look at your responses. I'm going to provide you with a little more feedback on charity and nest egg investing.

Charity is the Best Networking

I want to talk a little bit about the value of charity. Charity is the best networking. As I've said, almost every job I've secured, promotion I've enjoyed, business I've launched and capital funding I've received has come directly as a result of my service projects. Charity is where you find *your people*.

Even when you think you are not in a position to give monetarily, you are always in a position to give something, particularly when you value your time and your talent as a gift (which they are). Those of you who have read my books know that I was once a divorced and desperate single mother. I was getting a little bit of support and alimony from my ex-husband in the beginning, but it was less than half of what I needed to cover the bills that I had. As anyone knows, when you divorce, you now have two households to support. So, as a split family with two abodes now, your expenses almost double.

I was the primary caregiver, and my son was still only seven and really needed me around, particularly right after the divorce. I had to get creative. Following the conventional wisdom that you can cut out cafe lattes and balance your budget is just bunk. It didn't work for me, and it won't work for you.

What did happen is that I had chaired a major fundraiser for my son's elementary school the year prior to divorcing. Those women (and a few select men) who had made that project a success (more successful than the previous year, with a foundation that would continue that trend in the years to come) ended up being the initial advisory board, human capital, and Friends and Family capital that helped to launch the Women's Investment Network (the legal entity of NataliePace.com). In a very real way, my charitable contributions to my son's school actually provided the springboard into a better life for the two of us, even though at the time I received no monetary compensation, took six months off from active income and was solely in the *giving* (without any expectation of *receiving*) mode. That commitment also meant that I leapt up the career ladder to C-level, without going through all of the stages in between.

When you donate to multiple charities, trying to do the equitable thing where each one receives the same, you really won't benefit from this at all. It is when you hyperfocus on one area of the world that you want to improve, and make a solid and strong commitment to that, where you will *reap* more benefits than you ever *give*. Here's why and how. When you write a larger check, you might join committees or be on the board of the charity. When you donate your time, you are rubbing elbows with people who share common passions and interests. You will form stronger bonds in this community than you will in traditional networking groups where everyone is essentially there to sell you something or do a quid pro quo. As you work on the charity project, you discover the talents and passions of your new friends, which can be applied to other endeavors.

Nest Egg:

One term you'll hear a lot in this book, and all of my books, is Modern Portfolio Theory. The basic idea is that you need to always keep a percentage equal to your age safe in your investments, and you need to diversify the rest. In my system, I also avoid the bailouts, add in hot industries and rebalance annually. If you are depositing 10% monthly into your nest egg *first*, and you're doing the things I just outlined, then you should be making 10% return (or more) annually, on average. This is what stocks and bonds have done over the last 30 years. If you are using the outdated Buy and Hold strategy, then you keep losing half (or more) in every recession and then taking years to crawl back to even (if you ever make it that far).

Don't go *all in* on stocks, or bonds, or gold, or real estate. You need to be diversified across assets, and diversified within as well. You need to be safe, and also have your at-risk portion in the hottest areas. You need to have some liquidity (which is why you can't just be property rich and cash poor). You can't be over-levered, or using margins, options or hedging exclusively, which can seriously wipe you out.

Your strategy should allow you to buy low and take some profits, which is why annual rebalancing is key. I also teach limit orders at my retreats because the volatile marketplace we've been stuck in for the last 14 years provides multiple opportunities for the patient buyer and the opportunistic seller.

If you have more than $150,000 in your nest egg (IRA, 401K, pension, plus), then it is important that you really know how to use this system. Otherwise, you're riding the Wall Street Rollercoaster and more vulnerable than you know, particularly in today's Debt World, where bonds and high-debt, dividend-paying companies are vulnerable.

The Multi-Millionaire Game

If you make a million a month (and, again, that's *your income*, not the business sales), then your annual salary is $12 million a year. Let's put ourselves in those shoes.

Let's use the example of Brad Pitt and Angelina Jolie. Each of them makes (potentially) $12 million or more annually, through high film salaries and corporate endorsements. If you are earning $12 million or more each year, you are working very, very hard. If you have kids, then you will have a lot of help with them. You will be traveling a lot. You'll need a housekeeper, a gardener, maybe a personal trainer and even regular massages to keep the stress levels manageable. You may have a private chef. You might even need a private plane. Even before Elon Musk was ranked as a billionaire, he needed his plane to jet him up and down the California Coast, where he was the CEO of Tesla and the CEO of SpaceX *at the same time*. Having a two-hour security wait, or risking people mobbing you in the airport, is just not a time inconvenience that the over-worked multi-millionaire can risk.

Also, your nannies need to be pretty well educated because they are teaching your kids, and you don't want your children learning improper grammar. They are instructing your children all day long, in all things, while you are off working so hard to bring in $12 million or more a year.

So, remember this larger picture when you are playing on this level. You cannot possibly make $12 million dollars a year without a lot of support. You will also have a pretty big group of people who are relying upon you. Every time that Brad Pitt and Angelina Jolie green light a film, hundreds of professionals (and friends) in the film business leap for joy.

Spend Like a Multi-Millionaire

Here's what you will be investing and spending at this level *this month*.

1. $100,000 on your investments.
2. $100,000 on charity. (This is now a tax protection strategy.)
3. $100,000 on education. (If you have six kids, remember college funds.)
4. $100,000 on this month's fun.
5. $1,200,000 on this year's fun.
6. $500,000 monthly on basic needs. (Don't waste any of your time on this category, even though I want you to write down the number and be clear on it.)

Before you even start your investing (which is the auto-payment that you'll make), rethink your goals. Do you still have Buy My Own Island as the goal, or did you already achieve that? Is it time to set a new goal of Buy My Own Plane? What is the next thing you wish to achieve in this growing estate of yours?

Set the timer for five minutes, stop reading and spend your money. Be specific in each category. If you get stuck, give the crayon to the five-year-old within you and let her color outside the lines.

Feedback

Here are a few more things that come up pretty frequently when we share the multi-millionaire level in our small group settings at the retreat.

Fun

Some people have no problem spending $1.2 million on fun, and immediately buy their beach house or plan that trip around the world. Some purchase a plane.

However, a lot of people get very tripped up on fun, and this is usually an indicator that you are still suffering from the "money is evil" myth – that if you are making that kind of money, you are causing suffering in the world. Or that if you want to have that much fun, then you are just greedy. However, neither one are true. You could be a multi-millionaire, or billionaire, who is bringing a lot of good to humanity. We wouldn't have electric cars that are safer than

Volvos and can outrace Porsches without Elon Musk. And you don't have to spend all of that money on yourself to have a lot of fun.

Also, the career span of multi-millionaires can be much shorter than that of average folks. Mint.com reported in 2013 that 78% of NFL players are bankrupt within five years of retirement – despite making more money per year than most people make in a lifetime. In fact, if these players were following the Thrive Budget – limiting their fun budget to 20% and their basic needs to 50% – then they would have money for continuing their education after getting cut from the team and investments to cushion the landing.

If you got stuck on any of the categories at this level, then clear your mind of judgments. Remind yourself that this is just a game. Reset the timer for 4 minutes. Go back and add more details to each one of the columns. If you need to trick yourself to get the creative juices flowing (and stop the stewing of judgments), then think of your millions as something you won in the lottery. That way, you don't get stuck worrying about how you earned it and can refocus back on the game.

The Billionaire Game

Billionaire status means that you make $100 million or more a month. (With $79 billion in assets, Bill Gates is making more like $658 million a month.) If you are a billionaire, then you are the sun of your city. Your energy powers the whole region. Chances are that you are the largest employer. If you don't get up and shine every day, the whole area could descend into darkness.

You cannot own a Hummer big enough to drive through the ghetto to your mansion. (Just ask Gaddafi.) If you are not equitable, generous, serving the city well and empowering your staff and employees, then your business will not thrive. If you are not educating the city's youth, you won't have the next generation of workers. If your teams can't stay healthy, you won't meet your production schedules.

All of this matters. As you spend your money, you have to think with that larger vision in place. It's not all about you anymore. In fact, being a billionaire carries with it a great deal of responsibility.

Spend Like a Billionaire

Here's what you will be investing in and spending at this level.

1. $10 million on your investments.
2. $10 million on your charitable foundation. (This is now a tax protection strategy.)
3. $10 million on education. (This is now a community investment.)
4. $10 million on this month's fun. (This is now a community investment.)
5. $120 million on this year's fun. (This is now a community investment.)
6. $50 million monthly on basic needs. (Don't waste any of your time on this category, even though I want you to write down the number and be clear on it. If you have a good tax strategy, only $15-20 million, or 15-20%, of this goes to taxes.)

I can't stress enough how important it is to remember that this is just a game. Stop judging. Start dreaming. Don't get stuck. Play. There is a playful spirit inside your soul who used to look up at the sky and mistake the moon for a ball.

Whatever comes to the top of your brain, even if it is "I want to buy the moon and colonize it," write it down. Don't censor yourself. Dream it. Someone dreamed of going to the moon one day, and we did it. Someone dreamed of mapping out the genome. And we have it now. All of our conveniences and magnificent breakthroughs come from someone's crazy ideas, so dream big.

Pause reading. Set your timer for ten minutes. Spend your money.

Feedback

When Oprah has fun by giving out cars to everyone in her audience, General Motors is paying for it. Oprah takes audience members with her on great destinations around the globe. The expense is part of the production budget.

This is what I call living in in the Gray Zone. Once you get beyond basic needs and into the realm of creating your own world, and taking responsibility for those around you, the lines start dissolving a little more.

Investing is something that you have to pay attention to, not just for you personally, but for the city of people who rely upon you and your business for their own livelihood. If you don't have your own charitable foundation, then you don't have a good vehicle for transferring wealth to your children and you are paying too much in taxes. You will also be donating to universities, schools, hospitals and more, to ensure that your community is home to the best, the brightest and the healthiest staff in the nation, who are the Next Generation of your business. A lot of your fun might be writing a big check to the Central Park Conservancy or the Surf Rider Foundation to keep the beaches clean.

Much of what you must focus on is tax preservation, so that you aren't just blowing your billions keeping Uncle Sam fat and happy, without a say in how that trickles down to your own community, your passions and interests. You're going to need to educate yourself on *preserving wealth*, now that you've become a master at *creating wealth*.

Three Commitments

Look over your game sheet and circle the things that you would really love to be doing right now. From those, narrow it down to five that are the most important, and number them in order of greatest importance. Now, write down four commitments that you are going to do right now to start on the path to making your desires come true in each area of investing, education, charity and fun.

What commitment are you making to yourself surrounding your passive income and Buy My Own Island Plan?

What commitment are you making to yourself to have more fun?

What commitment are you making to being more charitable, and more mindful about how charity can create valuable alliances and partnerships?

What do you need to learn more about? What commitment are you making to education?

Some of your favorite things might lie in the billionaire category. That doesn't mean that they are completely out of reach. You can start fueling your dreams with your time and talent right here and now, even if you think you can't *afford it* yet. Volunteering for an international organization might make it fun and affordable to travel and be charitable. You might not be able to afford being a full-time student, but can you take a class at the local college? Just start somewhere.

You need to take action to make your dreams come true. And that's why these commitments are essential to write down and to do *this week.*

The bolder your choices to get your basic needs under control, the faster you'll have more money to thrive on. It's not more time or money. In fact, when you consider how much time you spend worrying about money right now, you know that getting a better plan will ultimately save both.

We've already discussed ways that you can reduce the costs in the big ticket items – in your housing, your insurance, your taxes, your car, your gasoline, the amount you spend on electricity, your food, your clothes, your education... With big, bold decisions, you will find a much healthier lifestyle that serves you fiscally and physically. You can firm up and beautify your bottom line.

A lot of the money that we are placing into the Thrive side of our Budget is being funded by money that we used to spend making other people rich. When you invest 10% of your income, you're paying less in taxes to Uncle Sam. When you set up a health savings account, you are taking money from the health insurance company and keeping it yourself. Charity is tax deductible, as are certain educational expenses.

I created the Billionaire Game so that you rub up against your own boundaries, fears and walls around money. I want you to break the box of thinking small, so that you can truly create the life of your dreams.

Another reason I designed the Billionaire Game is that I want to get at the core of who you really are and why you are here on this planet. Whatever it is that you would really love to do as a billionaire, you can be creating today. Maybe not as grand, large and spectacular as you can when money isn't an issue, but yes, you can start on that path today. Some of the greatest ideas on the planet were once outlandish – a farfetched dream and a small amount of capital. Muhammad Yunus launched Grameen Bank on $37.

When you are hitting your walls, don't think, "This is a dumb game." Think rather, "This is just a game!" Today's mantra is "Create." So, it's your job to color and dream like you never have before.

Remember how you used to skip and swing on monkey bars. "Lasso the moon." Walk on Mars.

A Few Examples of Aligning Expectations with Realistic Outcomes
Investing in Startups

If you are thinking that investing in your niece's cupcake startup business is a good nest egg investment, then you've got that in the wrong category. That doesn't mean that you can't invest in it. It just means that you can't invest in it thinking that it will be money while you sleep, earning a 10% gain. Startups have a high failure rate. If you think of this as education – that you might learn about launching a business – then you still have a return on your investment (education, not money) if the startup fails (and a tax write-off, too). If you think of your investment as charity, as helping out a family member, then every day that you see her smiling, even if she's struggling, then you are getting the exact return that you invested in.

Investing in Disruptive Technology

Greenies want to develop the next great alternative fuel or energy. Foodies want to promote organic food. Remember that there is a lot of power in your consumer dollars! However, investing in creating something new is not money while you sleep. Think of Edison! All of those years and all of that sweat and work! This can be your job, or your education, or your fun. But, even as you create a better world for all of us, remember to seed the ground of your own prosperity in your retirement accounts with low-risk funds, not high-risk startups.

A Few Stories of Inspiration

Grameen Bank was founded over 20 years ago by Professor Muhammad Yunus, with less than $50 given out to over two dozen women in Bangladesh. From that, Muhammad Yunus created an entire micro-lending program that transformed the lives of millions of Bangladeshi women (and their families). He became the first Bangladeshi (along with Grameen Bank) to win a Nobel Prize (the Peace Prize in 2006). In 2009, U.S. President Barack Obama awarded Yunus the Presidential Medal of Freedom and in 2010, he was the recipient of the Congressional Gold Medal.

Yunus' books will inspire you. He is an example of a man who paid attention to the world around him, saw a need, had a dream, created a solution and transformed the world with just $50 (initially).

Week 2: Exercise

Practice and embody the divine laws of prosperity and abundance

Day 8: Peace
Today's Mantra: Peace

Last week was our cleansing week. The goal was to get rid of thoughts, actions, patterns, beliefs and old ideas that no longer serve us, and replace them with the habits, mindset, skillset and actions that will empower us to achieve our highest potential in everything we do – particularly with regard to active and passive income. This week builds upon that foundation.

New habits are like a pathway cut through a dense forest of old growth and cobwebs. Tilling the soil and planting new vegetation requires good oxygen flow, good nutrition, vision, wisdom, best practices and some perspiration. Week two is all about exercising our new skills and getting better at them. That means discovering more about what we learned last week, while adding a new mantra each day that takes us further up the road to prosperity and abundance.

Today's mantra is peace. Think peace constantly. Create peace with your breathing and with your thoughts. Start your day by being well nourished in body and mind. Have a good night's rest and eat a healthy, organic breakfast. Take a morning walk or jog. Exercise to wake up the heart and get the blood flowing. Don't gas up on too much coffee or other caffeinated or sugary drinks. This is essential to having a purr in your engine. You wouldn't pour sugar in your gas tank. Become aware of what you are fueling your body with, and what kind of mood those chemicals create.

Though the words *peace* and *prosperity* are used together frequently, few people are aware just how romantically involved these two words are. We'll explore this relationship in this chapter.

Reject dramatic situations today all day long – not actively, but passively. In other words, don't trumpet your conviction; just do it. No matter how badly someone wants to engage you, from road rage to bickering, just say, "No." Don't stop to explain what you are doing. Your actions speak louder than your words.

Take your foot off the gas. Leave the battle cage. Walk into nature. Pick a flower. (Why am I reminded of that classic children's story *Ferdinand the Bull?*) Visit some of the happy places that you have rediscovered over the last seven days.

If someone you care about is demanding that you explain yourself in words, you can do that tomorrow. Forcing you to explain yourself is just another way of keeping you engaged in the conflict. Don't be fooled by all of the ways that our body, our mind and even our friends resist change – even when it is good for us.

The highest good is to be loving. Always. But that does not mean going along with everything that everybody says or does, or trying to make everybody *happy*. The Prince of Peace overturned the tables of the moneychangers, and the very seats they were sitting on, saying that they were turning a temple of prayer into a robber's den.

Being a peacemaker is not being a pacifist.

In life, there are all kinds of adversaries and obstacles. Understanding how to uplift the situation is not always easy. We see this with children on the playground – even as young as toddlers. One toddler will see a bright, shiny toy and grab it – even if it is in the hands of another. The baby who has been robbed will try to grab it back, even if that requires bashing the other baby on the head.

In this situation, the Dalai Lama recommends a Peace Zone, where the youngsters can contemplate more peaceful resolutions to their conflicts.

The Peace Zone makes so much more sense than having an arbitrary time limit and time-out, where no real reflection and learning occurs. In time-out, a child can actually exit the *punishment* space after XYZ period of time without any insight at all into how s/he is going to make amends and act differently going forward. The Peace Zone should be a comfortable sanctuary in the home, filled with books and pillows and meditation aids. When a child acts inappropriately they are there for as long as it takes to discover a more peaceful resolution to their problem – something that the environment itself helps to inspire. Whether that process takes 30 seconds or 30 minutes is up to them. When they have figured out the solution, they share this with the parent and make amends with the injured party. Having a child see you, the parent, sitting in the Peace Zone contemplating things is a great example for them. All of us have challenges that require quiet contemplation and rethinking. It is rare for the knee jerk response to be the right one – even when we have trained our bodies and our lizard brain to serve our highest good.

Today, step away from chaos and confrontation and into the Peace Zone, even if it is only a picture in your mind. If you smell anything that stinks of conflict, worry, doubt or fear, then snatch yourself by your own collar and lead yourself out into the fresh air of love, breathing, forgiveness, gratitude, faith, wisdom and conscious creation (the mantras of previous days). You don't have to *feel* these things about the situation or the person who fired up your adrenalin. Simply choose, for the entire day, to put aside that anger and focus on people, situations, possibilities, and feelings that build you up and make you happy. Whatever conflict needs to be resolved can wait until tomorrow.

Even though challenges can be urgent and require solutions, today your job is simply to create peace and harmony and calm and tranquility. New possibilities lie in the Peace Zone – things that you've never allowed yourself the time and the space to explore. Better ideas can't really break through when you are wrestling the bull of chaos. Relax and enjoy yourself.

You don't always have to confront things head-on – unless you are in a life or death situation. Sometimes walking away is the *best* strategy. The battle you win is the one you don't show up for.

That is not to say that there are not causes worth fighting, and even dying, for. Most of us are not martyrs, however. We are rather just following along in the status quo – thinking that what we are doing is normal, without realizing the power that we have to envision something better and make the change. Once we beautify our own world, then we can work on the rest of the planet. In fact, by improving our own lives, we are indeed making the world more luscious – at least our own home, family and community. If everyone did that, our world would look even more wonderful than it already does.

It's interesting how you can make this choice very quietly, yet the impact of it can be so loud. Traffic can be super stressful, particularly in Los Angeles. One morning during rush hour, on my way to grab some espresso in Santa Monica, there was a parking spot right in front of the coffee shop. I pulled in and, just as I was about to exit the car, another vehicle began backing into the space. The driver blared his horn and revved his motor, and it looked like he was threatening to ram my car.

Rather than honking back and creating a fuss, or simply parking my car and leaving – which would have been an easy, though passive aggressive, move, since I was already there – I looked in the rear view mirror. Miraculously, there was another open parking spot two spaces behind me. I maneuvered out of the spot I was in, pulled back into the other vacant spot and *then* jumped out to grab my coffee.

The other driver couldn't see past his own spleen to the easy solution. Who knows, he might have even wanted an excuse to yell at someone.

There was a small crowd seated outside enjoying their coffee and watching everything. The ringleader of the morning group was a very famous television actor. He immediately got up, ran over to me, patted me on the back and said, "Well done."

Now, that and $2 gets me my espresso, but in Los Angeles, creating traffic solutions every moment that you can is very key. There is a tremendous amount of road rage. (In fact, it would have been far better if I were on my bike… No conflict at all!)

I didn't avoid the conflict because I wanted a pat on the back from a celebrity in front of all of his minions. It was simply the first thing that popped into my brain. I've trained myself to focus on the positive and possibilities, which means that I immediately scanned the horizon for an easy win-win. This is how my brain is wired *now*. That wasn't always the case. I, like you, shifted my beliefs and patterns by embodying the very concepts that I'm offering in this book.

The aggressive bully in the truck looked like a dope for creating such a ruckus, and the coffee crew did indeed glare at him as he passed. By creating peace, I also ensured that the group would have had my back, if the aggressive behavior had escalated. There are strangers in every step of your life who will have your back when you need it – once they see that you are here *for good* on this planet. You will be completely amazed...

Just because I actively created peace doesn't mean that my spleen wasn't on fire. My adrenaline was racing and I really wanted to tell the guy off. However, I focused on the appointments that I was headed to, rather than the drama that I'd narrowly slipped away from. I didn't want to know who he was or what he looked like. That way, I wouldn't be tempted to give him the stink eye while he was standing in line. I knew that the quicker I could put the situation behind me, the more opportunities I'd see in the path ahead.

As Martin Luther King said, "Darkness cannot drive out darkness; only light can do that. Hate cannot drive out hate; only love can do that."

Even in the moments when you are not feeling love, and I definitely wasn't there with the road rage jerk, you can still create peace.

Taking ownership of your investments is another way of creating peace in your life. As I related in my first book, *Put Your Money Where Your Heart Is*, there was a stockbroker who, after he discovered that I had some cash from a successful real estate sale, began courting me. He wanted to *diversify* me into all stocks, which is not safe or diversified. (Always keep a percentage equal to your age safe in your nest egg, i.e. *not* invested in stocks.) He was saying this right before the Dot Com recession. The companies and funds that he was the hottest on included Enron, Global Crossing, AOL, technology and

Japan. I would have lost all of my money if I'd allowed him to manage things.

During our meeting, this commission-based salesman displayed the classic signs of an abusive relationship. He began by seducing me. He revealed secret charts (that he wasn't even supposed to share with me, according to him) displaying the magnificent gains that I would enjoy under the aegis of his adept stewardship of my estate – provided that I could come up with an additional $500/ month, since he was making an exception on the minimum deposit required to qualify for his expertise. Then, when I refused the pen that he had extended for me to sign everything over to him, he began *educating* me – enlightening me to understand why his way was the right way for me to choose, since he was the expert and I was, well, someone with very little experience in these complicated financial matters (even though I'd managed to make enough in real estate to attract his advances – and God only knows what his real financial experience amounted to). When I countered his suppositions with economic theories of my own (which turned out to be true), he began belittling and insulting me, and telling me lies.

Unfortunately, these methods of intimidation can be very effective. The first method appeals to greed and vanity. (You are *so smart* for hiring me! I'm going to make you rich, rich rich!) The second promises protection and security. (I'm an expert! You can't get any better than this. You sure don't want to lose everything by trying to do it on your own! You wouldn't *operate* on yourself!) Bullying works with those who feel weak and clueless.

I didn't know much about creating peace at that moment, but I knew that being reasonable was getting me nowhere. I'd just extricated myself from an abusive relationship, and saw the warning signs. I also believed strongly that I was right and he was wrong, and I was committed to educating myself enough to be certain that was the case. It was my money, and I was determined to increase it – not lose it after I had just earned it! I looked at my watch, and realized that I needed to get back to work. I never returned that broker's calls. The battle you win is the one that you don't show up for.

My actions that day saved my assets. But, it also saved much more. If I had lost all of that money, I would have lost the ability to provide for my son. God only knows where we would have ended up.

I can already hear the easy excuse the broker would have employed. "Who knew? Everyone lost money!"

I would have been in serious trouble. But, no matter how much he might try to console me, assuming he was still in the business, he would have been happy that he made his commissions. The percentage of broker/salesmen who leave the financial services business is extremely high – much higher than other professions, but pretty on par with the turnover rate of *salesmen*. The CMG Group quotes statistics that 75% of brokers entering the profession will exit in the first year, 35% in the 2nd year, dropping to 15% for brokers with at least four years of experience. In recessions, these numbers increase.

The peace and prosperity that I enjoy today is a direct result of having fortitude, wisdom and resoluteness in 2000. I preserved my assets in the top performing asset class of 2000 – Certificates of Deposit – and then went on to almost triple my money in stocks only eighteen months later in 2001. Incidentally, 2001, *as in 911*, was another down year in the markets. Boy, had I learned a thing or two to be able to make money in stocks in 2001, so much so that all of my girlfriends asked me to teach them what I know.

If I'd had blind faith that the salesman was smarter than I was, I would have never known my gifts in economic theory, or launched the Women's Investment Network, LLC. This book wouldn't exist. And odds are pretty high that I would be drowning in my own bile, hating the guy for suckering me in and then losing everything – all for a little extra commission. Just like all of the mortgage and real estate brokers who sold homes to people who couldn't afford them in 2005 and 2006, just so that they could make their own mortgages, this salesman was just *doing his job* and *providing for his family* – at my expense. Investors lost 75% or more in NASDAQ stocks between 2000 and 2002. Today, NASDAQ is *still lower* than it was back in

March of 2000. The Dow Jones Industrial Average lost over 50% in the Great Recession. *(The solution is financial literacy and wisdom.)*

Like *It's a Wonderful Life,* there are a million miracles that are born from optimism, hard work, kindness, wisdom and fellowship – and about thinking seriously about how our actions affect the person in our path. This is why, once you create more peace in your own life, the next step is actively creating more peace in our world. It's time to start adding up the ways that our personal choices impact those people we interact with, and with our world.

When we smoke, who are we making rich? The tobacco companies. A pack-a-day habit costs at least $2000 a year (more than $4000 if you live in New York City). Those who use recreational narcotics – from cocaine to heroine – should remember the countries (and cartels) who provide those products, and the thugs and gangsters who get rich on the addiction/vice. Afghanistan produces the majority of the world's heroin; Peru and Colombia are the top producers of cocaine. The Middle East is rich on oil. Who was that salesman who convinced a family to buy a home they couldn't afford in 2005? Is it really *right* to sell someone down the river just for the commissions – to make your own mortgage payment?

There is another addiction that *almost every American has,* which rarely gets talked about, unless there is a major catastrophe – our oil addiction.

The High Price of War (in Lives)

During the BP Oil Crisis of April 2010, during which oil gushed unfettered for 87 days, I don't know about you, but I felt greasy and disgusted every time I turned the ignition of my car. I knew that my addiction was the root cause of the disaster. If oil companies were drilling more than a mile beneath the ocean, using equipment that was not well tested, then sating my thirst for petroleum was getting more desperate than any CEO or politician – or I – was admitting.

In fact, the thirst for oil in America costs us about a billion dollars a day. That was the price tag of importing oil in August of 2014 – even though domestic oil production was higher than it had ever been, and petroleum consumption was lower than it was when President Clinton was still in office.

War puts an enormous strain on global petroleum resources and forces us to increase the amount of petroleum that we import. Since oil and gas are heavy fuels, they are too expensive to ship across the Atlantic Ocean to fight in foreign wars. Consequently, our trade deficits to OPEC and Saudi Arabia spike when we are involved in conflicts in the Middle East. During the Iraq and Afghanistan Wars (2003-2008), oil imports were at an all-time high – peaking at $450 billion in 2008 ($1.23 billion/day). By 2013, after the U.S. exited Iraq and began a pullout of Afghanistan, oil imports settled back down to $363 billion – about a billion a day.

In its 2009 report "Imported Oil and U.S. National Security," the Rand Corporation determined that the U.S. would save $83 billion in defense spending annually, if we did not have to patrol the Persian Gulf to ensure the supply and safe global transit of oil. According to Thomas Hicks, the deputy assistant secretary of energy for the U.S. Navy, who spoke to me at the Clinton Global Initiative in 2011, "For every 50 fuel convoys, we have one American killed or wounded. For us, that's just too high a price to pay for fuel." Bringing fuel into "the theatre" means sending convoys from Pakistani ports through insurgents and IEDs (Improvised Explosive Devices) to Afghanistan.

How many lives can we save by simply buying a more fuel-efficient car, an electric car, or by walking or commuting by bike? At least we are pointing our own choices in the right direction.

I know this is a lot of sobering data on a day when I want you to be calm and peaceful.

Don't freak out or start debating these issues. Just seed these statistics in your mind. They don't have to yield any fruit yet. In fact, if you plant them and forget about them – rather than try and make political sense out of the data, or to rationalize/justify things, or to get up in arms and on a soapbox – if you just allow this information *in*, that's a start.

Ultimately, we want to "be the change we wish to see," as Gandhi reminds us. However, before we can begin that process, we have to be aware of *our own role*. All too often, we're ready to assign blame to *them* for screwing everything up. We want to fix *them* or show *them*.

We are *them*. Most of us gas up. A lot of us commute by cars that are not very fuel-efficient. What kind of solutions and change can we co-create if we quietly reflect on the clear pool of that truth? What choices can I make to reduce my own oil and gas footprint on this planet?

Speaking of war, what if you, or your child, has a knee-jerk urge to hurt someone when you get angry? Even babies do this, by the way. And, sadly, if you grew up in an abusive household, you are more likely to be abusive yourself *even if you don't want to be that kind of a person*. You have to work to break the cycle of violence in order to not pass the behaviors that you grew up around down to your children. Soldiers returning home from war have a difficult transition, too. The rules are different on the battlefield than they are in the mall parking lot.

Therapy can be a piece of the solution because you do need to see different possibilities. However, training your body to *respond* differently to provocation is an action that is equally powerful. Our body can lead our brain into new ways of thinking. Think of how different the world looks and feels when you are in love – how the flush of those hormones inspires you to see everything in your world with new, rose-tinted eyes.

When my five-year-old rambunctious son showed signs of very aggressive behavior on the playground, I enrolled him in a hopkido class. The instructor was a strong man, who trained his young students to neutralize the energy of the aggressor with powerful grappling tricks. If someone kicks you, you are trained to grab their foot, twist it quickly and force them into submission onto the ground. A simple flick of the wrist can flip someone three times your weight onto his back.

Now, you might be thinking that this sounds aggressive. However, the point is to neutralize the aggression as quickly as possible, not to hurt the other person as much as possible before they hurt you (like fighters do in a mixed-martial arts cage). All the while that my kindergartener was gaining mastery over his body, and the confidence that goes along with that, he was also learning the value of peaceful resolutions. He was learning how *not to be the bully* because that was the person he was always neutralizing. The master of the class loved to quote peaceful aphorisms from Lao Tzu, Buddha and Confucius. This method of dealing with my son's aggression worked wonders. He needed his brain to learn from his muscle memory. No amount of talking was doing the trick with him.

Hopkido was a lot more fun than listening to my lectures or sitting in the principal's office. It offered my son an entirely new repertoire to employ on the playground during the rough and tumble play of young boys.

We become what we do the most... The practice and practice of Hopkido made the moves instinctive for him. Without even knowing it, actively creating peace became my son's reflex. It didn't make him a saint, but it was a giant step in the right direction, affording us both less time in the principal's office.

As we neutralize aggression, and the aggressive tendencies of our own mind to wrestle and wrangle and argue ideas endlessly without ever thinking up and enacting solutions, we take control of our mind, our body, our circumstances, our home, our community and, ultimately, our world. Sometimes the aggressor is someone who wants to "manage" our money. (There are a lot of ethical money managers who do a great job.) Or a colleague who wants our job. (There are a lot of co-workers who can be allies.) Or someone we love, such as a spouse, parent or a child. There are solutions to aggression. If you don't have the solution at hand, reach out and ask for help. There are others who have been in your shoes and have wisdom to share. (Just make sure that you are tapping the wisdom of a true wayshower – a shaman, not just a salesman.)

Today, rather than talk about "the news" I'm going to stay quiet. Listen to the wisdom of the wind and smell eternity in the trees.

We are *them*. We are *us*. We are U.S. As each individual transforms, so does our world.

Peace.

Daily Task & Action Plan:
1. Create a Peace Zone in your home. Grownups need them as much as kids do.
2. Attend a meditation, yoga, hopkido, martial arts or philosophy class.

Learning New Skills

Revisit the notes you made on days one and two, when you did your first meditations. Are you looking at things with the same attitude that you had then? What have you already learned? What issues are you still having? Write down your thoughts in your journal.

Additional Resources

Check out the writings of Confucius and Lao Tzu, and the book *The I Ching.*

Day 9: Vision
Today's Mantra: Vision

Vision is the antidote to fear, confusion and chaos. Vision – the ability to see a solution/path that others haven't conceived of yet – is key to success on any stage, from entertainment, to debate, to battle, to business, to life itself.

The essence of fear is a lack of vision – the inability to see beyond the obstacle before you. If you're frozen in fear you can't take a step forward. Once you can see the way, it's easy to walk.

When you can envision the solution to the problem at hand – or a better life despite whatever it is that is oppressing you – then it is easier to have the courage you need to create what you want. Sadly, many people around the world are preyed upon because they don't think they have the power or the courage to stand up for themselves.

When I think of vision over fear and triumph over harsh adversity, there is one person who immediately comes to mind. Malala Yousafzai. Here is a brave young teenage girl, who had everything to fear – and the vision and courage to stand up for what she believed in *at all costs* – even death.

She had read of Queens and Presidents in books, but Malala Yousafzai wasn't dreaming of grandeur, or of being on stage receiving the Clinton Global Citizen Award from the hands of Queen Rania of Jordan, when she rode the bus to school every day. She simply wanted a better tomorrow, to break the cycle of poverty and injustice that enslaved so many girls and women in her Pakistani village. It was something that Malala had no control over that catapulted Malala to fame and the stage at that special gala in New York City on September 25, 2013. It was the shot heard around the world.

On October 9, 2012, a member of the Taliban – a young man only a few years older than Malala – forced his way onto Malala's school bus, singled her out, shot her in the head, and said, "Let that be a lesson to you." He left her, presumably, for dead.

Thankfully, with the help of people in her village, great medical care and global citizens around the world, Malala lived.

It was a lesson indeed. As Queen Rania said in her opening remarks, before presenting Malala with the Clinton Global Citizens Award for Civil Society, "It was a lesson in how education triumphs over violence... And it was a lesson in how one person, one young girl, can inspire a global movement to create meaningful change."

In her acceptance speech, Malala described watching helplessly, in horror, for years as innocent people in her village, Mingora, were slaughtered. Girls were forbidden from going to school. Women were restricted from going to the market. Hundreds of schools were blown up. And the price of dissent was death. Amidst this danger and destruction, Malala dared to defy the Taliban. And she lived. In Malala's words:

We raised our voice. My father spoke. I spoke. And my friends spoke. We said that in this modern era, even disabled and special children are educated. On the other hand, we women and girls are forced back to the Stone Age. We raised our voice for the education of every child, and now schools are reopened and many girls are going back to schools.

Why is Malala fighting so hard for education? Because in many countries, including Malala's own village, girls are married off at the age of puberty – instead of going to school and getting the education they need to provide for themselves. In the poorest regions of the world, one-third of girls between the ages of 15 and 19 have a child. Two million girls under the age of 15 give birth *every year.*

Malala's mission is to save children around the world from poverty, from child labor, from forced marriages and from terrorism. Still a teenager herself and under five feet tall, she speaks firmly, with power and conviction, saying, "I know the issues are complex and enormous. But the solution is one and simple. That is education, education, education." She has already proven that she is willing to give up her life for this important cause.

Simplicity is another quality of *vision*. Malala firmly believes that books, pens and teachers are the best weapons against terrorism. While others wrangle their minds and try to inch their way toward solutions with an oppressor who is saying, "My way or death," Malala simply got on a bus and went to school. Yes, it's dangerous. But so is having a baby when you've just hit puberty. Complications from pregnancy and childbirth are the leading cause of death in teens in the developing world.

Through the Malala Fund, Malala vows to educate children, especially girls. With seed funding from some of the world's most recognized leaders and celebrities, the Malala Fund, in its first year of existence, was already educating 40 young girls, who were rescued from child labor.

Six of the seven visionary Clinton Global Citizens honored that night in 2013 are also transforming the world one empowered individual at a time, advocating, through their actions, that education is the best tool for peace and prosperity. Bunker Roy, the founder of the Barefoot College, is teaching grandmothers around the world how to power their villages with solar. Jessamyn W. Rodriguez, founder and CEO of Hot Bread Kitchen, offers her workforce the math and English necessary to break out of the lowest levels of the kitchen. Elias Taban, a former child soldier in southern Sudan, is building infrastructure, providing jobs and leading peace negotiations between warring tribes. And Adam Lowry and Eric Ryan, the co-founders of Method, are redefining how soap "fights dirty," by educating consumers on sustainability through their home care products.

Malala Yousafzai is one of the greatest examples the world has ever seen that the pen is mightier than the gun, and that vision and courage can be life transforming – even in the most perilous circumstances.

As Martin Luther King, Jr. said, "Cowardice asks the question, 'Is it safe?' Expediency asks the question, 'Is it politic?' Vanity asks the question, 'Is it popular?' But, conscience asks the question, 'Is it right?' And there comes a time when one must take a position that is neither safe, nor politic, nor popular, but one must take it because one's conscience tells one that it is right."

Young girls around the world now have hope, and someone to look up to, when powerful tribal leaders tell them to marry instead of going to school. With Malala's example, they can have the courage that they, too, might face down their oppressors, demand freedom and empowerment, and actually win.

The oppression you might feel is debt. Or feeling buried alive in bills. Some of the richest people I know, with the biggest bank accounts and possessions, feel the most oppressed by money because they worry that they could lose it. They feel that the taxes they pay could buy two or three houses every single year. (And they are right!) The Hearst Castle was once owned by William Randolph Hearst – not the State of California. There is always a way, no matter how much you are worth, that money can be oppressive.

There is nothing wrong with having less money, unless you feel "broke." There is nothing "right" about being rich, unless you feel free.

Being in the flow of prosperity can occur as easily in the widow with only a mite as it can with the business owner who employs most of the town. It is a mindset. The laundress who gave $250,000 to charity had the mindset of a philanthropist rather than a spender. That's why the Billionaire Game becomes important. One goal of the game is to discover how you would live if you had all of the money in the world. However, as you play the game, you start understanding that massive wealth is a *responsibility*. If you don't promote freedom, opportunity and even beauty in your village, if your future employees are not healthy and educated/qualified to work, and certainly if you don't provide a way for your employees/people to provide basic needs for their families, then you can end up like Gaddafi. Or Marie Antoinette.

How do you become a visionary? Start by imagining yourself in control of your life. How would you be living if money weren't an object? What do you need to get there? (Is it easier to achieve that than what Malala had the courage to fight for?) Surgeons go to medical school. What schooling do you need for your dream come true life? Who is doing what you want to do? Who invests well, or earns a great living, or enjoys a great home life with their family? Can you learn from them and achieve similar results?

You could, right here and now, if you so desired, volunteer to join the team of almost any politician or leader, or at least join the team of someone who is only a few degrees of separation from your Dream Team. I just searched for "volunteer for the Dalai Lama" and turned up pages of opportunities. The Clinton Global Initiative hosts dozens of staff volunteers at each event – whereas members pay $20,000 or more to attend. I have hundreds of qualified volunteers who assist me at my retreats. GLIDE hosts the annual power lunch with Warren Buffett. If you're not rich enough to buy the experience and training that you need right now, can you volunteer and get in on the action? Remember that even if you meet someone rich and powerful, you have to have the skill set to actually land the position that you want. No one is going to hire a gardener to do surgery on her.

Vision is something that we were exercising when we played the Fire Ritual – when you took your worries, doubts and fears and flipped them to the positive, including an action plan to create the solution. Mastering fear is not simply ignoring your feelings, or saying affirmations whenever your fight or flight gland starts pumping (although that might help calm you in the heat of the moment). It is addressing the root cause of the problem and seeking out solutions that prevent *what you fear* from being reality. If you fear failing a test, study – especially if the test is *life math.*

Let's use a sports example. If you are the striker on your soccer team, but you worry about someone stealing the ball every time you get it, the solution is to learn to run faster, handle the ball better and to practice scoring against defenders. The soccer player who worries everyone is going to catch him because he's a slow poke might also consider getting a different position where his skill sets shine. When you can't run fast, it's a rational fear to think that you're going to get creamed all of the time. Are you better at reacting fast? Would you make a better goalie?

Your fears are not to be ignored. You can actually use them to hone your vision. Because the stakes were so high for Malala, she had to think hard and seriously about why she was so committed to promoting education for herself and for her friends. She had to be sure beyond a shadow of a doubt that education was worth risking her life over. Now she has many supporters around the world committed to helping her cause.

When you have nagging doubts, it's your inner wisdom begging for more information or a better plan. Trust that your uneasy spirit *knows* something.

There were over 10 million homes in the foreclosure process between 2007 and 2012. Seven and a half million people lost their homes through short sales or by the banks seizing them. Millions more were able to negotiate a deed in lieu – a far better option if your home is seriously underwater. A lot of those homeowners had a bad feeling about the investment *going in,* but didn't study to pass the life math test. With a little digging, they would have discovered that they were buying at a very high price, and might get stuck with a money pit that they couldn't really afford. Some unscrupulous real estate and mortgage broker/salesmen were offering reassurances and projections that were unrealistic – with the underlying goal of just getting the commission. Financial literacy – knowing what the average returns of real estate *really are* – would have allowed for clarity of *vision,* instead of blind faith. Education makes it more difficult for others to take advantage of you.

Sometimes your fears are simply old baggage, and the vision you need is a new glimpse of who you really are. I'm from a very poor background. When I received my scholarship to attend the University of Southern California, I was embarrassed to think that everyone there would know that I couldn't afford to go to a private university. I was even worried that I might not make the grade, and that I'd lose all my scholarships and be forced to drop out. (Someone close to me liked to point this possibility out frequently.) This fear was pretty irrational considering that I was entering the university with a 4.0 grade point average from Santa Monica College.

The first day, as I stood in line at the Wolfgang Puck Pizzeria to grab lunch, the boy behind me noticed my watch. It was a faux Cartier – a gift. He said, "Nice watch."

My immediate response was something stupid like, "Oh. This? Um. Well. Errr. It was a gift."

I was terrified because I thought he must have immediately recognized it as a fake, and was mocking me! There he was smiling and making light conversation, and I was soiling everything with my own chaotic thoughts.

You can tell when someone is trying to insult you. They are usually not very subtle. And the smile is a smirk. None of this was present as the young man grinned at me and brushed his fingers over my wrist. Looking back, it was more probable that the guy was hitting on me. Then, however, I excused myself from the line and raced into a bathroom stall.

In actuality, I should have been very proud of winning the Dean's Scholarship and doing so well at SMC! How many of the students at USC were embarrassed that their *money and connections* had gotten them admission, when they really didn't make the grade? How many students sat blank-eyed when the classroom discussions flew far above their heads? Hadn't I just been in class that very morning with a famous college football player who was trying so hard to read a sentence of Shakespeare out loud that it made him cry? It was excruciating to watch. The professor was kind and helpful with sounding out the words, but it was seriously uncomfortable for everyone in the room to watch. I expected the football player to transfer out of that class as quickly as he could. Sometimes you don't realize that what *you have* is something others would pay a lot of money for. Maybe I should try tutoring for a little extra money on the side…

These are some of the things I told myself. Being at USC on scholarship was something to be *proud of* – not ashamed of. In fact, the only thing I was really ashamed of was the fake Cartier. It wasn't my style to be wearing a lie. I carried a see-through purse. So, I took it off and never wore it again!

By facing my fears in the bathroom stall, I was able to figure out the best solution. It was time to get rid of the thing that *wasn't me* and start embracing the *new me* that was emerging through education. I didn't feel completely at home at USC overnight. But, over time, I learned to embrace my own unique qualities and to understand what a blessing it is to feel as comfortable having tea in a castle with The Queen as it is to have a soda with my dad in his trailer. Maybe I could be a bridge between the worlds of the privileged and the hardworking – a messenger conveying important firsthand information from each side to the other.

Here's another example of how the vision that needed to shift was internal. A girlfriend of mine inherited a million dollars when her husband passed away suddenly and unexpectedly. It was a sad time, and there was $100,000 in debt to deal with, in addition to the mourning, the estate, the home, her children and the *things*. She pulled me aside a few weeks after the funeral and said, "After I pay off my debt, I want you to help me invest the rest."

My response to her was, "Why do you want to go from being a millionaire to a thousandaire? Why are you thinking about making the debt collector rich before compounding your gains and building up your own estate?"

Her math was simple. In her mind, she was paying 18% in interest, but would be earning nothing on the money.

If she were thinking like a millionaire, then she'd realize that she could pay off her debt with the first year's earnings – while keeping her million dollars of principal intact! 10% gain on a million dollars is $100,000.

Millionaires think first of protecting their principal, then of reducing their tax burden, then of earning a good, safe return on investment, then about reducing the interest rate on the money they borrow, and then about paying bills. (I'm not saying she should ignore her debt, mind you, simply that she should be thinking of how to pay it off without lopping $100,000 off of her million.) As she becomes more financially literate, then she can envision a whole different game plan. After she understands the tax benefits of depositing money into retirement accounts, and the compounding effect of 10% annualized gains, and the importance of protecting your own assets and principal first, and the fact that, as a millionaire, she can quite easily negotiate better terms for her debt through a different loan or credit card company, then a whole different future, full of the new reality of her *as a millionaire*, opens up. Her gut instinct was to immediately revert back to her comfort zone – out of millionaire status and back to broke.

As we learned last week, what feels normal is not necessarily good – particularly when we are challenging ourselves to grow. It certainly wouldn't feel normal for Malala to risk her life by riding a bus to school. She did it to transform her village. She is now a celebrity spokesperson.

Most people who are in debt are making the debt collector rich, at the expense of themselves. Some people are letting the fear of FICO score keep them trapped in paying debts that they should be restructuring.

In truth, debt is a vision problem that a lot of people have. Credit card companies use compounding debt to entrap people in a never-ending cycle of high interest payments to them. Investors can use the power of compounding to liberate themselves from the shackles of borrowing at high interest and overspending. If you want to reduce your debt, there are three things that have to happen. You have to increase your income, decrease your expenses and restructure the amount that you owe – whether that is through lower interest payments or restructuring the principal. Since making payments on time amounts to only 30% of the FICO score criteria, if this is your only plan, you could be increasing your indebtedness, lowering your credit rating, and digging yourself deeper into a hole if you focus solely on making your payments on time. Paying down debt is certainly a piece of the puzzle. But if that is all you see, then you are definitely making the credit card company rich at your own expense.

There is a Debt section in *The ABCs of Money*. The debt collector's vision is having a payment from you each month to report to her boss. If your vision is prosperity, it starts with financial literacy.

Here's An Annual Vision Dilemma: The Tax Refund

Each year, millions of Americans ponder on what to do with their tax refund. Should you pay down debt (ugghh), pay off your McMansion, fund your niece's cupcake startup, climb Machu Picchu or invest in Chipotle? The answers might surprise you.

Hmmm. What Should I Do with This Year's Tax Refund?

1. Pay Down Debt? Saving and investing are habits, just like spending and debt are. So, even if you think that paying down debt is the best idea – starting a new habit of investing in a tax-protected (and debt-collector protected) 401K, IRA or health savings plan is an even better plan. If you are honest about how long you've been trying to pay off debt before you start saving/investing, you know that the issue is more complex than just paying off debt. "Paying yourself first" really works, and that is why investing in Chipotle (or Whole Foods, or a solar company, or Google, or…) is a great idea. Transition out of debt consciousness (thinking first about making the debt collector happy) into wealth consciousness (thinking first about compounding your own gains and beautifying your bottom line) starting with this refund, here and now. Once you do that, then you can (and should) address why your budget is out of whack (which is why you are in debt in the first place) and how to reconfigure your life to become debt-free.

2. Take a Vacation? Did you know that Americans spend almost $3 trillion on health care every year? 75% of health related costs are from preventable diseases, which are aggravated by stress. Clearly, fun and R&R are part of the cure. If you're thinking that a vacation is the right answer, it is. A little time off and adventure could actually translate into more income. Could that infectious smile and empowered attitude earn you a raise and a promotion? Would clean air and exercise, along with some adventure, spark a fresh, new way of thinking about prosperity and abundance?

3. Should You Save Your Refund or Invest It? There are a million reasons to invest your tax refund, including the fact that if you started at 20 and invested $4,000 religiously (and smartly) every year, you'd be a millionaire before 55, thanks to the power of compounding gains. If you save your money (at 0% gains), you'll have $160,000 at the end of 40 years. If you invest it, and that earns a 10% gain (what stocks and bonds have done for the past 30 years), then you'll have over $2,000,000 at the end of 40 years. Get smart about investing so that you are protected, while profiting. When you invest in financial literacy, and know how to optimize your return on investment, you *can* achieve your goals.

4. Retail Therapy? When you spend your tax refund on shoes, you might end up living in one. Not so cozy. Just ask the Little Old Woman Who Lived in a Shoe. Yes, you have to look the part for the job you want, but don't use that excuse to justify being a shopaholic.

5. Paying Off Your McMansion. If you can qualify for a good, fixed loan, you might receive a historically low interest rate. (When I purchased my first home, I paid up to 12% interest on the mortgage!) Under 5% interest rates offer almost free money – which means there are not a lot of reasons to pay the loan off early – particularly if you think that you can compound your money at 10% annualized. If you have a high-interest loan and lousy terms on your mortgage, then paying off your home *could* be a great idea. A financial team (Certified Public Accountant and a Certified Financial Professional) can offer important tips. Your own financial literacy and wisdom are key to making the right decision.

6. Your Niece's Cupcake Startup. It's always tempting to take extra money and invest it in a great idea. However, most great ideas don't become great, lucrative businesses. If you think it might be *fun or educational* to fund a startup, then go for it, with the idea that this is money that you can afford *to lose* if the business doesn't make it. If you think it will make you rich, the odds on that payoff are pretty low! Steve Jobs and Steve Wozniak had to work long, hard, unpaid hours in Jobs' garage before Apple paid off. Investing in businesses, like Apple, after they are already profitable and traded on the big boards (the NASDAQ and the New York Stock Exchange) is a safe and steady plan, and a better bet, than starting a business in the hopes of striking it rich. Exceptional entrepreneurs, such as Bill Gates, Steve Jobs, Kay Koplovitz, Oprah, etc., make it their lifetime careers to overcome obstacles and create success. The road to riches in business is rarely easy. If you're ready for that kind of long-term challenge and commitment, then this might be the right answer for you!

It's easy to think that paying down your debt, particularly high interest debt, is the right answer, especially if you are being hounded by a debt collector. However, if that is the first and only thought that you have, then you are stuck in the "make everyone else rich" plan (debt consciousness). The debt collectors are not going to take up a collection to help you out if you lose your job or retire. So, it's your job to provide for yourself *first*, to develop a vision of your own prosperity *first*, and *then* make bold and effective adjustments to your budget, while addressing the best way to pay down debt – prioritizing the high-interest debt first.

And sometimes, the right answer is to reward yourself with a stress-reduction adventure, even when the numbers, on paper, don't seem to add up. Health is wealth! When you consider how much Americans spend on health care, a vacation becomes a great investment! And you can't make any payment on your debt unless you are healthy enough to earn a living.

Remember that a big piece of becoming a visionary is education, exercise, clearing out old clutter and eliminating the baggage of self-judgment.

As you shift your vision and the possibilities, lots of "issues" might come up. If you practice long and hard, your muscles might ache. You have to pace yourself to avoid injury. If your technique is a little off, as you adjust your technique, it will feel weird and you might not even make as many shots. Diligence, best practices and listening to your body are important. Overtraining – trying to push yourself too far, too hard, too fast, can injure you and actually delay your progress. (Options trading comes to mind, which is a temptation that is dangled in front of new investors quite often these days – because it is very profitable for the brokerages.)

When people who have never invested before start investing, the first thought they have is whether or not they have won or lost. When I make a sound choice about an investment and it decreases in value, my first thought is never, "I've lost." It is always, "Should I be buying more?" If I think I've purchased a great thing at an awesome price and I can buy it for an even better value, then I'm even more interested, rather than defeated.

Never expect yourself to be perfect. Have a plan that allows for the real world of imperfections. The best baseball hitters are only getting one hit per every three times at bat. You don't need to be 100% successful at everything you try in order to live a rich life and shift into wealth consciousness. Agility, the ability to roll with the punches and course-correct, while always keeping the goal in mind, is the hallmark of success.

As we talked about in Week One, there are certain exercises that you can do to start planting those visionary seeds in your own mind. If you wake up every day thinking of five things that you are grateful for, you are inviting more love into your life. If you get up every morning thinking about the five things that you hate about your life or what someone else did to you, and you've had nightmares about it all night, then you are creating more chaos in your life. A lot of the strategies that you are already learning are pointing you in the right direction and helping you to create the internal circumstances that will afford you a new way of thinking – new vision.

So, today and going forward, when you think of opposites, when you think of love and hate, understand that the negative side of the continuum of love – hate – is a signpost that tells you when you are headed in the wrong direction. When you experience fear, when you are afraid that something you don't want to happen *will*, envision and enact the solution.

You are training your mind, your body, your actions *away* from what you *don't* want to create, what you resent and what you hate, *toward* wisdom and best practices. Let vision consume your time and your thoughts. In each moment today, ask yourself, am I being a creator or a victim? Am I expressing love or hate? Am I breathing deeply and calmly, or hyperventilating and freaking out? Am I being contentious or calm and peaceful? Am I focusing on gratitude or resentment? Am I forgiving or drinking my own bile? Am I opening myself up to miracles or sabotaging myself by having blind faith?

We have to hack through a lot of old growth, a lot of old habits, patterns, beliefs, systems, propaganda and advertising, in order to seed the ground with new possibilities and see the sun, see the rainbows and glimpse that pot of gold again.

Daily Task & Action Plan:

1. Take a look at the solutions you wrote when you did the Fire Ritual. Did you envision the best solution? Do you need more information and wisdom in order to really solve the problem? Rewrite the action plan and initiate solutions that will actually work.

2. Write down the top 2-3 money problems that you have. Using the skills you learned in the Fire Ritual, what are the solutions?

3. Make sure that you have enough safe in your nest egg. Once you have it protected, then start envisioning what hard assets might preserve your estate better in the years to come than cash or bonds. Hard assets retain their value better than paper assets do in a Debt World.

4. Commit to an education project. Sign up now. Open up that College Fund for your kids. Take tango lessons. Enroll in an Investor Educational Retreat from a qualified investment mastermind, who has had a Ph.D. in results for more than a decade.

Learning New Skills

Many people in the U.S. are getting their financial information from salesmen, who may not be qualified or educated, and are incentivized to sell you more than you can afford. (The mortgage, real estate, bond and stockbrokers are all salesmen, as are the car salesmen, the retail associate, and the life, annuity and health insurance salesman.) Read the "Buyer Beware" chapter of *The ABCs of Money* to learn how to avoid the debt trap of being an unconscious consumer, and to embrace the life of an enlightened, empowered investor.

Additional Resources

Check out *The Queen of Versailles* documentary for an example of a vision, financial literacy and money problem in action.

Day 10: Fun
Today's Mantra: Fun

I keep repeating that health is wealth. Here's how that truth relates to fun. Fun is free endorphins. Endorphins are anti-oxidants. Anti-oxidants are very healthy for you. So, you are doing a great thing when you laugh, exercise and play around. You are contributing to your own health. You are making yourself a more enjoyable person to be around, too. So, you're contributing to the health (and reducing the stress) of the people who have to work with and live with you.

Your only task today is to make sure that you are having fun. Go *do* something that you really enjoy. Spend your short-term fun money (10% of this month's income) on something that you normally wouldn't do. Have fun in a *new* way – something that your heart has always longed to do. Maybe you have wanted to take that Spanish class, or salsa dancing lessons, or a spinning class, or to go to a concert or visit a museum. Answer your heart's calling. You never know where that will lead. However, since it's something you're likely to enjoy, chances are it will be healthy and good for you.

Since fun is healthy, and health is fundamental to wealth, every time you have fun, you should *envision* that you are putting money in your own wallet. Spend time generously – *invest* your time – on things that you enjoy, and honor just how valuable that investment is. Sometimes what you do for fun can also become the foundation of great abundance. Steve Jobs says that if he and Steve Wozniak had not sold free long distance (at the telephone companies expense), which began as prank, Apple wouldn't exist. If I had never had fun trading stocks on the side, I wouldn't be writing this book. And I have a few other similar stories to share.

One of the keys to abundance is to add value to other people's lives. People around the world love Apple products so much today that the company is worth over half a trillion dollars with over $178 billion in annual sales. I add value by offering forensic, investigative financial news, information and education, monthly teleconferences and my stock picks – something I enjoy doing very much. Subscribers and retreat attendees have made it possible for me to do what I love for the past 12 years. Daniella Clarke invented the sexiest jean the world has ever known. Wendy Robbins enriched our lives by co-inventing the Tingler – a tchotchke that massages your head, giving it, in her words, "a head orgasm."

The Tingler was the pet rock phenomenon of a few years ago. Something that was fun and funny became a cash cow for her – at least in the early days of the product. Wendy got a lot of publicity. Then she got a great distributor. Then the money started rolling in.

Of course, it's not quite as easy as that. You have to find a way to convince a few celebrities to put the Tingler on their head – something that Wendy made easier with the icebreaker opening line of, "May I give you an orgasm?" Before your first media stunt makes headlines, you have to make sure it's easy for consumers to buy your product. And after your product is the hit of the year, you have to battle all the fake Tinglers. But the possibility of having *the next big thing*, whether it is a Tingler, a smiley face t-shirt or a Candy Crush Saga game, is often sparked by play – not work.

Daniella Clarke launched a multi-million dollar brand off of a playful little thing that she liked to do with her jeans, as a teen. I met Daniella before she married Gilby Clarke (the guitar player from Guns N' Roses). We were all hanging together on the L.A. music scene. Daniella liked to rip the belt line off of her jeans and wear them super low. You might not like to see the plumber wearing his jeans this low and then bending over, but, trust me, when Daniella did it, it was super sexy. She was a gorgeous girl and this look was hot in a way that no one had ever dared before. (Now the super low hip pant has become mainstream – but it all started with Daniella.) Once Daniella's circle began to include famous celebrities, the girls all wanted to dress like her. She was smart enough to turn that into Frankie B – a fashion label that has changed the way we look at jeans forever. Daniella became as famous as her husband, Gilby.

Dreaming up sexy clothes is something that is fun for Daniella. Granted, turning that into a business requires a lot of effort and startup capital. It's pretty hard to become prosperous and abundant without focus, effort and funding, unless you are a trust fund baby. What might be surprising to you, before reading about these examples, is how large a role passion and fun can play in the mix.

Having Fun with Friends

When you surround yourself with people you enjoy *doing* things with, chances are that you'll get a lot more done. (Duh.) All of the words in that sentence are key. If you are just hanging out, getting high or drinking, and passing the time with gossip or light banter on television shows or movies, then days and years can pass pretty much the same without you noticing. However, if you are *doing something* with people you like, then, while you're chatting away, chances are your conversations will be more substantive, and you might find that those people will want to do other things with you as well. So, expand your idea of "fun" to include possible charitable projects, where you can rub elbows with people who have similar passions. You'll hear me say that charity is the best networking as often as I say that health is wealth.

Chellie Campbell says that the world is made up of two types of people – *your* people and *not your* people. You can use the fun factor as a gauge to whom you really should be working with. *Your people get* you. They understand your heart and soul, in addition to your words.

People who are not *your people* are difficult to be around. They make you feel inferior, or self-conscious, or, in the worst-case scenario, they outwardly put you down, belittle or oppress you. That's what makes family reunions and Thanksgiving dinners so tricky. In families, particularly extended families, there are very often people who are not *your people* in the mix. And you have to put up with it when everyone gets together. But you don't in your daily life. You can make a choice to start aligning yourself with people who lift you up, who encourage you, who help you and who make you feel better about yourself. They say that a true friend knows the ugly side of you and loves you any way. No one is perfect.

If you are around people who don't get you, who don't like what you do, who think that you are dumb and are always putting you down, chances are, if you achieve anything at all, it is after you throw the weight of all of that judgment off of your shoulders and out of your psyche first —something you'll have to do over and over again if you keep brushing up against the same negative energy. Imagine how much easier it is to soar if you don't have all that emotional baggage weighing you down. If you want to fly, you have to lighten your load. If you want to achieve great things, you need a good support team.

Your people are not sycophants; they are not *yes* people. They don't blow smoke up your ass just to win your favor or approval. (But you'll find a lot of these people hanging around, trying to catch your attention, once you do get rich and famous.) Your people will challenge you. They will have healthy debates with you. They will disagree with you on occasion. But they will still respect you and your right to your opinion – even if they think it is wrong. Undoubtedly you can think of someone right now whom you love and respect who has very different political or religious beliefs.

Many people find kindred spirits through events that they do for *fun* – after work. Hmmm...

Together you and your people can create great good. Our greatest achievements were a communal effort – from airplanes, to the genome, to the lunar landing and even agriculture.

Start thinking of fun in a broader sense. If you are deliriously happy with the people you work with, doing the things that you are doing, creating the products and services that you are co-creating, then you are already doing a lot right. If you're seriously unhappy with the things that you do for a living and with the people you surround yourself with, they really aren't *your people*. If you really aren't doing something that contributes to the planet, then you are selling yourself, and humanity, short. You shouldn't be doing it.

I'm not saying to quit your job tomorrow. What I am saying is that you have a limited amount of time on the planet. Your wealth is not as simple as how much money you have. Your ability to *enjoy that money* is a huge part of prosperity and abundance. A billionaire who can't spare the time to kick a ball with her child might be rich, but is leading a very time-shackled, impoverished existence. She will never be able to purchase those lost moments.

Happiness, like gratitude and forgiveness, is not something that you can chase down. Happiness is something that is born from sincerely letting your hair down, from long-sought-after achievement, from watching someone you love let their hair down, achieve something or just smile at you in a private moment. Happiness shows up unexpectedly, when you find yourself beaming.

Are you working at a job that is fun for you? Maybe you think that's not even possible. You might think, "I drive a bus. It's not that much fun for me. In fact, it's a real pain in the rear. Literally."

Well, of course, there are a lot of jobs that are challenging to enjoy. However, is it possible that a shift in your thinking might improve the situation? Have you stopped to notice just how many of *your people* are climbing on board the bus every day? Could you take pride in offering mass transit solutions to people who can't afford gasoline, or to greenies who like to use cleaner modes of transportation? What would happen if you offered a bright smile and a warm greeting of hello to everyone who comes on board? Would that be more fun for you and for the passengers? (Try it!)

One of my first real jobs was as a salesman for corporate health insurance accounts. It was at a time that was pre-Affordable Health Care and pre-COBRA. If you lost your job, you might become uninsured overnight, which, for a person battling a disease, could prove deadly. The health insurance company that I worked for had a policy of doubling the premium of companies that had workers with certain high-cost, chronic diseases, like AIDS. Although it was illegal to release the names of the patients to the employer, the company was allowed to send over claims reports. Many salesmen would white out the names but leave the social security numbers. As a result, the employer could identify the worker causing the claims, let that person go and, possibly, keep their insurance premiums affordable.

I'm not sure if this was legal, but, to me, even if it was, it was immoral. I certainly wasn't going to do that myself, and, further, I was not happy working for a company where that behavior was going on. It was probably *not* company policy, by the way. I'm sure that it was simply the way that salesmen got around losing their clients, due to strict underwriting standards.

I alerted senior management to the issue and was given the brush-off. Within a few weeks, I found myself in the human resources department defending myself. If I had been a little more sophisticated, I would have negotiated a better severance package, or maybe have even given myself time to find a different job. But I couldn't stand to be there even a day longer after I met with the human resources department and was asked to step in line more with the rest of my colleagues. The company response to my concerns over the rampant practice of revealing the social security numbers of sick employees to employers was that my hair was too blonde and I should try a darker shade. Some customers had complained apparently.

When I left (that same day), I didn't know where I would go or how I would support myself. I only knew that my salary felt like blood money, and I couldn't work there or spend that money anymore – particularly after the human resources person had belittled me for not blending in more. That decision was one of the most empowering choices I have ever made. And the fact that I left without a new direction opened up a world of possibilities to me that I would have never considered if I had simply moved to a different insurance company (where the practice was probably the same).

I ended up working in the music department at the Fox Film Corporation, where I met lifelong friends who are *my people.* One friend there, MaryAnne, was the first subscriber to the Women's Investment Network, LLC ezine. Another was one of the first investors. And, because I love music so much, this new job was a thrill for me! Imagine being able to help select songs for the dance sequence to a feature film, or watching movies to make sure that all of the music had been properly licensed. So much fun, particularly for a musician!

When you are in alignment with what you do *for a living*, the smile is not forced. If you're not having fun at work, then examine that carefully. Is it an ethos problem? Or is it an attitude problem? Can you be happy about earning an honest living?

If you're making nuclear bombs and you don't like that career, there are a few choices for you. If you are adamantly opposed to the product you are creating, then you could look for a job where your skills are cleaning up the planet instead of creating destructive devices. You could test the waters on another endeavor that is close to your heart – doing this initially after hours, until the time is right to leap into the new career. You might try educating yourself, or applying for other positions.

The issue here is that when what you *do* is in opposition to what you *want to do*, then you are at odds with yourself. If you want to enjoy life, then you have to pull yourself together and get more into alignment. Even if the transition takes time, you can start the journey now. You'll find that once you do make these shifts, then you will be far happier in the days to come.

You might believe in making weapons of war – thinking that is what the nation needs to remain secure. I'm not here to judge you. If you do what you think is important, and so do I, and so does the next guy, this world is going to be far more beautiful, even if all of us don't agree on every detail. When we are all benefitting the planet in our own way, and learning how to do that in ways that are less destructive to our collective humanity, everyone wins. As we get more microscopic about making these distinctions and commitments, we evolve and get closer to the truth.

What If Your Fun Factor is Actually an Unhealthy Vice?

If you think that everything that's fun is illegal, immoral or fattening, then you have developed some harmful ways of releasing happy hormones. The body's four mood-enhancing chemicals – endorphins, serotonin, dopamine and oxytocin – are easily accessible through good habits, too. Having a cigarette and a cup of coffee every morning can trigger dopamine, but so can winning an Academy Award or crossing the finish line in a marathon.

When I say to have fun today, I'm not saying to stay in your robe guzzling whiskey – even if you can justify that as *fun for you*. If vices are fun for you, then you'll just have to think far outside your own boxed-in thinking to remember things that you like to do that are good and clean – even if you have to try skipping, or something else that you enjoyed as a child.

Pleasure seeking is very different from creating happiness. An easy way to gauge which one you're addicted to is to be honest about the lasting power of the thrill. Something that lights you up for an hour (or less) is a vice. Things that lead to happiness are not so fleeting. I'm pretty stoked every day about my dream job, even the days that are challenging and daunting. I never felt that way about the health insurance company, unless I was buying cool looking clothes or a new car – fleeting joys. I always felt that way in the music department at Fox, even though it afforded me fewer retail-therapy days.

So, how can you make sure to get addicted to things that are good for you? The easiest way is to make sure that your vices are not habitual. Drinking a glass of wine here and there is different than guzzling a bottle of wine with every dinner, or starting your drinking right when the clock strikes 5 p.m.

If you're already embroiled in the daily drink, then mix up your schedule to escape the pattern. Do something else in the evening rather than have that big meal with wine. When I wanted to lessen my alcohol intake, I started tango lessons at night. It was a lot more fun. It was healthier. And since hardly anyone drinks while they are dancing tango, I didn't want to drink either. The social pressure *not to drink* helped tremendously. (It's smelly and you can't dance well if you can't balance.)

Here's where fun can help you shift out of vices and into smarter choices. Rather than *kicking* the bad habit, which is a feeling of deprivation, why not *replace* the bad habit with something that you enjoy *even more?* When I wanted to give up smoking, I asked my boyfriend to kiss me every time that I wanted a cigarette. That worked far better than a nicotine patch for me. In fact, I stopped in one day and never turned back! Lots of women quit smoking and drinking when they discover that they are pregnant. When your reason is important enough – or fun enough – kicking the habit is easy.

If you have a lot of bad habits or if your habit is a chronic addiction, then you will need to make the shift under the care of a physician or in a rehabilitation facility. Even then, do not underestimate the value of adding fun into the mix. Doing things that you naturally enjoy will make the rehabilitation process easier and more permanent.

Rediscovering Lost Passions

Take a look at the cover of this book. There was once a time in your life when bouncing a ball released endorphins for you. It is the cynical, jaded and weather-beaten side of you that adapted your own body chemistry to like the taste of cigarettes or whiskey, or got embroiled in the daily grind, instead of landing in the job of your dreams. The first drag off of a cigarette or slug of liquor is not pleasant. And that innocent, wonder-filled child within you is not dead.

There is something that you are here to do on this planet, and when you discover it, you will become like that child once again. And it will be fun. So, having fun now – not jaded fun, but something that feels like good, clean fun – is part of that self-discovery. So, is charity. Because whatever is calling out to you to make better in the world is going to release a lot of those happy hormones, too, once you start doing that. And the people you do it with are going to be bonded to you in ways that are far more lasting and enjoyable than just attending a "networking" meeting. Start acknowledging that on the opposite end of your drudgery and cynicism lies a world of possibilities. Rather than complain about *what is*, flip your thinking to imagine what *might be*. Dream a little.

Exercise – in a new way. Love – with renewed commitment. Break bread with someone. Laugh. Skip. Do something that throws your life a little off kilter. All of these create endorphins.

Some people say, "I spend my *fun* money on my home." They usually say this with a serious, pinched smile on their face. Hmmm. Trying telling your face that lie.

If your fun money isn't flushing you with endorphins then you're selling yourself short.

Sir Richard Branson says, "I try to find fun in everything I do, from business commitments to philanthropic ventures, to my personal life. You are far more likely to be inspired and have great ideas if you love what you do, and can instill that spirit of fun throughout your company."

Daily Task & Action Plan:
1. Have some fun!
2. Plan on something fun that you'll have to save up all year to afford. Set aside 10% of your income toward that goal. Write the date on the calendar when you are going to go and have that fun. Make any reservations that need to be made.
3. Count your blessings.

Learning New Skills
Be honest with yourself. If your idea of fun is narcissistic pleasure-seeking, and you've wondered for decades why you are still unhappy, then it's time to do whatever it takes to break the shackles of your addiction and discover a new passion. Personally, I think that rehab has such a miserable cure rate (and a high recidivism rate), because people are wallowing in their disease more than

immersing themselves in the pleasure panacea and the cure. I'm not saying that therapy and self-reflection are wrong. These are a necessary part of any personal growth. But growth tends to be *in a direction,* and if all that you are doing is reflecting, thinking and regretting, then you're stagnating.

Don't remain consumed with your addiction. As you endure the physical and emotional withdrawals, start healing with healthy thoughts and actions. Chronic regret about the time you've spent spiraling in the throes of alcohol, drugs, or some other temporary thrill, is still an obsession with the addiction. Rather, be sparked with possibilities of good uses of your time, brain power and brawn. Yes, you may have some apologies to dole out and some forgiveness to seek. However, investing your time and energy more wisely going forward is the best apology that you can give to anyone. Volunteering for a charity project might be a great alternative, or companion, to rehab. There are many different organizations that are in constant need of support, from Habitat for Humanity to missions overseas.

Additional Resources

Visit HabitatforHumanity.org or your favorite charity for volunteer opportunities. Whatever you believe should be helped and improved in the world, chances are there is a charity in existence right here and now that you can volunteer for. And if there isn't, then you have just heard a calling for you to step up and be the change you wish to see.

Research into that long-term fun project that you'll be immersed in a year from now!

Day 11: Abundance
Today's Mantra: Abundance

What kind of attitude do you have right now? Are you a person of constant sorrow or of constant celebration? If you are honest with yourself, are you spending far too much time whining and complaining about what is wrong with your life, or do you seed the ground of new possibilities? Do you celebrate your achievements, even as you climb to greater vistas? Do you have areas of deep longing in your life that have been unfulfilled for decades, or are you savoring milestones achieved and looking forward to more adventures? Are you leaning into the light, or are you casting shadows on yourself and others?

It's difficult to be abundant when you are the weed of your own garden, or if you spend most of your time hyperfocusing on the weeds, rather than fertilizing, watering and harvesting the fruit.

Are you taking ownership of your life and the fruit of your labor, or are you determined to prove that someone else always stands in the way, preventing your great good deeds and actions from coming to fruition? Is someone truly walking on your dreams? Controlling you or stealing your profits? Even under the threat of death, as only a teenager, Malala Yousafzai stood up to her oppressors and changed the landscape of possibilities for herself and her sisters in Pakistan and other developing nations. It took quite a while, far too long, but women and slaves won the right to freedom and to vote. What happens if you *demand* change in your own life? Chances are the downside of you standing up for yourself isn't death, and the upside could be the beginning of the life of your dreams. Literally. So many of us hold the keys to our own freedom…

Right here, right now, no matter what is happening in the world, there are those who find a way to manifest shelter, food, possibilities and profits – and this can be done without *taking* anything from anyone, without exploitation, and without nefarious dealings. Mother Nature doesn't have to steal from one tree in order to load both up with apples. With proper sunlight, nutrition and water, the entire orchard can flourish.

Different types of vegetation flourish in different settings. Every soul has her own geography – that place that will feel most like home to you. Don't underestimate the power of waking up each day feeling refreshed and renewed and excited about the possibilities that lie right outside your door. If your soul longs for the stage, then New York City theatre might be the answer. If you love bluegrass, Nashville. For some, home is close to family, where you grew up. For others, it's adventure. Would it be easier to whistle while you work if you woke up in a different environment?

Maybe your dour mood is as a result of watching too much television or reading too much "news."

If you're mainlining news 24/7, that is a weed in your garden. A lot of people ask me what news I watch. My answer is that I don't watch the news, unless I am preparing for an appearance on television and I have to research the anchors and people I will be interacting with. I do research, analyze and care about material facts of companies that I invest in. However, the source of that data is the original source – unpolluted by the opinions, biases, inexperience or censorship of writers and editors. I can assimilate 10 times the amount of usable and important information in one Stock Report Card™, and by asking the Four Questions for Picking a Leader and employing the 3-Ingredient Receipt for Cooking Up Profits, in the same amount of time it would take to read one article.

Some "news" websites and papers just reprint the press release, and many employ writers with too little time, experience or expertise to know how to put today's information tidbit into the larger context of what's really going on. Great, veteran writers are often furloughed before their retirement to make room for less experienced, lower paid labor. It's not a conspiracy. It has just been lean times in news – particularly print and online – for quite a while. (You might not realize that bloggers don't even get paid!)

If you want to be informed, the Internet makes it easy as a click to get quality information, although you need to be very judicious about the source of the information. Your best sources for financial information tend to be the government websites, such as:

1. The Securities and Exchange Commission (SEC.gov) for the company's earnings reports,
2. FINRA.org for ongoing investor education,
3. The Federal Trade Commission for Internet Scam alerts,
4. IRS.gov for questions on tax issues, etc.

I recommend that you take your favorite news source and do a few things. First, check out the headlines day to day – particularly with regard to the business and money pages. Do they fluctuate between euphoria and hysteria? Extreme emotions sell more advertising and capture more eyes. Over a 3-day period, and sometimes even a 3-6 month period, it's not uncommon for there to be a lot of volatility in the stock market that at the end of the day is right back where it started. The first day, if the markets drop 1%, you might see the headline, "Markets free fall on news of Russian tanks in the Ukraine." The next day you might read, "Markets soar for the 5th best showing this quarter." In truth, it was a rollercoaster and yesterday's losses are today's gains; however, that even-keeled reality doesn't make for a good headline.

Rather than reading headlines, it is a better strategy to just keep track of the relevant numbers. If it's on the front page, you're already late any way.

Also, who is penning the piece counts for everything. On February 6, 2001, *Fortune* magazine honored Enron as the Most Innovative Company of the Year, for the *6th* *time in a row* (just a few months before Enron declared bankruptcy). The following month, Bethany McLean, a reporter for *Fortune*, wrote a huge exposé, questioning Enron's accounting, writing, "The company remains largely impenetrable to outsiders. How exactly does Enron make its money? Details are hard to come by… Analysts don't seem to have a clue."

There were a few analysts during that time, such as Henry Blodget and Jack Grubman, who got into trouble with the Securities and Exchange Commission for giving buy ratings in exchange for various favors. This isn't the only reason why you shouldn't be relying upon analyst recommendations for your investment strategy. Basic supply and demand work against you when you follow analyst recommendations because whenever analysts say, "Buy," everyone buys, pushing the price up. When they say, "Sell," everyone sells and you could be trying to catch a falling knife – prices that are deteriorating so fast that your profits are evanescing before your eyes.

Bulls and bears often sort for the news that fits their strategy – ignoring anything that runs contrary to their opinions. The problem with this is that almost no one has a good track record of market timing. Euphoria and hysteria are hallmarks of boom and bust cycles. You have to be counter-intuitive to be on the right side of a boom and bust cycle – selling when everyone else is euphoric and seeing potential for rebuilding when everyone else is running out of the burning building.

If you try trading on an all-in or all-out crystal ball theory that the nation is going to hell in a hand basket – or on the faith that stocks (or real estate or any other asset) are the only thing worth investing in and you'd better jump in quick, while you can – then you are more likely to get burned than to get rich. Unscrupulous salesmen will use your fear to their advantage. Gold bugs often get sold expensive, semi-numismatic coins that are marked up far above the value of gold and silver – where the appreciation would have to be very robust just for the buyer to *break even* on the purchase.

There are ways of limiting your losses, protecting your assets, capturing your gains, getting hot, and avoiding potential bailouts and bankruptcies. A good financial plan that promotes abundance will:

1. Rise above the Wall Street rollercoaster,
2. Protect a healthy percentage of your assets at all times,
3. Rebalance and capture gains annually,
4. Avoid debt-laden, old-school companies and industries,
5. Add in hot companies and industries,
6. Lean in when Wall Street is hot and overweight safe when recessions are on the horizon,
7. Be diversified by size and style,
8. Discover what is safe in a Debt World, when bonds are vulnerable to credit risk and interest rate risk, and,
9. Protect your assets. Capital and principal preservation are the most important thing with regard to estate planning as you mature – before you even consider Return on Investment (ROI).

Boom and bust cycles are fueled by government policy and free, easy money, and the fires are fanned by the media. But they are also powered by greed. Those people who were watching late night infomercials in 2005 on how to buy and flip homes for a profit, and were in collusion with the mortgage lender and the real estate broker to buy property on speculation and flip it as quickly as possible for a profit, were at the eye of the storm of the subprime implosion and the Great Recession. There were a lot of false mortgage documents being filed in 2005 – and a lot of people involved in the ruse. Some homeowners were lying, saying that they lived in homes when they did not – and were actively looking for renters or a new buyer immediately after closing escrow. Other investors, realtors and mortgage lenders convinced friends and family to buy and flip homes and condos on their behalf, based upon promises of 40% gains (or higher) in less than a few months.

There were a couple of sick jokes in the industry at the time. One was that anyone with a pulse could get a loan. The other was The Biggest Fool Theory – that in the game of hot potato that was being played, with everyone trying to capture profits quickly, the person caught holding the hot potato when everything fell apart was just the person who turned out to be the dumbest. There are still data providers who chart where the Dumb Money is investing, versus where the Smart Money has migrated to.

No matter what the headlines and infomercials are screaming, or what sadness and tragedies are going on in the world, the foundation of your active and passive income can be ripe for abundance. Remember a few of the tenets that we've already learned.

1. Buy and Hold doesn't work when Wall Street becomes a rollercoaster.
2. Modern Portfolio Theory, which is the basis of my "Easy-as-a-Pie-Chart" investment strategies, has been performing far above the markets, through bull and bear sessions, for more than 15 years.
3. You have to know how to get safe in today's Debt World. Bonds are vulnerable.
4. You need to rebalance your nest egg at least once a year.
5. It helps to add in hot industries and to avoid the bailouts and bankruptcies. These are easy to identify when you educate yourself.
6. If you are a miserly rich person, you could be losing money every year. If you are generous with your time, talent and money – in a sustainable way – you'll attract a lot of freebies and partners.
7. A competent, qualified team of partners is essential to having a good return on any investment or business endeavor.
8. Stop making the taxman, the debt collector and the salesman rich. Start compounding gains with a solid *money while you sleep* strategy.

Remember Mario and his boss. Mario was worth a lot less and paid a lot less, yet daily he always received a lot more than his boss. His boss never received extra help, unless he paid for it, because everyone thought he was too cheap and that he never helped anyone but himself. Mario is happier than his boss, so he's more likely to live a robust, healthy, less expensive and more enjoyable life for a lot longer. If we measure wealth and prosperity as leading a rich life (including the time, talent, happiness and fun factors), then Mario is a lot richer than his boss.

It's not as easy as just being *nice*. In fact, if you are *too nice*, and are the person who always writes the check for everyone to have a great time, then you could bankrupt yourself.

Why Sports Stars Crash and Burn within 5 Years of Retirement.

Athletes and lottery winners, or anyone else who finds a pot of gold without getting the money smarts necessary to keep it, very often find themselves broke. We've heard about the most spectacular falls – such as Mike Tyson and Kareem Abdul Jabbar – but, unfortunately, this sad outcome is far from rare. In an article from February 22, 2013, Mint.com released an infographic declaring that 78% of NFL players are broke within 5 years of retirement – despite earning more in a year than most of us make in a lifetime.

In June 2014, FINRA issued an Investor Alert on promissory notes that relates directly to this problem. The latest victims of this familiar Ponzi scheme were current and former NFL and NBA players who invested $19.4 million with a bankrupt shyster. Restitution in the amount of $13.7 million has been ordered. That might sound like a decent outcome; however, the athletes are unlikely to see all of that money. Getting that judgment costs legal fees, so the amount actually returned to the athletes could be pennies or dimes on the dollar.

Earlier this year, I was having lunch at Elway's in Denver, Colorado (yes, *the* John Elway, Bronco quarterback), when a drunk guy (who was clearly *not* an athlete) stumbled in with a wad of hundred dollar bills in his fist. He blurted out, "I've never had this much money in my life!"

I shared a concerned glance with the businessmen in the booths next to me, knowing that he wouldn't have it for very long. In fact, he tossed a bill at me *just for being beautiful* (and for sitting in the right spot, I guess), as he shot back his whiskey and guzzled a pint of beer.

For some people, it's not just money, or their home and posses-sions, that they lose. Far too many suicides and homicides are money related. A few years back, in Santa Monica, California, a young foot-ball player, who had just been cut from his NFL team, drove his brand new Escalade into a tree. Those who loved him most, and even those like me who never knew him, wish that $80,000+ SUV could have been traded in for a new lease on his young life.

These are preventable problems. When a little information and education can solve the issue, that's the easiest, and the most per-manent, cure.

Here's a 10-Point Checklist to Ensure that You Walk on the Path of Prosperity and Abundance (no matter what your income is)

1. **Have a 10-Year Game Plan.**
2. **Live Within a Thrive Budget.**
3. **Know What You Own.**
4. **Learn the Basics.**
5. **Take Ownership.**
6. **Keep Players in Their Position.**
7. **Win, Don't Whine (or Sue).**
8. **Own Your Home.**
9. **Protect 10% of Income from Financial Predators.**
10. **Know Your Exit Strategy. Get Educated.**
11. **Write Your Will.**

And here are examples and details on each point.

1. Have a 10-Year Game Plan. The average career of an NFL player who makes the roster is only six years; the average career of NFL players in general (including those who get cut) is only *three and a half years* (source: NFL.com). Yet, the minute that first check hits their account, many start spending like a millionaire. A 3-year jack-pot game plan has a high probability of landing you in bankruptcy court. A game plan that makes sense before, during and after your heyday could set you up for a rich, fulfilling lifetime, using your talents as a team player as a great springboard.

2. Live Within a Thrive Budget. If athletes were operating according to the Thrive Budget, and limiting their basic needs expenditures to just 50% of their income (or less), they would be protecting 10% of their income in tax-protected, financial-predator-proof protected accounts (and paying less to the tax man). 10% would be set aside for education (offering a fantastic game plan for life post-pro sports and a Plan B for continuing education, if they get cut from the team). 10% would go to charity (tax deductible + the ability to build up a solid, diverse team of friends *outside of sports*). Fun, R&R, splashy cars, fancy clothes, expensive jewelry and fly-by-night friends would be limited to 20% of the annual income. (That's still a lot of dough to be able to blow.) Smart energy users can even save up to 90% on their electric bill. All kinds of freedom await you when you get money smart about allocating your income in a sustainable way, and stop making everyone else rich.

3. Know What You Own. Money managers, like doctors, can be dedicated and talented, or lazy and detrimental. Unlike doctors, money managers do not have to go through a decade of schooling to get licensed. Remember what Kareem Abdul Jabbar said: "I chose my financial manager, who I later discovered had no financial training, because a number of other athletes I knew were using him." So, don't buy into the sales line that money managers are "surgeons" of your money, without checking to see how much education they really have. The only way that you can ensure you have a good plan for investing your money is to truly know, and understand, the risks and rewards of what you own.

4. Learn the Basics. You don't have to build your own home to know how many bedrooms, bathrooms and square footage you need. You don't have to select every fund in order to ensure that you are diversified and have enough safe in your nest egg. Learn the basics.

Otherwise the money manager, just like the homebuilder, could be giving you far more than you need – just for the commissions and fees they receive.

5. Take Ownership. If someone loses your dough in a bad investment, it's your money, not theirs, that disappears. As Joe Moglia, the chairman of TD AMERITRADE always says, "No one cares about your money more than you do." Your future, which is seeded from the investments of today, depends on *you*. Make decisions. Do not just hand over your money and give another person the power to spend and invest it however they desire. If someone is managing your money, they should be providing you with quarterly reports on the performance of your portfolio, and meeting with you annually to discuss strategy changes designed to optimize performance in the changing landscape of the coming year.

6. Keep Players in Their Position. CPAs are tax specialists. Options trading pros are not trained to protect you and keep you safe. Brokers have both restrictions and incentives on what they can and can't sell you. You don't have to get a Ph.D. in economics to simply understand that you don't want your linebacker running downfield for the Hail Mary pass, or your CPA (who is hired to minimize your tax burden) trying to pick which investments offer the best Return on Investment (ROI). Your agent may be great at negotiating higher salaries, without knowing the first thing about building casinos in Atlantic City, or whether or not his buddy has enough experience to manage your estate.

7. Win, Don't Whine (or Sue). Trying to sue your way to victory is another sure way to bankruptcy. Lawyers are expensive. Make it your job to put together a winning 10-year budgeting and investing plan, with qualified financial partners who are committed to working together and doing an outstanding job, and stick to it. If you get cut from your position, or lose your job, act quickly to realign your game plan with the new reality, so that you can create a tomorrow that makes sense. Before you sue anyone, or hire attorneys for any reason, do a forensic analysis of what you stand to gain, versus the price of the pursuit. The best return on investment occurs as a result of great planning, rather than suing someone to gain back losses.

8. Own Your Home. Interest rates are at an all-time low. If your 10-year plan includes staying in the same city, then chances are that buying a home you can afford is a great investment – provided you don't purchase your home at too high of a price. Why? In many cities, it is as cheap (or cheaper) to buy than it is to rent. You get to write off the amount you pay in interest, offering a great reduction in your tax burden. And you have the potential to earn capital gains on the home itself. Make sure that your home purchase fits into the 50% to survive portion of your Thrive Budget. (You'll also need transportation, heat, food, clothing, insurance and to pay taxes, etc., to survive.) Real estate earns about 5% annualized, on average, over a 30-year period.

9. Protect 10% of Income from Financial Predators. According to Marion Jones, the Olympic all-star who declared bankruptcy in 2007, she lost a lot of her money on lawyers. "Bills, attorney bills, a lot of different things to maintain the lifestyle," she said in bankruptcy court, explaining why she was down to her last $2000. *Survivor* winner Richard Hatch went to jail for tax evasion. Living is expensive. The minute you hit the jackpot, you get very popular with Uncle Sam (taxes), the debt collector (credit cards), the utility company (all those late night raves), the cell phone company (get a better data plan), the bank, the county tax collector, money managers, attorneys, unscrupulous scam artists (who trip on your front porch), fair-weather friends and more. **That is why it is important to protect your money *first, no matter what,* in IRAs, HSAs and 401Ks, because that money is yours to keep forever – *no matter what.* No one can sue you to take it away.** This is another call to get money smart, so that you can employ all of the legal ways of reducing taxes, compounding gains, protecting your assets and limiting your financial exposure.

10. Know Your Exit Strategy. Get Educated. Athletes are not the only professionals who need an Act 2 in their career. Most of us are switching jobs every eight years these days. No matter how secure you feel in your job, keep up your commitment to lifelong learning and that 10% of your budget that supports it. Education is the highest correlating factor with income. The more you know, the more you earn and the less likely you are to be unemployed in the years ahead. The more you know about financial literacy, the easier it will be to protect your assets, compound your gains and avoid crippling (or bankrupting) losses.

11. Write Your Will. European Royals have kept their estates in the same family for centuries by starting the legacy process early and by training their kids to assume the stewardship of carefully distributed assets. Educate yourself on gift taxes. (This is one click and less than ten minutes on IRS.gov – or perhaps an eight-minute discussion with your CPA.) Set up a trust or LLC whereby you can start transferring your assets to your children and grandchildren, under the gift tax threshold and annually, so that by the time you pass away, *they* are the owners – without any estate taxes or disputes. Primogeniture has worked to preserve various dukedoms intact in Europe over the centuries. In America, too often the family members co-own, bicker, sell and then split up the profits. Consider assigning separate assets to each individual, according to their skill sets, and make sure they know your wishes. If this child or grandchild gets *this* and another gets *that*, they are less likely to cut everything in half to share.

Your Financial Team

I want to give you a few examples of why it's important to know the skill set of everyone on your financial team, and why you should not allow (or expect) your team members to crossover into areas that are not their expertise. The truth is that a lot of people are *thinking* about abundance, and then simply selecting the wrong people to handle things for them. This mistake is one of the most expensive mistakes you can make.

Relying on an Accountant for Investing Advice

There was a man who invested in Sun Microsystems at $10/share. By 2000, the stock was over $100/share and the holdings were worth more than a million dollars! He consulted with his accountant, who told him to gift the stock to his three kids, rather than sell it and give them the cash. The gift was structured to avoid the capital gains taxes that would have been assessed if the stock was sold and the gains were distributed to the kids.

The accountant was right to be concerned about the tax consequences. However, he wasn't considering what would happen if Dot Com stocks were in a bubble and the share price imploded. And that is exactly what happened.

In only two years (by 2002), Sun Microsystems was trading for under $10/share again. The gains were gone.

Had the man sold the stock, paid the taxes and gifted the money to his kids at the level of under $14,000/year (to avoid the gift tax level) every year, then his kids would have each received $333,000 tax free (over the course of a 24-year period). Alternatively, he could have used the money to buy vacation property that everyone could have enjoyed, and then transferred ownership to his kids gradually – again, under the gift tax level. As it was, the kids received nothing –because no one had the prescience to consider possibilities beyond simply avoiding taxes.

Relying on a Broker/Salesman for Investing Advice

I know a couple who were caught up in real estate fever in 2005. They were approached to buy a home, in cahoots with a real estate broker and a mortgage broker. Both broker/salesmen were promising that the home would be flipped within three months and that the couple would make a profit of $40,000.

As the wife was going through the fine print of the documents, she noticed that the salesmen had already checked off a box saying that she would be living in the home – which was a lie. The wife went ahead and signed off on the lie because she felt that she had promised everyone on the team that she would participate in the investment. (This is an example of NOT TAKING OWNERSHIP!)

The ruse went through as planned, and the couple did indeed make $40,000.

The team wanted to do it again immediately. This time, the wife said, "No." She wasn't going to lie again.

That's when the real estate market started to fall. Had she done the second deal, she very likely would have been stuck with an over-valued home, an underwater mortgage and a liar's loan with an adjustable rate mortgage that she wouldn't have been able to refi-nance. Chances are high that she would have paid a lot of money every year to try and keep the home to keep her FICO score high, or would have lost the home to foreclosure, ruining her credit rat-ing. It was in Las Vegas – the area of the country where real estate values plummeted the fastest.

With all of the taxes, mandatory insurance, housing, food, transportation and clothing costs of modern life, if you don't have a solid, time-proven, effective plan for your budgeting and invest-ing, then it's far too easy to just make others rich. You can pray for abundance. But if you want to actually achieve it, then you've got to be financially literate and be the architect – the decision maker – of your money house.

Budget like a Rock Star to Become One: How to Get Creative about Cutting Costs

How do rock stars have it all – the hottest dates, coolest awards and a globetrotting, jet-set lifestyle? It's not because they are the wealthiest people on the planet. The great ones with the most stay-ing power inherently understand that living in the band house is more affordable when you're starting out. Many have one or two clothing pieces – leather pants or signature sneakers – with little else hanging in their closet. They are investing in their dreams, not their basic needs and doing a lot of other things that you can model to have more fun in your own life.

So, if you're stuck in the rut of just trying to survive, remem-ber that the solution lies in simply increasing income and decreas-ing expenses. Young rock stars might win Artist of the Year at the

Grammys, return to the band house for rehearsal in the garage the next day, walk to the Hari Krishna Temple for a bite to eat, and then moonlight on a session gig for extra dough.

Where are you investing your time and money? Spending, spending, spending has a low payoff for the long term, whereas education has a high return. So when/where/how/what you spend determines how much you enjoy your life, how rich you can become, as well as how *rich* the life you are living is.

Are you ready to get a roommate? To downsize? To carpool? To walk to work? To get that high-deductible health and car insurance plan?

The Flow of Prosperity and Abundance

The flow of prosperity – giving and receiving – lies at the heart of all abundance. When Daniella creates her fashion, she's giving. When someone buys her clothes, she's receiving – which allows her to keep giving. When a bee, hummingbird or a butterfly sucks nectar from a flower, they are also helping the plant pollinate and create more life. Getting the flow right is tricky. Many of us are, by nature, either *too* stingy or *too* giving.

Another truth of prosperity and abundance, which is worth repeating, is that every cent you own and every moment you spend is always an investment. Invest more time in the bar stool than on the kids' soccer field and your family might leave you. Invest more money in looking rich rather than being valuable and your car and home might be repossessed.

The "rules" below help us to achieve more balance.

People Who Give Too Much

Givers give because they believe it is the right thing to do. And it is – in balance.

How do you know if you are *over giving?* It's not as simple as asking yourself whether or not you feel taken advantage of. Some rich people feel used, and berate themselves for giving away too much, based on how much money, rather than the percentage. When a multi-millionaire gives away a thousand dollars, that's a rounding error. When a laundress gives away $250,000, that's impressive.

Oftentimes the person who thinks they are over-giving is someone who is really giving far less than they could. It's the attitude, not the amount of money, that needs adjusting. And when it does, you become more like Mario and less like his boss. When you give, others want to give back to you. Giving 10% of your income to qualified charities is tax-deductible, in addition to the other benefits you receive from helping others.

Is the laundress over giving? Or is it possible that being able to donate that money is the mission of her life – that which gives her the passion to work at a rather mundane job? In a very real way, she is *receiving* – even when she gives. Her charity gives meaning to her life.

Many givers worry that they'll run out of money – and they will if they are giving away more than 10% of their income, or throwing money excessively and impulsively at people and things without any plan. (That's part of the issue with sports stars and lottery winners.)

When you are a worried *giver*, it's impossible to enjoy the lap of luxury, even when you are sitting in it. The truth is that chronic givers will indeed run out of money because they never remember to fill back up before they attempt to give again. Also, when you are hyperfocused on something that you fear, you create it!

"I don't want to be broke!" givers think, largely because they are stuck in a habitual downward spiral that they *know* is going to bankrupt them! The fear is justified! The right action would be to stop over giving, not to pray for a miracle to save you from yourself (while you continue to deplete your own estate).

Givers who don't know how to receive will eventually tap themselves out. You've got to be able to afford guitar picks, if you want to give it all on stage for your fans.

Graft, Greed and Grifters

The takers of the world are stingy #$%^&*! types that rape, pillage and end up screaming, "A horse, a horse. My kingdom for a horse!" The stingier and more greedy you are, the quicker your demise, and usually unpleasantly. This has been true throughout history. (Think Hitler, Idi Amin, Richard III, Muammar Gaddafi, Marie Antoinette, etc.) The more you love money and will do anything for it, the less you are beloved and the quicker people want to get rid of you, or topple you to take your throne.

People must thrive under your leadership in order for them to wish you continued success! Something must be going very right in their eyes in order for you to remain at the top of the pedestal ...

Getting the Balance Right

What stingy people don't understand is that it is not all about the money. Money won't buy you life if you have to drive through a war zone to get to your guarded palace.

What givers don't understand is that receiving is necessary to fuel your growth and replenish your supply. True sustained prosperity and abundance is a flow between giving and receiving, between nurturing and being nourished.

Here is the general idea. When you add value, you prosper. When you add beauty, you enjoy the bounty. When you sing a great song, your fans buy your CDs, which gives you the gas money to drive to the next town, with more t-shirts and music for your fans to buy. This is true in all areas of life and living. It is the law of flow and abundance.

21 Days Off The Grid

21 days is a great start toward creating a new habit. When you're stuck in a rut, it's hard to see beyond your own walled-in circumstance. How hard would it be for you to take 21 days out of your normal routine, and venture into strange circumstances and a whole new setting? Whatever challenges you face, a fresh, new look can afford you possibilities that you'd never dream up otherwise. Everyone should try 21 days in a foreign land – where no one speaks a language that they understand – at least once in their life, and preferably, at least once every twelve years.

Qualities of Abundance

True abundance never lies, never steals and never hoards. Start envisioning your life as an orchard full of peaches, where the bounty is so plentiful that you have enough to eat, package, preserve and sell around the world. Picture yourself working with talented, honorable partners who are creating great things in your life, your neighborhood, your city and around the world. Understand that you have the ability to be brave, complete, confident and successful, and that you when you are, you will attract others to help you. Everyone loves a winner.

Phil Knight, the founder of Nike, talks about this from a purely business standpoint, when he says, "Never underestimate the value of a free t-shirt." In my business, I gift 10% of my retreat seats to individuals who would have little hope of attending the retreat on a paid basis. I mentor schoolgirls from slums in Africa who are the first in their family to go to college. Some of my best testimonials and my greatest success stories come from my charitable giving. Better than any advertising I could ever purchase.

Daily Task & Action Plan:

1. Do a final analysis of your budget and investing plans. Are your 401K, IRA, health savings account and any other tax-protected retirement account set up to have 10% of your income auto-deposited? Are you diversified? Have you selected the best funds and brokerages? It is important to consider taxes, trading fees and whether or not your money market accounts are FDIC-insured, as part of the process of selecting the brokerage that is right for you.

2. Go through the 11-point checklist. Implement all aspects and make all necessary changes.

3. What would you be doing right now, right this moment, if you had all of the money in the world? Can you do something that starts up that pathway? Can you experience what you desire even in a small way? Should you start saving for it now? What's stopping you from taking the first step?

4. Abundance consciousness is a state where there is more than enough. To reinforce the fact that you have more than enough time and money, donate at least one hour of your time today to someone or some cause. Make plans to do this at least once a week. You can afford to donate up to 10% of your time and money to charity. More than that is over giving. Less is stingy.

Learning New Skills

1. Where would you be living if you had all of the money in the world?
2. Where would you like to live in 15 years?

Journal freely on these ideas. Start the creative process of brainstorming.

Additional Resources

I host Investor Educational Retreats. Oftentimes, that's the easiest way to jumpstart your financial literacy. At the retreat, you'll walk in without a clue, or with a cracked nest egg, and walk out with a plan that works immediately and for the rest of your life. We play the Fire Ritual and the Billionaire Game at the retreat as well, so that you can learn how to solve money problems and live according to the Thrive Budget.

Day 12: Yes

Today's Mantra: Yes

"There's a dark and a troubled side of life, but
there's a bright and a sunny side, too."
This is from the traditional folk song "The Sunny
Side," written by Ada Blenkhorn.

Today's mantra, yes, has a lot to do with keeping on the sunny side. The idea of "yes" is simple. *For one full day,* eliminate all negatives from your thoughts and speech, and focus on the power of possibilities. When you are tempted to say "No," find a way to say "Yes." When you think "Stop," find a way to think "Go."

I'll give you two examples of how this works. When your teen asks if she can ditch school to go surfing, today, rather than just say "No," try saying, "Let's go surfing on Saturday. Where would you like to go?" While this isn't a direct "yes," it's the spirit of yes, and you get my point. You've created a possible alternative rather than just shutting everything down.

If you are a mother with fidgety five-year-olds at breakfast, rather than saying "Stop doing that," over and over again to no effect (except making the people around you crazy), you might try, "Would you like some crayons and paper to make a cartoon?" Or, "Do you want to go pay the bill for us?"

Today's "yes" day is another exercise to get you problem solving, rather than stuck in the problem. If you are trying to lose weight, instead of saying to yourself, "Don't eat *that,*" think, "I can snack on *this* or *this,* or maybe I can take a walk in the park at lunch." If you are a smoker, rather than think, "Don't smoke" (which only makes you want to smoke all the more), when you get the urge to light up, think, "Hmmm. I'd like to have a kiss!" Even if your loved one isn't around to kiss you, you can call or text her and get a thrill from the playful interaction. This is not intended to replace a diet, or rehab or an anti-smoking regimen. It's intended to put you back in charge of your urges, emotions, mind and body.

If you are a shopaholic, instead of saying, "Don't buy *that*," think "I'll invest in *this*." If you think of the money you spend as having the power to be worth more tomorrow than today, how does that change what you purchase?

Censor your words and your thoughts all day long, and drink in the power of focusing on possibilities and the magic of *yes*. Carly Fiorina, the former chairman and CEO of Hewlett-Packard, says, "There are people who focus on the limitations of the situation, and there are people who focus on the possibilities. The people who focus on the possibilities always achieve more. See what's possible!!"

Every time you are tempted to say a negative, flip it to its opposite. If you're accustomed to noticing what's wrong, instead of what's right, then this is going to be a tough day – full of forensic self-adjustments.

I want to share the way that the book cover for *The Gratitude Game* came into being. I contacted Bryan Zee, who is a very talented artist, and asked him to do a mockup based upon the photo of Davis, the name of the book and the templates that I'd used in previous books. The first draft that came back to me was so far from what I wanted that I honestly thought I'd need to find help elsewhere. Bryan reached out and said, "What changes would you like to see?" That invitation sparked me to write down seven things that I'd like for him to try fixing. The next draft was so much closer to what I was envisioning that I sent over a list of 10 more changes. Within just a few days, we had a cover that I *loved*.

It's very difficult for anyone to make the necessary changes if you are only pointing out what they are doing wrong. And it's surprising how far and fast change can occur when you communicate what you want clearly. (Not always, of course, but often.)

When you believe in someone, they are emboldened. When you criticize someone, they shrink – or they challenge your stand and bickering might break out.

Some of us have been raised in an environment where criticism and negative critique is the way that we were programmed. I'm not saying that you shouldn't notice when things are wrong, or when people are doing things that they shouldn't do. I'm saying that in every instance, you can convey that message in a way that invites positive change, rather than merely splash more mud (negativity) on the problem.

Past mistakes are useful as a map to dodge future potholes. However, sitting in the mud day after day talking about all of the dirt on your clothes doesn't help anything. Better to get up, brush yourself off, wash your clothes, give thanks that you're still around to sing a new song and continue on up the path to greater health, wealth and wisdom – avoiding similar pitfalls, as you go. Keep on the Sunny Side of Life.

A few months ago, at the Farmers Market in Santa Monica, California, I saw a hip, young mother shopping with her adorable 5-year-old daughter. The daughter reached into her purse, pulled out a five-dollar bill and paid the vendor for a basket of organic strawberries.

The vendor was smiling ear to ear, and asked her, "Wow, you buy your own strawberries?"

The young girl glowed, as she nodded, smiled at the farmer, pulled out a strawberry and took a bite.

"She earns her own money, too, by making her bed and helping with the dishes," the mother responded. "Now see!" she said as they walked away, "Aren't these strawberries going to be delicious? Better than candy!"

There are so many great messages here, almost too many to count. But, here are just a few. And all of these lessons were taught in a positive, empowering way.

1. **Money doesn't grow on trees.**
2. **Experiences teach more than words.**

3. **Yes is more powerful than no.**
4. **Money grows on deeds.**
5. **Pay for grades.**
6. **Life math.**
7. **A pocket full of change.**
8. **Be charitable.**

And here are the details…

1. Money doesn't grow on trees. We've all seen a tired five-year-old screaming for candy in a store, and an exasperated parent scream-ing, "No! I said, No!" one hundred times in a row. When the child carries her own purse, the question can be, "Do you have enough money to buy it?" Putting your kid in charge of her own purse – filling and dispensing it – can be a real lifesaver when your cranky child is at the grocery store, and later on, when she becomes a teen.

2. Experiences teach more than words. There's no candy on sale at the Farmer's Market, but any candy lover is going to be seduced by the sweet smell of ripe strawberries. Creating experiences where your children can make good choices, and then complimenting them, builds self-esteem, good health and a healthy relationship with food and money.

3. Yes is more powerful than no. The strawberry experience was even more profound because before shopping at the Farmer's Market, I had breakfast at my favorite Mexican restaurant. There an exasperated, tired-looking mother must have repeated, "I need you to stop doing ___ (fill in the blank)" to her two young boys a million times. The befuddled and deflated boys couldn't win. They weren't eating fast enough. They were fidgeting too much. Everything they did was *wrong*. The meal was a horrible experience for everyone involved, including those patrons who were sitting close by.

In the same circumstance, my own parents would have given me a twenty and told me to go pay the bill. (I was the fourth child, and they had learned a thing or two by then.) That task, for a kid, can eat up a good ten minutes of parental feasting time. The waiters and owners knew the family, and would have been delighted to assist the children in paying the bill. (It would have been so much more enjoyable than listening to the berating – for all of us.) Your eating experience can be a lot more fun if you remember to bring the crayons, blank paper *and* a few twenties for the tab (not just the credit card).

4. Money grows on deeds. An allowance reinforces the myth that money grows on trees, whereas earning money by doing "jobs around the house" reinforces the truth that providing value in the world is the way to earn a living. Money grows on deeds. The more people value what you do, the more you'll get "paid." At its heart, money is just another way of saying, "Thank you!" (This is something I discussed at length in the introduction of this book.)

5. Pay for grades. Why pay for grades? Because education is the highest correlating factor with income. The better your child performs academically in kindergarten and the years to come, the less money she will cost you in the decades to come and the more "money" she will earn as an adult. She could even earn scholarships for college – as I did – which make her cost of a degree a small fraction of what most people pay.

Of course, different kids need different school environments in order to "perform" well, so if your kid isn't "making the grade," then it's time to get creative about what environment is going to be a match for your child's talents and passion. Don't be stuck on the thought that the only achievement worth acknowledging is academic – particularly if that isn't your kid's forte. It might be sports, or the arts, or a charter school, or smaller classrooms, or digging in the dirt, but somewhere there is an environment for your child to excel in. My parents attached my allowance to practicing the piano for an hour every morning (before school). Also, there is a difference between all and nothing. For a five-year-old, an A might be worth a dollar, a B seventy-five cents, a C fifty cents, a D twenty-five cents, while the F is worth only a nickel. Give them something to aspire to, assistance in achieving the goal, and reward them for the effort as well.

6. Life math. I know so many educated men and women, some who are in charge of the complicated calculus of getting spacecraft on Mars, who were never taught the basics of life math. College students get credit cards that they don't know how to use, and by the time they graduate are already embroiled in a cycle of debt that could take decades to untangle. Giving your 5-year-old life math, such as buying her own strawberries at the Farmer's Market, is a 1-2-3 leg-up that will multiply over a lifetime.

7. A pocket full of change. A pocket full of change and a pile of penny rolls can be fun and instructive for kids. Have a jar where you dump all of your change, and then once or twice a month, maybe while you're doing your own housework, have the kids create stacks with the coins and then fill the rolls. Get creative about what this "found money" can purchase, whether it is a family miniature golf night, or movie night, or saving up the change for a trip to Disneyland or Yosemite. Have fun with your spare change!

8. Be charitable. Just as charity is a simple way to reinforce the message that you are living in the overflow, that there is more than enough, it is also a valuable skill for your kids to learn. 10% of their allowance is both sustainable and doable. This simple habit is one that will bring you the most unexpected gifts – one of which is creating a more compassionate child. Your five-year-old might be saving up nickels and dimes, which by Christmas could be enough for a great toy for a child in need, which she can purchase with her own money. In my household, during Christmas, we spent as much money giving gifts to underserved families as we did on our kids. My son was in charge of selecting and purchasing the gift.

The more personal you can make the giving, the better, for everyone involved. Don't overlook the fact that a child in need can be very close to home. Is it the child of the person who bags your groceries at the grocery store? Or of the teacher's aide in the classroom? Or even a cousin? (One of the most fun holiday gifts that we gave was to take a family, whom we were related to, to Disneyland.)

We lose sight of the fact that Money Grows on Deeds in our chase to accumulate enough of it to buy the life of our dreams. But, one young mother and daughter, on a sunny morning in Southern California, with only five bucks and a basket of strawberries, were setting a great example of the power of yes, and the healthy, abundant relationship that these magic tokens of gratitude that we call money, can bring.

If you want to criticize someone and tell him all of the things he is doing wrong (whether this is self-criticism, or aimed at your kids, or at an employee), stop yourself. Remember those five-year-olds in the restaurant who were supposed to stop fidgeting and stop fighting, but were never given any guidance or options on what they *should be doing.* Compare that scene to the five-year-old who was in charge of her own purse, in a setting where all of the choices are healthy ones. Think of how surprised I was when I sent over seven changes on a book cover that I really didn't like, and was sent back one that I liked quite a lot.

Are you even sure that those people whom you are most thankful for in your life know this? Do your children know what you love most about them? Does your companion?

Your life right now may be more beautiful than you are allowing yourself to think, particularly if you've slipped into the bad habit of focusing on the negative, instead of the positive. Is the sun shining outside? Do you have your health? Are you in some way, in some part of your life, really fulfilled? If you are not, then you need to examine your Billionaire Game and start implementing some of those areas that will allow you to thrive right here and now. Every day, there should be something that you are doing for yourself that makes you feel beautiful, whole, complete and healthy. If you don't fertilize and water your own tree of life, then you can't provide beauty and sustenance for anyone else.

Bless others with the power of yes today. Bless yourself as well.

Saying "yes" today is also giving yourself permission to follow your heart. Today, say "Yes" to your heart's desires. Let life be different from the average daily grind. When you get a whim, follow it. See where that leads, as a curious observer. You might be pleasantly surprised.

Focus on What You Want Rather Than What You Don't Want

Right after college, I was interested in giving back, and I signed up to teach to kids in the inner city on a substitute basis. One of my first jobs was a complete disaster, because during our physical education hour, I had an impossible time getting two fifth-grade boys to line up and come back into the classroom. I called to them. They ignored me. I walked over to get them. They ran away. Pretty soon, I was on a wild goose chase that should have been a segment on a comedy show. I was the only person who wasn't laughing. *All* of the kids were – even those who were standing obediently in line.

Fortunately, during a weekend training session, a veteran teacher gave me a classroom management tip that changed everything. Rather than chase the two boys who are doing the *wrong thing* – which was bound to result in frustration and a trip to the principal's office, why not reward the 29 kids who are doing the *right* thing? Once there's no audience, 99% of the time, the prankster steps offstage and into line.

When students know that they will get the attention they desire by doing the right thing, they are more likely to do it. When you believe in someone, they are more confident and will work even harder to impress you.

This simple trick worked like magic. By pointing out and rewarding the behavior that I did want, I never had to chase down the behavior that I didn't want.

Just last month, I applied this practice to a young niece. She was three – just past the Terrible Twos. Lydia was confident and athletic. She was climbing all over the monkey bars and slides. There was another little girl who kept getting in her way. Her first instinct was to push her out of the way, and say, "Move! Stop getting in my way!" The other little girl started pushing back.

I wasn't sure that it would work because I hadn't been around Lydia much, but I called out to my niece, saying, "Lydia. Try saying, 'I'd like to slide. Will you please move over so that I can?'"

I waited while Lydia paused and thought about it. Then she repeated what I said word for word. The other little girl responded, "I want to go first." She slid quickly down the slide before Lydia could say anything back. Lydia slid down after her, giggling the whole way. Problem solved. The two little girls repeated this dance a few times, and then began playing together.

Follow Your Heart Today

In his 2005 Stanford Commencement Address, which I recommend that you watch, Steve Jobs talks about three major vicissitudes in his life and his unconventional approach to success. One major life event was when he dropped out of college. Another was when he was fired from Apple. And the last was when he was diagnosed of pancreatic cancer. According to Jobs, the thread that runs through each of these was that he was following his heart. Jobs said, "You have to trust in something – your gut, destiny, life, karma, whatever – because believing that the dots will connect down the road will give you the confidence to follow your heart, even when it leads you off the well-worn path."

Steve co-founded Apple, enjoyed great success there and was then stripped of his job by the CEO, John Scully, whom he had hired to steer the company into the future. Can you even imagine how maddening that would be? At that point, Jobs could have given up, or been eaten up by his own indignant anger. (And, honestly, perhaps he was for a time.)

What does a "yes man" do in that rare circumstance that he is fired from his own great company? Jobs founded a new company – NeXT Computer – and co-founded the best new animation company in existence – Pixar. Pixar became so successful in children's animated film that Disney purchased the company, making Steve

Jobs the largest individual shareholder in Disney – with more ownership than Walt's nephew, Roy Disney.

By 1996, nine years after Jobs left Apple in 1985, Apple was in real trouble, and Jobs was recruited to save the company. At the time of writing this book, Apple is worth $602 billion and is the most valuable company in the U.S.

Following his heart didn't always feel great and it didn't save Jobs' life. But it certainly added up for him and for us.

When you follow your heart, you will appear to be lost to some. It's hard to imagine Jobs' parents being loving and understanding that he was dropping out of college so that he could "drop in" on *calligraphy* classes. Someone, whether it was Jobs' himself, or Wozniak, or Jobs' parents, or a mentor, was encouraging him to keep launching businesses from his garage.

Following your heart might seem like you have no map or North Star. You might feel lost yourself, even as you step bravely forward into the great unknown of tomorrow. However, at the end of the journey, you will have enjoyed your life. And the divine pattern will reveal itself to be a masterpiece. When you have your nose stuck so close to the canvas of a map, you cannot see the larger work. You miss the magic that might be only a few steps to your left or right.

Daily Task & Action Plan:
1. Say "yes," all day long. Find creative solutions and ways to turn all of your negative thoughts and your "no's" into yes.
2. Start the process of getting your basic needs expenses down to 50% of your income (if you aren't already there). Housing is the first thing that you should address, since it is the biggest expense in most budgets. Oftentimes, the right answer is to think bigger. Can you bring in additional income by buying a quadraplex or an apartment building? By renting out the garage or a spare room?
3. Is a health savings plan right for you? If you are paying an arm and a leg for insurance, then it's worth it to consider a HSA. Research IRS.gov to learn more. Can you reduce the

amount you spend commuting to work, on your electric bill and on gasoline? Do you need that expensive insurance policy or annuity? Could you earn a better ROI more quickly in your own IRA? (These savings will go a long way to getting your basic needs expenses under control.)

4. Look at your pie charts. What are your 10 funds? What are your four hot slices? Get hot, get safe and avoid the Bailouts. If you don't know how to do this, commit to learning how to do this now.

5. For most people in today's Debt World, the challenge is to get safe and to know what is safe in a world where bonds are vulnerable. Start the process of educating yourself on this subject, and dreaming up hard assets – whether it is a second home or income property – that you think you might like to invest in.

Learning New Skills

Visit the Bond section of FINRA.org to learn more about bonds. Become familiar with the difference between interest rate risk and credit risk. Review any Investor Alerts that FINRA has issued on bonds.

Additional Resources

Search for the Stanford Commencement Address that Steve Jobs gave in 2005. Other great commencement speeches include J.K. Rowling speaking to Harvard graduates in 2008 and Larry Page (the co-founder and CEO of Google) addressing graduates at University of Michigan in 2009. You should be able to view all of these videos online without any problem. Jim Carey's 2014 commencement for the Maharishi University of Management is worth listening to, too! And, if you're reading this book 20 years from now, in 2034, I fully expect Davis Lau's commencement speech at The New School to rock!

DAY 13: HEART

TODAY'S MANTRA: PUT YOUR HEART INTO IT

I'm sitting in Union Station in Kansas City, Missouri, as I write this chapter. Honestly, I can't imagine a better setting. This building is celebrating its 100th anniversary this year. The ambition of this transportation hub is much quieter than in years past. It's in preservation mode, trying to find its soul and recapture the heart of the community. But the relics of Westward Expansion are ensconced in the architecture – in the vaulted and gilded ceilings, the massive chandeliers, the arched windows, the limestone walls, and the observation deck of the main restaurant, where it's easy to imagine women and children scanning the disembarking passengers for fathers and sons, who are returning from war or business on the rail. Since 1914, many families have reunited and many lovers have kissed sad farewells, while Harvey House waitresses scurried to deliver burgers and pie in time for everyone to catch their trains.

Today Union Station is trying to be a cultural gathering spot. There is a Science Center for kids, a U.S. Post Office, a coffee, chocolate and tchotchke shop, and, this month, an impressive King Tut Exhibition.

Yesterday, we talked about the value of yes, and of following your heart. It is synchronicity that has led me to this moment.

A few weeks ago, I was looking for something interesting to watch on Netflix, when I ran across the history of Highclere Castle – a popular destination in England due to it being the location of the beloved historical drama "Downton Abbey." After a long day

– another 12-hour workday – I wanted to relax for an hour before bedtime, and this documentary was the perfect length. I expected it to be boring enough to put me asleep. However, close to the end of a surprisingly interesting feature, I was introduced to the 5th Earl of Carnarvon and his wife, Almina, who was an illegitimate daughter of the banker Alfred de Rothschild. These two very privileged English Aristocrats were quite extraordinary! During World War I, Lady Carnarvon turned the Castle into a hospital, funding the operations with her own money and nursing the soldiers herself. Lord Carnarvon, who was ill and disabled after a car accident in 1901, was sent by his physicians to the arid climate of Egypt – where he ended up funding the discovery and excavation of the tomb of King Tutankhamun.

It was only two weeks after seeing this documentary that I found myself with family at Union Station, where we stumbled across the King Tut exhibit. We hadn't come for the exhibit or even known it was there. However, when I saw that it was the feature, I knew it was important to go in. Why? I certainly didn't know *exactly* why, and honestly I still don't – although I suspect it was simply to tell the story of Howard Carter in these pages. He is an exemplar of putting his heart into something.

Lord Carnarvon was the financier of the King Tut exploration; Howard Carter was the mastermind archaeologist. And this is where the heart of our story begins.

Howard Carter was a gifted English artist who was hired, at the age of 17, to document artifacts that were discovered on archaeological digs in Egypt's Valley of the Kings. Early on it became clear that Carter was a man who had something special to offer the archaeology community. He didn't just copy and catalog the relics the way others had. He actually improved the methods of rendering and mapping how the pieces were arranged in the tombs and sarcophaguses.

By the age of only 25, Carter became the First Chief Inspector of the Egyptian Antiquities Service. Now, he had the money and labor needed to conduct *his own* search parties. His grid-block method of searching for new tombs revealed two new pharaoh burial grounds – which, sadly, had already been looted. Carter remained convinced that there were untouched tombs buried in the Valley – and he was determined to find them. With his position, his power and the capital of the Egyptian Antiquities funding, he was in a great position to keep searching.

Everything skidded to a halt, however, when a group of French tourists bickered with Egyptian site guards in the Valley of the Kings. It's difficult to know the exact circumstances that led to Carter's resignation. The Saqqara Affair has been described as a "noisy confrontation."

From 1905, when Carter resigned from his post, until 1907, it appears that Carter was having the worst three years of his life. He was broke and unemployed, scuttling up a few bucks here and there as a tour guide. His dream of discovering a tomb intact was out of reach. At the age of 29, Carter was at rock bottom. And that was when the fates decided to throw a wild card in his pile. Carter was introduced to Lord Carnarvon, who had a fascination for Egyptology, was wildly wealthy, and had been banished to the desert by his doctors for health reasons.

Between 1907 and 1914, Carter supervised expeditions in the Valley of the Kings for Lord Carnarvon. World War I brought an end to the search for something extraordinary. Carter resumed his steadfast, tireless digging after the war, in 1917. But, over the next five years, his crew had still not discovered anything monumental. Lord Carnarvon gave Carter notice that 1922 would be the last year of his patronage.

Can you imagine that moment when Carter heard the news? His entire life's work – something that he had been toiling under the hot Egyptian sun for his entire adult life to discover – was about to slip like sand through his fingertips – unless a miracle happened.

It is recorded that a water boy was digging in the sand *with a stick* when he discovered the steps to King Tut's tomb. On Nov. 26, 1922, in the presence of Lord Carnarvon, Lord Carnarvon's daughter and others, Howard Carter used his lucky chisel to carve out a hole and peer into the chamber. Carter describes that day as "the most wonderful that I have ever lived through, and certainly one whose like I can never hope to see again."

After three decades of following his heart, and pouring everything he had into the endeavor, Carter was looking at the most astonishing and spectacular archaeological discovery the world had ever known. What words could describe what he felt? Certainly happy, grateful, astounded, humbled, relieved – dancing on the ceiling time.

When you follow your heart, and put your heart into it, and forge ahead in the heat, and refuse to be stopped by war, barriers and obstacles, then, one fine day, a miracle arrives. It reminds me of the famous Thomas Jefferson quote, "I find the harder I work, the more luck I seem to have."

You might think, Who has the time for that? I've got to make a living to support my family! I barely have enough hours in the day to sleep and recover!

There's nothing wrong with that. There's nothing wrong with having less money, unless you feel broke. And there's nothing wrong with being normal, unless you want to be extraordinary.

The laundress who donated $250,000 to charity was extraordinary. The banker T.S. Eliot is one of the world's most beloved poets. Howard Carter will stand that test of time as one of the most important archaeologists the Earth has ever known. Anne Bradstreet, the first published poet in America, had eight children and failing health – at a time in the 1600s when the life of a mother was arduous and endless manual labor. Gandhi gave up a very privileged and comfortable existence to set an example of inclusion and to free India. Some of these great achievements were single-minded labors, while others were passions that were squeezed in between the daily grind.

Think of that "Think Different" Apple ad from 1997. Jobs said: "Here's to the crazy ones… The people who are crazy enough to think they can change the world are the ones who *do*."

You don't have to change the world. The goal of this 21-day program is simply to change *your world* for the better. If you part your heart into your work, even if your work is as a teller at the bank, you'll find that life will spark more opportunities, and yes, even miracles, your way. (Remember the Currency of the Smile and Mario's story.) Everyone notices when someone shines. Your customers will greatly appreciate the extra care you take to ensure their satisfaction, whether you own the business or are just a cog in the wheel.

I am often greeted by people who quiz me on how I achieved my high performance ranking on Wall Street, and secured the endorsements of Dr. Gary Becker and TD AMERITRADE chairman Joe Moglia. (Gary and Joe wrote the forwards to my first two books.) They do this because they are looking for a short cut, or the magic formula – hoping that it's as easy as asking me for the recipe and then baking up some bread one lazy afternoon.

It's a rather simple formula, but it's not easy to duplicate because I earned those achievements. How did I earn them? The same way Carter did. I spent decades toiling in the hot sun, pouring over strategies and possibilities late into the evening when others were out playing around and drinking. Adding a splash of green to Wall Street and transforming lives on Main Street is my heart's desire – as much as finding King Tut's tomb was Carter's life passion. When something isn't working right, I dig into the problem and fix it. I study, read, examine, course correct, dig, process, question, fix. When there's not enough revenue to keep the expedition going, I find a way to continue on nonetheless. I don't do this with the idea of "winning" in mind. The accolades and achievements are the *outcome* of me putting my heart into my work.

Great actors don't dream of Academy Awards. They dream of iconic characters that they can drill into the heart and soul of, and convey something so rudimentary to life's struggle that we all become invested in and transformed by the story.

Another side effect by fueling your work with passion is that passion drowns fear. When you are so into something that you are immersed in it, you're not afraid. You're engrossed. When you worry about winning or losing the Academy Award, you'll be staring in the mirror trying to find the best angle, worried about whether or not you've used enough Botox to cover the wrinkles. The considerations are skin deep. When you are consumed with conveying the truth of someone's experience, you'll be drilling into the nuances of that person's soul, and the only winning or losing that comes into the mix is whether or not you've succeeded in understanding and dramatizing the dynamics enough to draw the viewer in. The Academy Awards are given to great actors, not "success" junkies.

When you are afraid, you are *trying* to do something (while fearing that you're not doing it well enough to be applauded). When you have your heart in something, you are *doing* it. Howard Carter wasn't *trying* to find King Tut's tomb. He spent three decades of his life digging and mapping, then digging some more and remapping. Over and over again. Carter was *determined* to find it.

Rosalind Franklin did not *try* to photograph the DNA helix. She kept at it until she got it right. Meryl Streep didn't attempt to portray Margaret Thatcher; she *became her* onscreen. As Yoda says, "**Try** not. **Do** or **do not**. There is no **try**."

The difference between trying and doing, between putting your heart into it or being sabotaged by fear, vanity or greed is exhibited by two strikers who played on my son's soccer team. Jose had passion, skills and commitment. On the sidelines, he would teach the other players how to do the sombrero, where you kick the ball over the opponent's head (making them look like a dope) and then catch it on the other side and score. He practiced his bicycle kick and ball control constantly. The other striker, Mikki, had speed and skills, too, but he joked around on the sidelines during practice and was more concerned about being popular than he was about being good.

During games, when someone kicked a through ball to Jose, he had a high percentage of dribbling, juking past all of the defenders and scoring. If the ball came to Mikki, most of the time he was caught and stripped of the ball, even if he had a clear shot. What was the difference? Mikki ran while looking over his shoulder to see if anyone was catching him. You can't run nearly as fast when you have your head cocked behind you. Your body wants to follow your eyes. Jose's eyes were always on the goal, even when he was maneuvering around a defender. Like Kobe Bryant, Jose's focus was solely on scoring. And he'd trained his body so well that he has a dozen different ways to achieve that.

Joe Moglia believes that when you discover what you are good at, and what you have a passion for, that is what you'll be great at. He's great at coaching football *and* leading TD AMERITRADE.

You can't read a book on success and become legendary. Great people carve their own path. Edison didn't invent the light bulb from reading a how-to book. Rosalind Franklin didn't photograph the DNA helix by reading white papers. The DNA helix was so far outside the conventional wisdom that Rosalind didn't even know what she was seeing when she looked at her own photograph.

Oftentimes, innovation comes from people who lie outside of the field because it requires a fresh, creative mind to think up something that hasn't been dreamed up or discovered yet. I am not formally trained in economics; however, my theories have worked very well over the past fourteen years – through bull and bear markets, at a time when most of the banks in the developed world had to be bailed out. That doesn't mean that I've never cracked open Schumpeter's *Capitalism, Socialism and Democracy*, or Simone Weil's *Oppression and Liberty*. I read earnings reports constantly and have frequent conversations with the most respected economists, policymakers and business leaders in the world. I'm not asking how I can be successful. We're discussing our mutual passion, and the problems and issues of our industry that are on the plate in front of us. Rosalind Franklin worked closely with Frick and Watson, sharing her photographs. Gertrude Stein's artist salons and support of Picasso, Hemingway and Fitzgerald are legendary.

What happens if you put your heart into your own health? Into the health of your Thrive Budget and your Buy My Own Island Plan? When the healthful choices of eating right and exercising are *the way life is*, then putting your heart into physical fitness is as easy as breathing.

The same thing goes with healthy fiscal choices. That is why it is easier for wealthy people to stay wealthy than it is for sports stars to become the next billionaire. The Kennedys and Annenbergs have grown up being steeped in the tradition of being stewards of their family estate rather than spenders of their income. Prince William has been trained for his entire life to be The King of England. First, he'll become The Prince of Wales and The Duke of Cornwall (along with other titles and dukedoms), where he will be expected to hone his skills even further.

Even now, Prince William is studying agriculture. Why, you might wonder? Surely he won't be a farmer! While we don't have the privilege of listening in on family conversations, his father, Prince Charles, owns one of the world's most sustainable estates and organic home farms, where he raises endangered breeds of livestock and protects the integrity of a variety of rare, organic seeds. This all goes to William when Charles becomes The King of England. Why should the state of the Home Farm be left to chance? Just as you should be the CEO of your money, even if you don't manage every dime, Prince William will be the decision-maker at the Home Farm, even if he doesn't dig up his own carrots.

Nothing with regard to the family estate will be left to chance – which is exactly how the family has retained its land and status over the centuries. (In the United States, a nation that doesn't have a legacy of wealth traditions, like primogeniture, most of a family's wealth is, sadly, squandered by the third generation.)

Prince Charles has proven himself to be one of the world's most visionary leaders on sustainability and organic farming. In my blog, I refer to him as Nature's Prince. Perhaps in the years to come, Prince William will, too.

How will you throwing your heart into your work change those around you? Kaiser Permanente began a campaign to promote health a few years ago – with their Thrive advertising campaign and by paying for wellness visits. Health is the best health insurance. Who decided to make this the new focus of the company? Can you have that kind of impact on your business? Can you be the seed of a great idea in the company, simply by embodying and living a particular way?

Sometimes it works differently. You start manifesting at a higher and more holistic level, and the place where you are at isn't *sympatico* anymore. This could happen with a company, with co-workers or with a companion. I needed to leave the health insurance company. Malala no longer lives in her village. Once abused women learn the Cycle of Violence and start standing up for themselves, they often divorce their abusers. Putting your heart into your life forces positive change.

Let's say you are a pastry chef who, for health reasons, decides to eliminate sugar from your creations. You're not going to get hired at a donut shop. However, your delicacies might attract a line at the raw vegan restaurant.

Putting your heart into your work is yet another way to attract *your people.* Just like Howard Carter won the support of Lord Carnarvon, there is a team waiting to cheer you on and help you achieve your goals.

Daily Task & Action Plan:

1. Make a new commitment and goal to work on this week in the categories of budgeting, investing, charity, education and fun. How are you going to reduce your expenses? Increase your return on investment? Where are you going to donate your time and money? What do you need to learn more about and where are you going to get the training? What new adventure awaits you?

2. Write three pages in your journal based upon the title "The Life of My Dreams."

3. With regard to business, think of yourself as a partner. If you work for a company, your job is more secure, and you're more apt to get a raise and promotion, if you actively promote the health and profitability of the enterprise. If you're a struggling small business owner, can you share overhead expenses with another entrepreneur to cut costs and increase profit margins? Should a group of clothing or furniture shops, or restaurants, locate themselves on the same street to attract ten times the traffic? (That's what malls do.)

Learning New Skills

Learn more about your favorite person. It's always best to read about them in their own words – so look for firsthand autobiographies and quotes. If the person is living, do they have a blog?

Additional Resources

Check out the blogs of Ben Horowitz and Marc Andreessen at BHorowitz.com and Blog.PMarcA.com, respectively. These two guys actively blog and are considered to be two of the most successful tech entrepreneurs alive today. Kay Koplovitz has a blog on Koplovitz.com. Springboard Enterprises (at SB.co) offers capital resources for businesswomen.

Day 14: Beauty
Today's Mantra: Notice, Acknowledge and Create Beauty.

When I think of beauty, the first thing that comes to mind is an old, outdated, politically incorrect joke. A boss had the choice of two women for his executive assistant. One was nothing to look at, but could type 100 words a minute without a mistake. The other was beautiful. Guess who gets the job?

Women can be seduced by physical beauty, too – and quite easily. However, as you become more aware, more enlightened, you come to realize that beauty is, *at its core,* sourced from something far deeper and richer than what we *see*. Beauty is not just skin deep. Eyes can be penetrating or piercing, judgmental or vacant, kind or predatory. Which do you find attractive? Why? Is it a healthy attraction?

Beauty can be one way of experiencing heaven. As you walk throughout your day today, look for things that delight you. Look for angels. Look for signs of the divine. Is it in the butterfly? The cherry blossoms?

Close your eyes for a moment, and remember the most beautiful thing you've ever seen and the most delicious moment you've ever experienced. Whether it is your children sleeping in the next room, your husband or wife, a celebrity, or a stranger on the street, Rome, Machu Picchu, the Lincoln Monument, your first car or home… Take a moment to tell yourself why that person, place or event came so immediately to mind. Resonate with the feeling that you get just by revisiting that moment that was so wonderful to you.

When you *create the life that you love* you get to experience that feeling more and more and more. A lot of people say, "I'm happy," but they are really just describing a few moments here or there that are segregated from the rest of their life. When the way you feel in church, or yoga class, or when you read a book to your child is the way that you feel most of the time – even at work – then you've integrated your daily routine with your Sunday routine. That's where magic and miracles are born. I felt ugly at work at the health insurance company. Leaving made me feel beautiful.

When you are at peace with yourself in an integrated, holistic way, then it's easier to live larger and gaze calmly, curiously and confidently at the world outside yourself. There's a lot of beauty to behold, and of course, there's a lot that needs to be beautified. Once you are part of the beauty – once you've got your entire life, from the nine to five, to the family, and beyond right where you want to be – then you can go about beautifying things that require teams to rehabilitate. Brad Pitt is rebuilding the Lower 9th Ward through his Make It Right Foundation. Doctors Without Borders assists people without access to medical care.

Beauty isn't limited to any age, or time, or mold. Beauty can be present in anything. In tango, it is pleasing to watch the passionate dance of two people connecting to the music and each other – regardless of whether they are 70 or 20. In fact, if the 70-year-olds have a flow, ease and mastery, then they might be a lot more enjoyable to observe. Sometimes, when you look closer you might find that you've been admiring two men or two women dancing together.

James Watson described the DNA double helix as "so beautiful it had to be true."

Buckminster Fuller said, "When I am working on a problem, I never think about beauty. I think only of how to solve the problem. But when I have finished, if the solution is not beautiful, I know it is wrong."

Beauty is something that makes us try a little harder, connect a little deeper, skip a heartbeat and see things in a new way. Beauty is a muse. We catch insights and respond to the world around us very differently when we are swooning under a flush of endorphins. Road rage is impossible when you are lost in the dream of rolling, green meadows spotted with grazing horses, as you cruise along, or noticing the stores and homes along your commute. Maybe it's time to exit the freeway.

At my retreats, I always add beauty to the equation. When we play the Billionaire Game, we relax on an empty beach early in the morning before the tourists arrive. The setting alone invites limitless thinking, as we gaze far out to the horizon line on the Pacific Ocean. When we do the Fire Ritual, we're looking out at a 180-degree view of the Santa Monica Beach coastline from The Penthouse restaurant – it's one of the most stunning settings in the world. A gifted Shakespearian actor often hosts our artist salon.

It might sound like we get no real work done; however, these off-site activities are specifically designed to promote wealth consciousness, so that when we are working in the boardroom, the insights are deeper, more profound and more permanent. The laughter and the joy relax us, and begin the process of associating passive income with pleasure and ease.

I touch pleasure points intentionally in my work. Most people have fear and loathing around money – bad experiences that have scarred them, or worries and doubts that prevent them from being successful. Too many investors are making their decisions with bile, stomach acid or adrenalin. They either want to stop the pain and confusion of losses, or jump in quickly on euphoria. When you understand budgeting and investing, then you are confident that the choices you are making are smart and sound, and will bring about a better tomorrow. When your hard work affords you fun, charity, investments, education and vacations, instead of just paying off credit cards, student loans, mortgages, cars, gasoline, utilities, your cell phone and insurance, then your life can feel beautiful. In other words, the thirteen mantras that you have been working on, and the seven that are yet to come, can add up to the life you've always wanted to live. Your results will be in direct proportion to the effort you put in.

Think about the food that you love the most. If your palette is pure, then you'll enjoy a piece of organic fruit more than Pop Tarts. When you are healthy, your body craves nutrients, not junk food. Excessive consumption of sugar, like habitual reliance on drugs, pornography or alcohol, is simply pleasure seeking, and always results in a short thrill, a steep crash, and the Sugar Blues. So, part of experiencing beauty is cleansing your own body and soul.

Who are the people that you find attractive? As you dig deeper into your own ethics, and celebrate the gifts, talents and integrity of others, you'll find superficial airheads quite unattractive. The poet John Keats wrote, "'Beauty is truth, truth beauty.' That is all ye know on earth, and all ye need to know."

What If the Ugliness in Your Life is Your Job?

Kicking a bad habit is in many ways easier to do than kicking a bad career. If you smoke or drink and you want to quit, it's pretty easy to get help. There are a lot of programs. It might even be covered by your health insurance policy. When you think your career is a cancer, where do you turn? Most people think that earning a living is good – however you can legally do that – even if you have ethical issues with it.

If I had assembled a committee to advise me on whether or not I should quit my job at the insurance company that was releasing the names of sick employees to their employers so the company could fire them, there would be a lot of people who would justify keeping the job – even if it meant stepping in line and not ruffling any feathers with management. No one likes a whistleblower. I found zero support within the company – not even with my "friends." No one would have dreamed that if I quit and slept on friends' couches for a month, I'd find a great job at 20th Century Fox Film in the music department!

That career crisis, which happened when I was in my early 20s, gave me the courage to follow my convictions. From that point on,

I knew that what lies beyond such a moral crisis – one that we fear the most because it hits us right in our wallet and could put us out on the streets – can be beauty beyond our wildest dreams. It gave me the insight that the ethical high road is easier to follow than we think, even when we can't clearly see where the path is leading. I can't imagine how ugly I would feel about myself if I had just gone along with the ruse – like *all* of my colleagues were doing, and would continue to do in the decades to come.

At the end of the day, beauty begins with how you feel about yourself. Look in the mirror. Frown at yourself. Tell yourself you are ugly. See how that manifests. What does the face that stares back at you look like?

Now, walk away from the mirror and tell yourself ten things in a row that you love about yourself or that you think you are particularly talented at. Then tell yourself you are beautiful. Go back and stand in front of the mirror. You'll find that it's a completely different person smiling back at you.

When you are honest with yourself about your work, is it something that makes you ashamed or something that you are proud of? Is it an honorable way to make a living? Is there a way for your job to reward you monetarily *and* emotionally? It is, after all, what you do most throughout the day. What needs to change in order for your job to fulfill you? Your attitude or your job?

I am a much better business owner, mother, musician, writer and artist as a result of being charitable, healthy, holistic, free, educated, athletic and adventurous. Part, but not all, of the solution lies in what you do outside the office.

I *feel* younger than I am. I am happier than I have ever been. My heart is full of love. My smile is genuine. And tomorrow is another grand adventure. Many women my age go under the knife, or shoot Botox into their face, to try to *look* the way I *feel*. You've seen what that looks like. The smoother skin becomes a mask, where the stark truth of the person's essence still spills through. Happy people are more attractive than miserable people. Smiles are the best face-lifts.

There are a lot of ways that we can sell ourselves short and lose a piece of our beauty. When a peacemaker builds bombs for a living, or a struggling screenwriter sells pirated DVDs to pay rent, or a career woman neglects to have children until it is too late, or a spouse stops working to please her partner, or a father works 12 hours a day at the office to afford private school for the kids – whom he's too tired to play with. Most of us don't feel that we've chosen these things, but, rather, that life has thrown these cards on the table.

When what we *do* and what we *believe in* are out of synch, we don't feel beautiful or happy. There is no thriving. In the worst-case scenario, we'll even take our unhappiness, stress and angst out on those we love most. Abusive people don't act that way because they are delirious with delight.

Many abusers are ashamed of their actions, at least in the beginning. An abusive husband once admitted to me that his father was a tyrant to his mother. He hated him for it. I couldn't bring myself to ask why he hit, screamed at and spit on his own wife then. It was obvious that he hated those actions in himself, too.

His wife loved him very much. But she had a young son. And she wasn't going to pass the cycle of abuse down another generation. She left her husband in order to create a home for her son where everyone was respected, where conflicts were resolved with love and where frustration could be released through sports and activity. She left her husband, so that her son wouldn't grow up thinking that abuse was normal, or that hitting women was okay. The couple divorced.

Sometimes that kind of strong action will result in separation and alienation, and sometimes it will jolt the abuser into changing their ways, sparking the possibility of reconciliation and building a new foundation of love and respect. Another abusive husband whom I know was so shocked to discover that he might lose the wife he loved and have only limited access to his kids, that he made a vow never to threaten or hit her again. Over twenty years later, and he's kept this promise. The last time I saw this couple, the wife joked that she had too much of a good thing. Her husband was doing the dishes every night because it made her so happy. He jogged with her so that they could release the stress of the day. It was an amazing transformation! And it was only possible because the wife was brave enough to stand up for herself, and demand that she be treated with respect.

Is there something or someone that you need to stand up to? Is it possible that when you do the outcome might be far better than you imagine?

One of my subscribers worked at a defense contractor (a company that supplies the U.S. military with war planes, bombs, etc.). He was at odds with it because he's very active in a community of peacemakers. Should he quit his job? Look for engineering work within a different industry? Retire early? The right answer will be different from one person to the next. However, asking the questions and answering them honestly is the only way to start discovering what's right for you.

Our country was built on the actions of the Boston Tea Party – when early colonists refused to pay taxes to The King of England. America the Beautiful – the land of the free and the home of the brave – was a revolutionary rejection of the idea that luck and chance should determine your lot in life. I am proof that a poor girl from a rural town can access the resources that are necessary to graduate summa cum laude from a private university (the University of Southern California), and rise to the top of one of the most competitive industries in the world. When I think of what Malala Yousafzai has gone through, I'm even more grateful to have been born in America.

Repetition of bad (or justified) choices that are out of synch with our highest self pounds these behaviors into the core of our being – scarring the essence of who we really are. These compromises mar our self-perception and pollute our passions. They chip away at our innate beauty – much like the lead character in *The Picture of Dorian Grey* by the great Oscar Wilde.

When we honor our ethics and our heart's pure desires (which are quite different from our pleasure-seeking vices) and stay true to our soul, then we are on a sustainable beauty regimen. This is much more affordable than cosmetic surgery! But we have to be courageous enough to live our dream life in order to laugh freely.

You can't create beauty in this world if you despise your job, or if you feel that you are buried alive in bills. In the wake of my divorce, sharing a home with another single mother was the financial springboard of support that I needed to launch the career of my dreams. Once you understand that your retirement dollars are invested in the companies that you believe are harming our world, you will feel emboldened and empowered by taking ownership and investing, instead, in products and services that are creating a better tomorrow. Yes, it takes a little effort to set these things up. But once you do, this wonderful existence becomes *the way life is*, and you get to relax and enjoy it.

When you think of your job, ask yourself, "Is this beautiful or is this ugly?" When you think of how you spend and invest your money, ask yourself, "Is this making everyone else rich, or is it beautifying my bottom line and compounding gains?" When you think of your 401K, ask yourself, "What companies do I own? What products and services am I supporting?"

In 2007, retreat attendees would justify their choice to invest in Altria (which is just a name that Phillip Morris tobacco company gave itself to appeal to investors) saying, "The dividend is beautiful, even if the product is deadly. I'll do something good with all of the money that I make." A few months later, under the weight of the Great Recession, Altria lost more than 45% of its market value. Once the losses turned ugly, people sold off in droves – selling low (losing money).

At the same time, if there was a product or service that you really liked, you might want to *buy in* at the low point of the Recession. Let's say you like discount travel (Priceline type companies) or smart phones (Apple) or Internet companies (like Google). If you invested in any of these companies at the low point in 2009 (March), then you would have more than doubled your money. When you are true to your own ethics, then your emotions become allies.

"When you grow up you tend to get told that the world is the way it is and your life is just to live your life and try not to bash into the walls too much... Life can be much broader once you discover one simple fact. Everything around you that you call life was made up by people that were no smarter than you... Shake off this erroneous notion that life is there and you're just going to live in it versus make your mark upon it." Steve Jobs

Life is beautiful when you are living your dream in your daily life. When you've aligned your job, your career, your spending and your investing dollars with what you consider to be a beautiful world, that is the pinnacle of personal happiness. It is something to envision, to create a blueprint for and, then, to actively implement. What a gift you give your life companion and your family when you do this.

Daily Task & Action Plan:
1. Write down 10 pluses and 2 wishes – 10 things that you love about you, and 2 things that you'd like to improve on.
2. Design the cover of a magazine where you are the star of the cover. Is it *Forbes*? *Rolling Stone*? *Time* Magazine's Person of the Year? What would you be doing if you had all of the money in the world? Since today's celebrities make headlines for their philanthropy, their vacations and their investments and endorsements (passive income), include those snapshots in your collage (or painting). Once you dream it, and fill in the details, then you can start actualizing it.
3. Take a walk. Notice three unusual things on your walk. Write them down in your journal, along with any other thoughts that you might have about these oddities. Was there anything attractive about them? This is designed to get you observing the world around you more closely.

Learning New Skills
Be inspired by the blogs, speeches and interviews of people whom you admire. Successful people generally like talking about

themselves, so it shouldn't be hard to do a search and find something interesting and valuable online.

Additional Resources

The Picture of Dorian Grey, by Oscar Wilde.

The Double Helix: A Personal Account of the Discovery of the Structure of DNA, by James D. Watson.

The poetry of John Keats.

WEEK 3: PARTY.
INVITE FRIENDS TO THE PARTY!
PARTNER UP FOR
EXPONENTIALLY BETTER
RESULTS.

Day 15: Sacred Union
Today's Mantra: Be the Soul
Mate You Wish to Attract

John Keats wrote, "I am certain of nothing but the holiness of the Heart's affections and the truth of the Imagination."

The holiness of the heart's affections is a big piece of the puzzle to sacred unions. However, our culture, from *The Bachelor* television shows to romantic comedies, still teaches love in a storybook way. We fall *in love* with someone magically – often within minutes of meeting him. There is, of course, something *wrong* that we have to overcome. He's the owner of the big bad department store chain that is bankrupting our small business. Over the course of half an hour, I learn more about leveraging up. He learns the value of walking barefoot in the grass. And then we live happily ever after.

On screen, and far too often in real life, we are a "couple" before we really even know each other. The film *Maleficent* exposes this myth when The Prince's kiss of "true love" fails to wake Sleeping Beauty. Maleficent's kiss does work, however. The Prince has only met Aurora twice and hardly knows her. Maleficent has known Aurora all of her life. Over the years, Aurora's radiance has managed to melt Maleficent's bitter heart and turn revenge into true love.

We all want a soul mate – that person who completes us. And yet, rather than seriously considering what *kind* of person would complete us, or what qualities matter most, or where and how we are most likely to meet the perfect partner, we count on love striking randomly, like lightning, when we least expect it. We imagine that we are loveable and would make a great partner just as we are and that, sooner or later, as fate decides the storms and rainbows of life, some stranger will race in from the downpour, right into our arms.

As we mature, we discover that the easiest way to attract a soul mate is to *be* a soul mate. When I exude loyalty, confidence, stability, fun, adventure and wealth, and I put myself in circumstances where others can see these qualities in me, then I'm more likely to meet someone who appreciates these attributes. If I'm looking for someone to have these qualities when I don't embody them, then I am looking for someone to save me from myself – to be more to me than I am willing to be to him or to myself. That's dependency – not a soul mate.

All of the things that you have been doing over the last 14 days are leading you closer to your sacred beloved – by bringing you closer to the sacred within you.

We've talked about replacing fear with solutions, about having faith that, with smart choices, you can become wealthy. Financial literacy and a healthy relationship with prosperity and abundance are important to sacred unions because the thing most couples fight about is money. Oftentimes, we are soiling the holiness of the heart's affections with bad choices in daily life.

Start with Great Seeds and Soil

You'll hear couples who have been together for a long time talk about giving 110%, about watering the garden of their love regularly, about appreciating each other, about not taking one another for granted. This worked at a time when tradition and religion put the idea of divorce completely out of the picture. However, today, when the unionizing glue of religion and tradition isn't so sticky, the pressures of life are more daunting and temptation is always just a credit card away, having a deeper and more soul-centric bond before you make the commitment is critically important. You'll still need to care for your partner and cultivate your relationship. However, the richer the soil, the better the seeds, the finer the care, the better the harvest. With this plan, you can have a sacred union, instead of just someone to plan family vacations with.

I got all of this wrong in my early relationships. My soil (soul) was depleted, and the sun didn't shine very much in my sliver of the field. (My self-esteem was more like a dark path that was wedged between two buildings). I bought seeds without the slightest notion of where they'd come from. With regard to watering, I was assiduous, but uninformed. Inevitably, I either drowned or starved my seedlings. And when it came time for harvest, the seven or eight strawberries that managed to spring up were promptly eaten by spiders. (Or, perhaps, the spiders were preying on the critters that were eating the strawberries, one of the two. I didn't want to get close enough to find out. Some spiders jump!)

It takes a good U to make a good *us*. As I align myself with the principles of prosperity and abundance, and learn to live a rich, fulfilling life on my own, I am giving the 110% of myself that is necessary to create a sacred union with all of the partners in my life – my parents, my children, my companion and my business partners. Smart farmers have natural ways of fertilizing their fields, rotating crops, replenishing soil, guarding against pests, pruning, weeding and watering. They don't throw their kids into the management of the farm without teaching them all of the industry tricks that are necessary to cultivating plentiful crops and harvesting the abundance without losing too much to pestilence.

In some countries, parents still select spouses for their children. It seems unfair and unjustified, but I'm not sure that the way Americans select partners is any better. As a teen, my girlfriends and I all *said* we wanted a soul mate; however, every Friday night we would hang out in bars, hoping to find him. It's a bit like trolling ponds for frogs that will become princes. Princes don't hang out at the local watering hole, or when they do, they are acting more like frogs for the day (and hoping not to get caught). I'm sure there were girls who met Prince Harry in Las Vegas a few years ago on his wild weekend there.

Where is your perfect partner likely to be found? What passions will he have? Are you more likely to find him building a house for Habitat for Humanity than at the local pub?

When my friends and I went out drinking, how often did I bring along my list of qualities that I'd like to have in a life companion? Honestly, beyond the physical, I don't think I had given it much serious thought. I simply preened, primped and played coy to attract the most attractive male I might run into that night! If he slipped closer to buy me a drink and whispered something original that didn't reek of being a stale pickup line, my heart might skip a beat! I wasn't selecting someone based upon qualities that I admired. I was relying, quite literally, upon a shot in the dark. Compared to that scenario, a couple of well-meaning parents would do a much better job of selecting their daughter's life mate!

Imagine going to the grocery store when you are starving, forgetting your list, getting so low on blood sugar that you just stuff a handful of doughnuts down your throat to stave off the hunger pangs. If you take an extra dozen doughnuts home with you, you're doomed! The next thing you know, you're fat, bloated, unhappy, addicted to sugar and ready for Weight Watcher's rehab!

Are we looking for a Master of the Light sacred companion, or just *someone* so that we don't have to be alone with ourselves? Starving is no way to start any love affair. If we are full and complete as individuals, then our companion is the icing on the cake – a delightful dessert!

Fill yourself up with a rich life. Have a clear idea of the person who will enhance a world that is already pretty amazing.

Now, here's another sad reality. When you have a cynical belief about something, it becomes a self-fulfilling prophecy, largely because that is the only possible outcome that you are capable of seeing. As a young woman, because I'd had some many traumatic experiences as a child, I honestly believed that there were no good guys out there. Because that was my overriding belief, I always looked right past the nice guy and found the loud-mouthed, narcissistic, abusive, jealous blow-hard who was elbowing the nice guy out of the way.

I've heard men describe their wives as someone to hide the credit card from. I've known women who lost their family homes because their husbands leveraged it in a business deal without telling them.

It took a lot of meditation, fasting and personal work for me to discover that there is a better way. I never opened myself up for true intimacy when I thought that all men were troglodytes. How often are we sorting for the sad outcome that we've already scripted? Why is it that men who believe that women want them for their money end up with gold diggers, and that women who believe all men cheat date unavailable or married men?

In the process of cleaning up my own life and becoming a "soul mate" myself, I become a soul mate magnet. While I'm soiled with my own thoughts on how unsacred love can be, somehow, someway, raucous, complicated, hurt-filled affairs are all that show up for me.

The perfect relationship begins with a solid look in the mirror. Am I the wonderful, well-rounded, loving person that I want to be? Do I exercise and eat right? Am I interesting? Is there something about me that is uniquely lovable and vital to the world? Does my soul shine? Am I trustworthy, honest, engaging and interested in a calling higher than this year's fashion statement?

One of the most successful songwriters and rock stars of all time, John Lennon, went to an art exhibit one day, climbed up a ladder, peered into a very small box and saw simply the word "Yes." According to John, that was the moment he fell in love with Yoko Ono. And what better way to describe a soul mate than that person who says "Yes" to you when you dream of a higher calling for yourself.

While John Lennon and Yoko Ono were together, John composed two of his most beloved songs, including "Imagine" and "Happy Christmas (War is Over)" (which John co-wrote with Yoko). John admits that Yoko's book *Grapefruit* was the inspiration for "Imagine," going so far as to say that the song should be credited as both of theirs. Does your spouse inspire you? Do you inspire him?

John and Yoko believed so strongly in the peaceful opposition to the Vietnam War that they spent their honeymoon in a Peace

Bed-In at the Amsterdam Hilton. (There you can still sleep in the John and Yoko Suite, if you wish.) They used their celebrity platform to host "bed-ins," talk-show appearances and other glitterati events to promote peace and equal rights, particularly for women. Yoko became the highly visible executive of the John Lennon estate during their marriage. In an interview for *Rolling Stone*, John bragged that Yoko's returns on their combined estate were more impressive than the money managers he'd hired previously. She was infamous for selling *a cow* for a quarter of a million dollars.

Their relationship wasn't perfect. We're all human. But there was a lot that was sacred about their union.

Is your partner a master of the light? Do you have a common vision? Are you dedicated to causes that are bigger than your companionship?

Or is the relationship toxic and soul killing?

It is very easy to have a "story" about how difficult your life is, or to have very good reasons about why you are cynical about the opposite sex, or to be focused on attracting your mate through physical beauty. (I admit that I've made all of these mistakes, as a young woman.) My mother died when I was seven. I was raised by a series of foster parents. I was sexually abused as a child. I was finally emancipated as a minor, at the age of 16. It was easy to dress nice, work out a little, lose a few extra pounds and attract some attention. I was the talented, complicated, small town girl, who should be pitied a little bit. Now, outside of me relating those facts in this book, those are stories that few would ever guess about me. I lead with my strength, not my weakness – my light, not my darkness.

During those early, complicated relationship years, when I did have a boyfriend, I focused on fixing *him*, rather than fixing *me*. One or two or three years later, we'd finally come to the conclusion that we weren't right in the first place, and that we'd endured enough drama, and then we'd live through some ridiculously painful breakup. Remodeling is not as easy as you think – particularly when you think you should be reroofing your neighbor's house, instead of your own when the rain comes in. In love, dare to choose the best partner. Dare to *be* the best partner. You never want to have buyer's remorse in your sacred union!

Fixer-Upper Projects

If you are in a relationship that you would like to improve, as I was prior to my divorce, start with healing/improving/remodeling yourself first, before you try to "fix" the relationship or fix your spouse. My ex-husband and I spent nine years trying to fix *him.* Our relationship changed when I realized that *I* needed to work on *me* first. In any partnership, it only takes one partner to change the dynamic.

After lifting your own psyche up to your higher calling, you will be in a better position to evaluate the health of the relationship in general and your partner's level of love, support, affection and ability to make your relationship more intimate, loving and sacred. Understand and accept that the two of you created the relationship that you are currently in, and that by shifting your side of the equation, the dynamic changes. Unbelievable growth and improvement become possible, even if you are the only one doing the work.

Visualizing and Creating Sacred Union

I have a drawing that I refer to for inspiration on the perfect Sacred Union. It is a heart, with another heart slightly overlapping. The Sacred Union is the foundation of the family. Around this, I draw another heart. The heart closest to the Sacred Union is reserved for children and the Sanctuary Home. Then I draw another heart around the family that is reserved for parents, siblings, friends and close loved ones. Then another, larger heart for the people I work with or go to church or school with. Then a heart for those in the local grocery store whom I run into. The hearts keep getting bigger and bigger on the page until all you can see are arcs that resemble the rippling effect of a stone skipping across a pond.

The heart drawing reminds me that my kids come before everyone else, but after me, my sacred companion and our foundation. A great relationship starts with a strong, enlightened individual.

We are first and foremost responsible for ourselves. We must make sure that whatever we are here on the planet to do, which we are uniquely qualified to do better than anyone else, actually gets done. I must feed my soul with wisdom and truth, and walk on that path daily. The first commitment I am making is always to honor and love myself, and to stay true to my life's calling.

My second commitment is to honor, love, cherish and respect my sacred companion, and support him in being true to his life's calling. We are two separate individuals, with a strong, sacred bond.

Sacred Union: Sanctuary Home

A sacred union of two enlightened, divine individuals is the soul of the home, the foundation of the sanctuary. As a couple, the sacred union must share a common and deeper understanding of the meaning and goals of life – a faith in something (even if we are non-believers in "God"). If the home is to become a sanctuary, we must be diligent in our own special calling, and treat one another with great respect and dignity at all times. While our missions and careers might be different, we share a common vision and commitment, a moral backbone, and we say "yes" to one another's dreams.

The sanctuary home is the center for celebration for the family. It is a place of nurturing, forgiveness, mistakes, love, learning, safety, celebration, joy and healthy routines (healthy, regular meals, family time and moral learning).

That doesn't mean that there will never be frustrations, conflicts or confrontations. It means that the individuals learn how to resolve their differences peacefully. The Dalai Lama's Peace Zone is a great room, or at least a corner, to set up in the sanctuary home.

The Ripple Effect

If there is a sanctuary that is full of truth, love, healthy routines and celebration, then the individuals who live in that home walk into the world strong and full of beauty, light and love to share. They make the world a more beautiful place simply with their presence. They are inspiring and inspired.

Where there is no sanctuary, the individuals walk into a world depleted and needy of finding their worth through the opinions of others. They are more vulnerable to an emptiness and hole in their own self-view that is fed, but never filled by, addictions (sex, drugs, rock n' roll, etc.). These individuals suck up the resources from the world, but have trouble giving and creating beauty. With seven billion-plus people on the planet, we need to be creators, not parasites. Giving up addictions is very difficult! Giving up old ideas is painful! Sacred union/sanctuary home is the gift we give our children and ourselves.

All actions have consequences and a ripple effect, even when we think we are not acting. I cannot merely think and meditate on becoming the person I *wish I were* or *will be* soon, when this or that thing in my life gets fixed. I must be, now, the sacred partner who respects and appreciates my beloved companion. I must act exactly today how I *would be acting* tomorrow, if life were easier.

Life challenges us frequently to deal with stressful situations with grace, and to keep up our healthy habits even when the going gets tough. If I have only ten dollars, I am still tithing one dollar to charity. If I'm working 60 hours a week, I'm still going to take an afternoon to help a friend or family member. I realize that it can't possibly be any easier to tithe $100,000 to charity when you have a million than it is to tithe $1 if you have $10. So, I'm just going to jump in and develop the right habits. Now. Here. No excuses.

Be the Change You Wish to See

I'm expanding my view of what being a soul mate means. It doesn't just mean to be someone special to one person – my beloved. It means to be a special person to the world. If I appreciate beauty, then I exercise, get ample rest and eat right so that I can present myself with my best foot forward. If I want political change, I volunteer for causes that are close to my heart. If I have an economic theory to share with the world, then I publish it. I form more sacred unions with my children and my parents.

Love People Where They Are

It takes a lot of effort over time for someone to change their core personality traits, so if I truly love the soul of my companion, I am likely to love him despite how much money he does or doesn't make, despite his choice of career and whether or not having kids is a dream or a nightmare for him. And more importantly, if I find the man whose *soul* I *love*, I am far more likely to be dating a person who feels the same way about me.

On the other hand, when I find myself embroiled in a relationship with someone whom I fundamentally do not respect or who treats me with less respect than I deserve, I do not expect that person to perform above their current skill set. As Maya Angelou said, "When someone shows you who they are, believe them. The first time."

It's impossible to create a sacred union with a drug addict, a sex addict, a shyster, a scam artist or an abuser. When the situation is toxic, you must leave. You don't have to rush straight to divorce, but you need to leave the environment in order to heal, to find your light again and to shine. Your old partner might rise to the occasion and make the shifts necessary, once you make it clear that you're not going to live with insanity.

If a toxic person is harming others, then I consider what actions are needed to protect the innocent. If they are harming themselves, I offer my support and help. More often, however, when the interaction is unhealthy, the only thing really needed is for me to stop expecting them to be different than they are. It's better to release someone with love in your heart, than hold them close with resentment on your tongue. Endless arguing never resolves anything. When someone wants to change something, very few words have to be spoken.

Attracting a Different Kind of Person

The universe doesn't always roll out a red carpet for you when you decide to change the road you're on. When you decide that you want to have a different kind of love relationship than what you've known in the past, you still might have some attraction for the old pattern. That's what's comfortable. So, you can't just trust your instincts. Until being a soul mate becomes the *new normal* for you, you'll probably not be on the lookout for the enlightened partner of your dreams. You'll have to work for a while before your taste changes.

Actions Speak Louder than Words

I've seen self-proclaimed "healers" abandon those in need for their own quick dose of pleasure. I've known successful movie producers who call themselves "spiritual" but date naïve, young ingénues who are just off the bus. Don't take anyone at her word. Pretend that life is a silent movie and just watch what people do, as an indicator of who they really are. Going sober to a party is another great way to see things clearly.

As I seek to distinguish between a self-proclaimed "nice guy" and my soul mate, I simply look at how I *feel* about what he *does*. Do his actions in the outer world add up to a man whom I respect so much it makes me glow? Or, do I justify not really liking his actions with the thought that he's trying and will eventually get it right? If I really believe in my lover's intentions and actions – his mission – then I can be the kind of partner to cheer him on.

The way to know the difference between addictions and food for the soul is that you always come down from addictions.

YOU GET EXACTLY WHAT YOU SETTLE FOR. Settle for a dream come true.

Creating Sacred Unions with Business and Financial Partners

Extend the idea of sacred union to *all* of your partnerships and friendships. You want all of your close encounters – your interactions with people in your inner circle – to be sacred unions. Your core values should be in alignment or complementary to one another. Think partnership, not one-upmanship.

Co-creating great things requires partnering with competent, successful individuals who are aligned with your goals. When we pool our talents, great things occur. Certainly it's easier to raise kids with a parental partner, but our lives can be so much easier with partners in every walk of life. This decade may well be the Age of

Room-Mates. With incomes stagnating, while the cost of gasoline, electricity, housing and food is multiplying, it's almost impossible to make ends meet without a roommate. If that roommate can be a soul mate, then we have a shot at creating a sanctuary home – even if we're living in a dorm room.

A lot of people get into financial trouble because they start thinking of their business and financial partners as "friends" or they rely on their friends to do the due diligence. Recall that quote by Kareem Abdul Jabbar where he admitted, "I chose my financial manager, who I later discovered had no financial training, because a number of other athletes I knew were using him." You wouldn't let your parents pick your spouse, so why are you having blind faith and letting your friends choose the second most important person in your life – the person who manages your money?

A lot of brokers try to become your "friend." If you believe that your stock broker is a friend, then rather than asking important questions, such as, "Am I keeping enough safe?" and "Why is my nest egg flat, when the markets have doubled?" you might spend time telling him or her about your kids, or asking about the last golf game. With real estate "friends" and car "friends" you might end up purchasing a home and vehicle that you can't really afford.

A CEO wouldn't do that with her CFO. If the Certified Financial Planner is hired to manage your money and to achieve certain financial goals, then you should focus on results, not golf and kids. It's your job to know what kind of home and car you can afford.

In 2014, it was common for CFPs to brag about their gains. I can't tell you how many times I heard that someone's broker had earned him 20% annualized gains. NASDAQ had earned **38%** annualized since the Great Recession, so the boast wasn't warranted at all. The brokers were earning half of what the general "market" was doing. And if the broker had all of the assets at risk to earn that gain, then chances are that the portfolio still hadn't fully recovered from the losses of the Great Recession.

That is why it is important for you to know *The ABCs of Money* – for the same reason that Prince William needs to know agriculture. He needs to know what best practices are in place so that he can be a more effective CEO of his estates, and hold his team accountable for achieving outstanding results, based upon the legacy of organic and sustainable farming that he inherited from his father, Prince Charles.

If you know that Buy and Hold doesn't work in today's Debt World, and that Modern Portfolio Theory, with a few trademarked tricks, does, then you can examine and gauge the efficacy of the system set up to increase your assets and compound your gains. You can make adjustments as necessary. You can understand that bonds are vulnerable in a world of low interest rates and high credit risk. The charts in front of you will make sense, and if they don't, then the answers to your questions should. When the mutual goal is protecting and providing for your future, then the sacred union between you and your financial team is aligned with that mission – not brushing aside that important discussion for banter on trivial, unrelated matters.

When your partners make it easy for you to understand the answers to your questions, then they are actively promoting your wisdom and empowering you. When they are tearing down your self-esteem, making you feel dumb, or complicating things, then chances are that they have something to hide.

Like it or not, you are the architect of your life. When you select competent, ethical business and financial partners, based upon results that they have achieved for a reasonable period of time, and they communicate with you clearly and professionally on a regular basis, your life is easier and far more blessed – not just for you, but also for your family and life companion. Since money is the thing couples argue about most, imagine when your assets are protected, your gains are compounding, your bills are paid and there is no high-interest credit card debt to worry about! This scenario is worth investing the time it takes to get it right. Until you do, the foundation of your family life is cracked, which makes it difficult for any union you have to be sacred.

Asian Americans were exploited and underpaid a century ago. Today, they are the top-earning ethnic group in the United States.

That impressive shift was achieved through a strong family commitment to send the children to college and onto medical school or for their Ph.D. Parents and kids alike gave up having their own rooms and cars, and lived in cramped quarters in inner cities, in order to propel the next generation to the top of the income ladder. What brave choice can you make today that will allow for the investments that will create an easier, more fulfilling tomorrow?

As you lift the light, you will become more attracted to (and attractive to) those who are shining as well.

Daily Task & Action Plan:
1. Make a list of the partners in your life. Which partners are lifting the light? Which partners need to be examined more closely to see if they are really qualified to be in their role? Who needs to be replaced?
2. How can you create a more sacred union with your spouse? With your CFP? With your CPA? With your colleagues at work? With your kids and parents? Do you need to consult an expert?

Learning New Skills

As a parent, I resorted frequently to the books and office visits with my fantastic pediatrician, Dr. Jay Gordon, and the child development books of Dr. T. Berry Brazelton. What wisdom do you need to become a better partner with your life and business partners?

Additional Resources

20 Ways to Get Good Karma, by the 14th Dalai Lama of Tibet

Check out *The Square,* an Academy-Award nominated documentary about the Arab Spring uprising in Egypt.

DrJayGordon.com is a great resource for parents.

Day 16: Sing
Today's Mantra: Sing

Sing in the shower. Whistle while you work. But most importantly, find *your* voice and the song that *you* are meant to sing during this very brief moment (in geological time) that we call life.

There have been times that I tried to find some hope, and the only light was my cigarette. I felt so despondent that I had no conviction that anything would *ever* save the day. I have had many, many moments in my life where I had to rely upon these mantras to find my way back to the realm of possibilities, where all solutions lie.

Singing is the quick-start button to that place because it opens up your heart and gets the blood flowing. Voila! Welcome to the ability to soar above the treetops of the dark forest.

In some of my darkest moments, I even played the Fire Ritual begrudgingly, facing my fears and forcing myself to dream up solutions that were so outlandish and so far out of reach, that I rolled my eyes and cursed as I wrote them down. It's far easier to be cynical than optimistic when you're backed into a corner. So, I played the stupid game, scribbling fairy tale solutions with even wilder abandon. The fact that the answers to my problems were delightful only inspired a sneer. Yet, even then, because I had dared to dream, the solutions showed up.

So, what kind of trials and tribulations did I need to overcome? Certainly nothing as horrifying as a boy soldier in Africa faces. But I have seen and experienced a lot of things that I never wanted my own children to have to live through. Gazing at my mother in a casket, when I was only seven years old. Running away from home at the age of twelve. Getting kicked out of high school just a few months before I should have graduated, and then, a few years later, creating a way to attend the University of Southern California on scholarship.

I'm a survivor. However, the way I got through the rough times in the first part of my younger life had nothing to do with a plan. I just worked hard and kept putting one foot in front of the other. Many times, I added months and years of misery to the equation simply because I didn't know any better.

Once I developed this 21-day Walk to Wealth program, it didn't eliminate the challenges I faced, but it did supercharge the solutions. There's one story in particular that I want to share with you.

By 2008, I'd had nine years of a great track record at picking stocks, and anticipating the bull and bear markets under my belt. My first book was penned. A Nobel Prize winning economist *and* a world-renowned spiritual leader had both signed on to write the forward. One of the most respected publishers was giving an A-list release of *Put Your Money Where Your Heart Is*. I was on television regularly. Tens of thousands of people were receiving my emails, reading my blogs, following me on social networks and checking out my ezine.

There was only one problem. If I were managing money, I could have been rolling in the dough of my management and performance fees. But, I had decided that I would never be happy waking up each day to make rich people richer. Instead, I wanted to add a splash of green to Wall Street and transform lives on Main Street. I wanted to empower millions of Americans with the basics of financial literacy, so that they could save their homes and nest eggs, compound their gains and provide for their future – now that we are all in charge of our own tomorrow.

Companies used to offer pensions and medical care throughout retirement, but that policy was replaced with employee-directed 401Ks in 1980. By 2007, more than 40 million Americans – more than 10% of our population – were uninsured. That has changed now with the Affordable Care Act; however, it has not reduced the amount of money *spent on health care*, or made us a healthier nation.

One third of Americans are obese, and, as a result, we spend almost three trillion dollars annually on health care. The U.S. spends more on health care than any other nation in the world – with some of the worst results in the developed world.

Health is the best health insurance; fiscal health is the best pension plan. These are messages needed on Main Street, and this is where I want to be of service. Taking charge of our own future is easier than you know. It is a necessary ingredient in personal freedom. When corporations are in charge of this, they *must place corporate interests in front of retiree interests* in order to stay in business. The retiree gets shortchanged. We've seen this story repeat itself in the airline and auto-manufacturing bankruptcies, and it's starting to show up in municipality bankruptcies, too, such as Stockton and Detroit.

But selling financial education isn't nearly as lucrative as managing money. In fact, at the time in 2007, (and most of the time, when we are honest about it) most people wanted to get their financial education from their money manager or bank or brokerage *for free*, rather than pay for it from an independent source – even one with my track record. Wall Street was setting record highs every day, so no one felt any need to get financially literate. It was a bull market, and everyone was making money and having fun.

I had cut costs within my company, was working 12-hour days, was just months away from a major book release, but the online news and education business had dropped to free. As a result, my partners and I were writing checks to keep the lights on.

Now, those loyal subscribers who were reading the ezine in 2007 were doing great – far better than the markets. They were sending in notes that their investments had doubled! In January of 2008, I issued a red flag investor alert warning of the Great Recession and advising everyone to make sure that they had a percentage equal to their age safe *plus* an additional 10-20%. Over the next year, the Great Recession deepened, Lehman Bros. failed and the stock market plunged to half of its value. In addition to feeling great that I'd saved my subscribers' assets, we had ample testimonials of people who saved their homes and nest eggs using my Easy-as-a-Pie-Chart Nest Egg Strategies, and by reading my real estate warnings prior to the Bubble bursting. Surely this would guarantee major book reviews and headlines! Who wouldn't want to feature Bill and Nilo talking about how happy they were that they were *making money* in the Great Recession, rather than losing half of their net worth!

However, at the height of the Great Recession, the television and radio networks stopped discussing personal finance. They would talk about rises and falls in the market, or the tragedies of millions of people losing their homes, or the high unemployment rate. But no one, and I mean not one of my editor/producer friends, were allowed to write a review of my book or put me on-air to discuss how Bill and Nilo (and others) were both protected and profiting, and how their viewers could do so, as well. The media outlets weren't going to take on the liability of featuring anyone's solutions because they didn't have the time to research what worked and what didn't work. (This is understandable. Think of the heat that Oprah took for featuring James Arthur Ray on her show and promoting *The Secret* so heavily.) And frankly, a lot of their advertisers were in trouble, and a few had been mentioned by name in my book. (I'd given General Motors a bad grade and warned of imminent bankruptcy, at a time when GM was one of the top advertisers on television.)

By 2009, with a book that had been overlooked and ignored, and a business that was eating me out of house and home, I was so beaten up that I couldn't see any solutions. I still had to publish my ezine monthly, write a mid-month update and host my retreats to keep the revenue flowing and the business running. Meanwhile, I consulted with my partners to decide whether to shut things down or find other ways of bringing in revenue. Most of my partners advised me to throw in the towel.

At a retreat, during the Fire Ritual (yes, I play with the attendees), I wrote down the problem: "My business is cash negative and has been for seven years. My book that was supposed to save the day is a failure. And I'm too worn out to know what to do, particularly since I believe that Americans need financial literacy now, even *more* than ever."

For the solutions side, I wrote the opposite. "I'm so thrilled that my business is making money and paying me a great salary! My *next* book is wildly popular! And all of this came about because…"

How in the world was I going to achieve this? If I hadn't found a way with my #1 ranking, a Nobel Prize winner's endorsement, the best publisher in the world placing my book in bookstores across the land and real-world testimonials that were astonishing, what other bag of tricks was going to conjure up cash and success?

I wrote down, "Because I took 21 days out of my routine to go to Europe and dream up new possibilities." Why did I write that? Because that trick had worked before. Force yourself out of your routine for 21 days, and you'll find that all kinds of new possibilities come creeping into your mind.

I had taken 21 days to visit Greece and England when I was 26. I had been stuck in a rut then with a stalled music career and a boyfriend that I knew I had no future with. Seeing the Acropolis, standing in the shadows of Ionic columns that had stood for thousands of years, drinking retsina and sailing to unchartered islands in the Aegean Sea – all of that inspired the *new* me that would be married with the love of my life – my newborn son – in my arms within a few short years… (If you think this cost a lot of money, it didn't. Greece is one of the most affordable vacations in the world, if you do it right.)

So, even though the business couldn't afford to send me to Europe, and hadn't paid me a salary in a decade, I wrote it down *just to write something down.* There was no part of me, zero, that believed there was any way that it would come to pass.

Sometimes, however, these slips of paper sail on a wind, and the Great Unknown decides to blow you back a miracle.

Less than two months later, one of my volunteers was helping me by opening up mail. She found a letter from the State Treasurer advising me that I had almost $10,000 in a retirement fund. I had no idea that fourteen years before, when I was substitute teaching, a retirement plan had been set up and funded for me. While normally, it's no question that the money should be rolled over into a new self-directed IRA where it can continue to compound, this situation required a different analysis. *I'd had no time off and no extra money for fun for seven years. Everything* had been about investing, ongoing education, charity and retirement plans, with no emphasis placed upon fun and replenishing *me* – to the point where I couldn't see anything beyond the darkness of all of the problems. I was so depleted that I had become suicidal. If I rolled the money over without getting a new business plan, I feared that I'd just be draining it dry to fund the cash-negative business in a few months.

I cashed the check, bought a ticket to Italy, put a vacation auto-responder on the business email, meditated every morning in the Sistine Chapel and wandered through the streets of Rome and Verona in the afternoons and evenings... Singing. And exploring. And praying. (Opening up my heart, peering into the great unknown and calling in divine inspiration.)

After a month, I returned with new hope, a new plan, a big, fat smile and unbridled energy. I attended the Clinton Global Initiative for the first time and began mentoring schoolgirls from Kenya. My agent called, encouraging me to publish my second book. More and more people started signing up for my investor educational retreats. I even was invited to spend three weeks in Paris, as a kind gesture for my philanthropic efforts. Whoa! More soul renewal! Yippee!

As of the writing of this book, *The ABCs of Money* has been at or near #1 Investing Basics on Amazon for over 18 months – for free, so that those who need it most can get the information. We've gone from tens of thousands of people knowing about this work to hundreds of thousands of people. This is without advertising and without any major media book reviews – solely through social networks and by word of mouth. Over 50 readers have given *The ABCs of Money* a 5-star book review online.

Thank you. I'm so grateful.

My new mantra is: "If not me, who? If not now, when?" Yes, there's not a lot of compensation in financial literacy education and forensic, investigative financial journalism, particularly when you want those who need this information most to have access to it. However, if I don't do it anyway, how will it ever get done?

This work is too important for me to be concerned about the small *me*. It's about **us**. It's about the U.S. – and our beautiful world. You should not be getting your debt reduction strategies from the debt collector, or your *save your home* strategies from the bank you owe money to. They are, of course, concerned about the vitality of their enterprise – even if it is at your expense. We should all receive this important information in high school. I have a lot of work to do to get this done. I'm thanking you now for all of your help and continued support. Your support makes my work possible, and it is only through you going the extra mile that this information will go viral.

Thank you in advance for all that you do.

What I've come to realize is that every time I step up to feature something or someone I believe is important for the world to know about, something magical happens that is beyond my wildest dreams.

When I began my journey in stocks, I would have never thought that a Nobel Prize winning economist would write the forward to my book. Or that Joe Moglia, the chairman of TD AMERITRADE, would pen the forward to *The ABCs of Money*. Or that Kay Koplovitz, truly one of the most dynamic, visionary and successful women I've ever known, would open the pages of *The Gratitude Game* with her compelling words. Or that I'd enjoy a private tour of one of the most sustainable homes in the world – the Home Farm of H.R.H. Prince Charles, The Prince of Wales. I knew none of these people when I started. I met them on the journey.

The challenges of offering financial education remain. But I am now strong enough to see through and beyond them. And I can't wait to meet the partners and volunteers who will join me on the way. As you read these pages, you are now part of the team. Thank you.

This mission pays me in ways that a business never could. I live a life that is priceless.

What song are you meant to sing that no one else, but you, can hear right now? If you were to ask yourself the question, "If not me, who? If not now, when?" what would you be doing? Can you do that at least for an hour each week, as part of your charitable giving? Will it lead you to the life of your dreams, as my life mission has done for me? What kind of miracles and astonishing surprises will bless you? You'll never know until you start calling them in with your good deeds.

Slave Spirituals

You don't have to only sing happy songs for the experience of singing to be transformative. Slave spirituals sport some of the saddest lyrics you'll ever hear. But the experience of singing the blues is more empowering than you might realize. A traditional song such as "Poor, Wayfaring Stranger" is actually saying, "I'm traveling through this world of woe, but there's no sickness, toil or danger in that bright land to which I go. I'm going *there* to meet my loved ones!"

When you are stuck in hellish circumstances, it is empowering, even thrilling, to have a destination, even if it is only a dream – no matter how far away it is. It gives you a direction to walk in. As Winston Churchill said, "If you're going through hell, keep going." Slaves sang in the cotton fields to transport them out of the sweltering sun. Today, slavery is outlawed. Miracles happen.

If you're really down, try putting your own lyrics to a blues melody and singing your heart out. What you'll probably discover is that the process makes you stand taller, breathe deeper and that the tones resonate in your lungs, offering a tingling sensation. You are being enlivened. Something within you is waking up.

If you don't feel comfortable writing your own song, try singing (or listening to) "Summertime" or "Amazing Grace," or another popular blues tune or slave spiritual. Did the slaves know that one day their progeny would be freed when they opened their mouths to sing? Did they have any hope at all? Certainly the foul-mouthed slave trader John Henry Newton would have never imagined that he would become an Anglican cleric (priest/healer) and compose one of the most touching slave spirituals ever written – "Amazing Grace." Newton spent the latter part of his life fighting for the abolition of the slave trade in England, which he lived just long enough to see (in 1807).

How many of us were lost and blind, but now can see? Even now, there is some insight waiting to show up for us. What is it? How will we clear away the clutter and sharpen our own insights to catch a glimpse? Even though Rosalind Franklin photographed the double helix, she couldn't *see* its structure. Watson and Crick could.

We can all, in at least one way, feel "enslaved." Most of us – as heartbreaking as some of our personal tragedies are – experience nothing close to slavery. However, chronic disease, losing a loved one unexpectedly, losing a job and the ability to provide for ourselves, losing a home to foreclosure, working so many hours that you never get to spend time with loved ones – these major, tragic life events can *feel* just as imprisoning. Music can be part of the healing and part of the journey to a cure. Singing can be transformative.

When my son lost his best friend in a car accident in high school, there was a song that helped the healing – Israel "IZ" Kamakawiwo`ole's version of "Somewhere over the Rainbow." To this day, when that song plays, I feel Dillon next to me, and when I want to think about Dillon, I listen to it. It doesn't *bring him back*. It keeps him next to me, present in my life.

Think of how a song defines certain moments in your life, or how just hearing one of your favorite tunes makes you feel. If it's been a while since you've felt a certain sensation, try to remember what song was playing during that moment. Playing that song again is the quickest transport back in time.

Many people are still carrying anger, fear, worry, doubt and loathing in their attitudes about money. In today's world, it's easy to have a story – one that you've personally lived through – that supports that point of view. The statistics are not good. Millions of people have lost their homes. Most sports stars are broke within five years of being cut from the team. Most. People who try to get rich quick – from lottery winners to rock stars – are more likely to end up broke because they don't learn the tricks of the trade. They never embody the sustaining values of prosperity and abundance. They can. You can. I can.

People wonder how you can have all of that money and go broke. If you win a million dollars on *Survivor*, you're paying at least $400,000 over night in taxes – unless you get smart and sophisticated about charitable contributions, tax-protected retirement accounts and business expenses. Everyone calls you a millionaire – but Uncle Sam is happier than you are the next morning when you realize that you ate leeches for only $600,000 – 60% of what you'd been promised.

You have to do something different in order to break out of the norm of making the taxman, the debt collector, the insurance company, the oil company, the bankster, the lawyer and the utility company rich at your own expense.

We are free, but we are shackled, too. The chains of today are simply chains of misinformation and ignorance. Financial education is the key to freedom. Sing a new song about the possibilities. Get educated and live your way into the answers – just like so many on the right side of the equation are doing. The smart get richer in America.

When you experience a negative emotion, particularly when it is recurring or persistent, think of it as a red flag on some deficiency. When your house is cold, you turn on the heat. When your tea is too hot, you add an ice cube. When it's dark, you light a candle. Hatred is a deficiency of love. You can learn how to love more, and in the process find that you automatically hate less. Vengeance is a lack of forgiveness. When you exercise your ability to release the debt, even if you don't *feel forgiveness yet*, then you are still focused on giving instead of taking or extracting revenge. There's not enough time in the day to focus on both.

If you are underwater on your mortgage, don't hate the bank and the broker who sold you your home. Instead:

1. Learn the average returns of real estate, so that you don't buy high in the future,
2. Educate yourself on deeds in lieu, short sales and foreclosures to expand your options,
3. Keep contributing to your 401K, IRA, HSA and other tax-protected, financial-predator-proof protected retirement accounts, so that you have a life boat of assets to swim away with in the worst-case scenario,
4. Do a cost-benefit analysis on your housing options and search for solutions to the predicament that you are in,
5. Sound ideas from new sources, such as the Federal Trade Commission's debt restructuring pages, the Federal Reserve's resources for distressed homebuyers, and the Housing and Urban Development's consumer information pages.

When your persistent, recurring problem is money, the solution is always to get educated and informed – from an independent, respected source that is not there to profit on your vulnerability. Learn what a rich person would do in your position. They would never let the bank design the solution to their mortgage problem. Or put the debt collector in charge of their income. Or ask the real estate salesman how expensive of a home they can afford. Or let the car salesman determine whether they should buy the new or used car. Or let the mutual fund salesman put them all in on stocks.

Sing a new song. Tomorrow is the great unknown. When you step on a new path, wonderful experiences and opportunities await you – particularly now that you are driving with a map. No more reckless driving, or stumbling in the dark, or giving the wheel to someone who is going to drive you on their lot and sell you something you don't need, for their personal gain. As you encounter darkness, you flood it with light. As you battle fear, you win with wisdom.

Singing with your own unique and true voice means that you become one with the symphony of solutions in the world. You no longer parrot bad lines from stale television comedies, or believe that brief physical thrills are happiness.

Main Street owns Wall Street. Take ownership. Which businesses have earned the support of your hard-earned retirement dollars? Which companies are going to be stripped of your support? Why?

Part of the new song is that you will no longer check off boxes in your 401K without knowing what you are invested in. Rich people don't do that. Cronyism flourishes when your money flows into their pockets without you ever realizing it. It's easy as a search to learn which companies are owned in the Gigantic, Conservative, High-Yield World Fund, which is one of only a handful of options in your 401K. Sing a new song of freedom – freedom of choice for where your money is invested – and keep singing until the day our retirement plans are invested in the companies that we believe are making the best products and services in the world – not the companies that have the most connected, powerful cronies on their board.

Our consumer dollars and our investment dollars make up the companies in existence today and the world as we know it. When you don't like GMOs, it's not enough to just raise consumer awareness. It's not enough to be an organic foodie who pickets GMOs and solicits signatures, while you profit from the very company that you are boycotting.

Nothing will change a corporation faster than thousands of investors selling the stock on the same day, or thousands of employees migrating over to the organic food production facility. There was a time when typewriter companies flourished, and before that, when horse and carriages were the transportation of choice. Even today, aging nuclear power plants are being decommissioned across the United States because they can't compete with the lower costs of renewable energy, like wind and solar. (When you factor in the Fukushima Power Plant meltdown and subsequent contamination of food, water and land in Japan, it's hard to imagine *any time* when nuclear was affordable.) Create the solutions. Support the solutions, instead of the problems, with your retirement dollars. It's faster and more effective than battling the company through a legislative process that is far too influenced by corporate dollars.

Without your retirement plan funding, the company has no hope of remaining in business. We have so much more power than most people realize. Our voice, our song, can be heard.

Cronyism economics flourishes when good people are so busy in their daily lives that they sign over their livelihoods and our collective future by checking off boxes without really understanding who they are giving the money to. Dare to wake up. Dare to find a way to make your voice heard in a world where the powers that be have made it far too easy for you to be silent. Do not give your power, your voice, your song and our world over to greed.

Sing.

"You might say that I'm a dreamer. But I'm not the only one. I hope some day you'll join us. And the world will live as one." John Lennon.

My dreams inspire my direction. But my footsteps take me there.

Daily Task & Action Plan:
1. Ask yourself the question, "If not me, who? If not now, when?" What would you be doing if time and money weren't an object? Do that for at least an hour this week, as part of your charitable giving.
2. **Know what you own.** Research the companies that are the Top 25 Holdings in the funds that are invested in your 401K, IRA, annuity, trust, insurance plan, Health Savings Account, etc.
3. Make sure that all of your past retirement plans are in a self-directed IRA at a brokerage that allows you the entire universe of stocks and bonds to invest in. Ask your human resources person if there is an option, or a qualifying event, that allows you to rollover your 401K into a self-directed IRA. There you can choose to invest in the companies and funds that you believe are making the best products and services today.

4. Do you want your insurance plan or pension to be secured by a company that wouldn't be in business if we hadn't bailed them out in 2007-2009? Who really insures your insurance plan or annuity? Most companies are owned by someone else. Find out which company is really in charge and accountable. Ask yourself, "How safe is my future in the current hands? Can I do a better job for myself by investing and compounding my gains in a retirement account?"

Learning New Skills

Most of us put off learning about tax protection strategies, investing and smart allocations in our 401Ks because we think we don't have the time or expertise. Since your passive income can build up to more money than you earn in 7 years and earn more money than you do within 25 years, it is well worth it to learn about how to keep and compound your money. Once you learn, it's part of who you are and the way life is, which means that your kids are more likely to know this stuff naturally.

Learn about taxes from IRS.gov and about investing from FINRA.org. FINRA also has a lot of valuable information on bank, insurance and annuity products. FTC.gov has key information on debt, restructuring and bankruptcy.

Additional Resources

Do a search for NataliePace.com Tips for Visiting Italy, or search the archives at NataliePace.com for the August 2009 ezine (vol. 6, iss. 8) to learn about my adventures in Rome and Verona. You can check out my tips for visiting Amsterdam, Ireland, France and royal destinations in England in other ezines since then.

Day 17: Shine
Today's Mantra: Shine

Following your morals and passion requires courage. It can sometimes feel like it "costs you." But in the end, you get what money can't buy – happiness. And that happiness is the best antidote for dis-ease.

That happiness. Those smiles. That wisdom. That forgiveness. That gratitude. That love. That creativity. These are attractive to others who embody these traits (and to those who do not as well). If you want to attract a soul mate, be a soul mate.

Shine.

When we played the Billionaire Game, you got a taste of the responsibility that goes along with wealth. If you are a billionaire, chances are that you are one of the largest employers in your community. You become like the sun. If you don't get up and shine, the entire city suffers. If you are not a master of the light and your business is not offering a viable, beneficial popular product or service while turning a profit, then your city could face the problems that we've seen in Detroit and Stockton. Prior to its bankruptcy, General Motors was facing unsustainably high costs in materials and labor at a time when Toyota created fuel-efficient cars that the world, including Americans, liked better. Toyota surpassed GM to become the number one auto manufacturer.

Incidentally, if you didn't notice all of the Toyotas showing up on your street and add up the consequences of that in your head, you could have accessed the information that you needed to prepare and protect yourself quite easily. All of this information was available with an investment of about five minutes of your time and a couple of clicks on your computer. If you were just watching commercials, or applauding Oprah for giving away a GM car to each of her audience members, then your attention was being drawn away from the facts. No major financial news outlet was reporting that General Motors owed more than $100 billion and was losing tens of billions annually. However, this information was publicly available to those who knew where to look.

You might be surprised to learn what another American automaker still owes. It's worth your time to do a checkup on your bond portfolio and make sure that you are keeping the credit quality high and the terms short. GM bondholders were surprised and shortchanged, but they are not the only ones.

Being the Sun of Your Village

Rich people can't earn millions on their own. They need a team. They have a lot of partners and employees. As a rich and powerful person in your community – the sun of your village – if you don't educate the kids, you will not have tomorrow's skilled workforce. If the only thing that people can afford to eat are fatty foods, mystery meat and sugary drinks, then your city will spend a lot more on health care than the community that has easy, affordable access to farm-to-fork organic meat and produce and fresh, clean water. A healthy work force gets things done; a sick work force has a lot of paid, unproductive days off.

If you maintain robust parks and multi-use trails for people to play, hike, bike, commute and exercise in, you'll spend far less on pharmaceuticals, dialysis machines and gasoline and oil imports, too. Colorado, home of a lot of multi-use trails and one of our nation's most beloved playgrounds, enjoys the leanest, healthiest population in the United States.

If you install LED lighting in the public areas and government offices, and incentivize people to do this in their homes, you'll have savings of up to 85% – dramatically reducing the amount of energy that you have to generate to light things up. Those savings can deepen with other energy efficiency upgrades and lifestyle choices.

This is cleaner for the environment, more sustainable and helps everyone to pay less on her utility bills.

When you break down our nation's problems to the community level, it's easier to see the solutions.

Almost everything that we are doing can be done smarter and more efficiently. Otherwise we'd still be washing clothes on washboards down at the river and galloping our horse from coast to coast for business meetings. Or making edits to our emails with Wite-Out.

Whether you are the CEO or the chief widget maker, you are the sun of someone's world – even if it is just the light in your own family and home. So shine.

Leaders Are Light Houses of Truth

During a Friday evening dinner party last year, some friends got into a high-octane debate about leadership. Someone suggested that there are leaders and followers in this world, and that the majority of people just want to follow. Examples were given about how excited Ivy League grads are about working at Goldman Sachs. The premise put forward was that followers are short on ideas, and need smart Pied Pipers to whistle a tune and lead them around.

The party guests were either intentionally or unintentionally slapping hubris-laden insults on hardworking people, many of whom I know on a personal basis. And the catchall definition of a leader as anyone who has people working for him sparked a fire in me. American banks would be out of business if we'd not bailed them out during the Great Recession, and here, less than five years later, a banker and a marketing executive were already back to singing the praises of them. (Yes, I know that Goldman was able to borrow money from Warren Buffett. However, if the banking system had frozen up, if AIG had gone belly-up, and if insurance companies had been forced to pay out the claims that had been levered up, it's hard to imagine anything but a Depression or anarchy in the U.S.)

"By your definition, Bernard Madoff would be a 'leader,'" I roared. Madoff was the President of NASDAQ, and the envy of the hedge fund industry for well over a decade before he became the poster child of Ponzi schemes. Ivy League graduates were stamped-ing to work with him. And not out of stupidity or complacency or herd mentality. Out of sheer greed. Foundation fund managers and multi-millionaires alike bragged of their ability to get into his inner circle and participate in his astonishing gains – until the truth of the scam was revealed.

Henry Paulson was the CEO and chairman of Goldman Sachs *before* the banking crisis in the U.S. Paulson was at the center of the U.S. banking system, *at the top* of one of the preeminent investment banking establishments. It's fair to say that his business policies, along with those of his close colleagues, blew up the U.S. economy, resulting in the worst financial catastrophe this nation has seen since the Great Depression.

When it became clear that a meltdown was eminent, Paulson was recruited by President George W. Bush to oversee the banking bailouts (and the Lehman Bros. bankruptcy) as the Secretary of the Treasury. "Leader" is not the word I'd use to describe Paulson, or any of his colleagues who were heading up the U.S. banks in 2005-2007. "Janitor" might be a more apt term. You know just how far you've fallen from the ivory tower, when you agree to be hired to clean up your own mess, at a pay scale that is a rounding error of your prior salary.

So, I was getting a very, very, very bad taste in my mouth listen-ing to this debate on leaders, particularly since one of the dinner party guests making these claims had come from a working-class background before choosing his career in banking. Investment banking was his ticket out of poverty. Just like so many other Ivy League recruits who want to work for Goldman Sachs, he had cho-sen his career primarily based on money, not because he was an avid fan of this or that CEO or because he needed someone to follow. He just wanted to earn a living – a good one – and better than the living that his father provided for his family.

Over his career, since he is a man of morals and conscience, this banker has attempted to provide a service to the world and to democratize capital, but the truth is that a lot of his day is spent chasing deals. When he is in a more lighthearted mood, he has humorously described his job as the chastity belt between drunken sailors on leave and prostitutes wearing their best perfume.

Aren't most people getting a job to *pay bills*, rather than because they love the leader of the company or need someone to follow? For many of us, a simple math equation called *providing for our family* is the most apt description of why we get a job. In fact, all across the land, there are people who vote and yell at the political ads on their television. Americans are smart and opinionated. We are not always told the truth or given all of the facts, so not all of our choices are as well informed as they should be. However, every day that we learn something new, we are stepping in the right direction.

I couldn't hold my peace any longer, and finally blurted this out. "Let us define leaders when their contribution holds up over the centuries – not over the decade."

I used Galileo as an example. The "leaders" of Galileo's time wouldn't allow him to publish his wisdom that the Earth rotated around the sun. The Vatican tortured him for even suggesting this. But by my definition, Galileo – not his oppressors and murderers – is the leader. They won in the short term; his contribution is what ultimately counts.

By this definition, Jesus is a leader – not Pontius Pilate. By this definition, Malala Yousafzai, not the Taliban, is a leader. Those who promote sustainable business and financial literacy, and teach people how not to be taken advantage of by financial predators, like Muhammad Yunus, are the leaders – not the multitrillion dollar banking industry that is funded with our bailout money, and is thriving now by taking advantage of financially illiterate customers. Not *dumb people* and not *followers*. Hard-working people who are struggling to live the American Dream and are getting smarter day by day on just how to achieve that.

Obviously, I'm still heated about this.

After my shout-out suggestion on the best definition of a leader, the "other side," who cared more about winning the debate than absorbing a thing or two, explained to me that my examples were not really "leaders." It's pretty hard to classify Galileo and Jesus as followers, so they coined a new term for the debate – lighthouses. Galileo, they said, was not a leader. He was a lighthouse. The pope was the leader. It was the pope after all who held the power to imprison and torture Galileo. Galileo's students, the powerful Medici, didn't come to his rescue. Nor did the people of Italy.

Hmmm. Well, if people know that they can be killed or fined for speaking, they think twice about speaking up, even if they believe the person in power is a buffoon, megalomaniac, murderous tyrant. This happened during the Inquisition. It happened in Hitler's Germany. It happens during the reign of the Taliban in Afghanistan and Pakistan. By my friends' definition Muammar al-Gaddafi is a leader. Idi Amin is a leader. Hitler is a leader. By my definition, these men are just, frankly, corpses. I suppose it is noteworthy that I remember their names. That's slightly better than the pope who tortured Galileo, whose name I had to look up.

Even in the Dark Ages, "truth" finds a way, ultimately. And the visionary leader who screamed the truth from the rooftops is remembered and revered – even if s/he is martyred.

Why would we remember the person who led humanity off of a cliff? Surely only to ensure that we don't fall for Madoff's pyramid scheme again, or drink Jim Jones' cyanide Kool-Aid.

Throughout my travels, I've met many regular folks. Not one of them does their job mindlessly. Some enjoy the daily grind more than others, but we all do it to earn a living. Most of us have similar goals, no matter which color we vote. To live a decent life. Enjoy it the best we can. Take care of our family. Add value through our work. Make a positive contribution, where we can, to others. And collectively, as a nation, co-create something that we can be proud of.

In America, we are so worried about the corruption of power that we limit the time anyone can be President. By my definition, "leaders" carry the wisdom of the divine – that which will be treas-ured for centuries and centuries to come. We can easily think of

U.S. Presidents who meet that standard. George Washington, who led a revolution to break free from monarchies and founded a nation where any citizen can become the head of state. Abraham Lincoln, who ended slavery. John F. Kennedy who championed the Civil Rights Movement.

Far too many of today's leaders, including politicians, businessmen and celebrities are not symbolizing anything of value. They will be exposed. They will be forgotten. Tyrants pay a high price for the time on stage that they steal. In the case of the Madoff family, and the Gaddafi family, and Hitler, and and and... you can see that the price of tyranny is not worth the brief period of caviar and diamonds and sycophants.

Jesus never lived a luxurious life. Galileo died a broken, tortured man. Mozart was buried in a common grave. Malala Yousafzai is very fortunate to just be alive and continuing her education. But their vision, their contributions to humanity, their symphonies live on forever.

A leader is a lighthouse that shines in the darkness. Even when the jerk in power tries – but never succeeds – to extinguish the flame.

We are not a nation of followers. We are a nation of free-thinkers.

Don't fade away. Don't drift out to the sea. Don't sleep and never wake. Don't lose your destiny. Nothing in this crazy world is free, but strawberry dreams.

Wherever you are and whatever you are doing, step it up. Step out.

Shine.

Daily Task & Action Plan:

1. Shine in everything you do – in your charitable giving, in your education, your *Buy my Own Island Fund*, in your fun and your basic needs.

2. Write down the things that must shift in order for you to thrive. Prioritize them. Commit to doing the first thing on your list now.

Learning New Skills

There is a difference between all or nothing. Don't get paralysis by over-analysis. That's why simplicity is always your friend.

Most things take longer than a day to do. Put your goal in motion and start on the path to achieving it. Have more than one thing in progress at the same time.

You can set up an hour for your charitable giving that can be done in a few days *and* start figuring out how to reduce housing costs. Should you get a roommate? Downsize? Rent out the big house and get a smaller place closer to work (to save on gasoline, too). Should you ride a bike to work? Purchase an electric car? While you are brainstorming on the solutions to your big-ticket expenses, you can set up the auto-deposit of your income into your retirement plan, and roll-over old 401Ks – even if you don't know which funds to buy yet. You can register for an investor retreat that you'll be attending in a few months, and plan to use that time and space at the retreat to select the funds that you wish to invest in.

Start these balls in motion. That calendar event does come to pass.

Additional Resources

My monthly ezine includes a monthly teleconference where you can get answers to your questions. Get more information on how to save up to 85% on the subscription on the Join Now page at NataliePace.com.

Day 18: Imagination
Today's Mantra: Imagination

"What is now proved was once only imagined," William Blake. I've given you quotes from a lot of different leaders – who dream up great new worlds for us to enjoy – and many of the quotes are from speeches that you can search for and view online. At the 2013 Clinton Global Initiative University in St. Louis, Missouri, my own son, Davis Lau, was featured in a video, in a moment that was, for me, far more beautiful than any I could ever have imagined. And yet, it didn't surprise me at all. Because when you are living in the zone of prosperity, abundance and gratitude, and your daily meditations are asking to be of service to the highest good, magic beyond your wildest dreams has a way of showing up unexpectedly.

When you believe in people, and expect and encourage them to do great things, they have more confidence in themselves and they want to *do you proud*. In short, they have the fuel to experiment, to actualize things that exist only in their imagination, and in so doing, amaze themselves with what they are capable of. (When you belittle people and make them feel bad about themselves, you're urinating on their dreams and poisoning their potential.) You can teach your children well with the power of "yes" and empower them to excel.

Davis has a major passion in life – poverty alleviation. He developed a plan to achieve this that is quite innovative, which he will share with the world in his own time. Davis submitted that plan to CGIU when he was a senior at The New School in New York City, and, as a result, was invited to attend the conference with about 1000 other students from around the world. Some of the sessions were taped, including a Question and Answer session with President

Bill Clinton and Stephen Colbert. Davis managed to be just one of three or four students featured on-air in that segment. It's only a few minutes; however, this is also only the beginning of his journey with this social business that he's launching. And such an auspicious start! Particularly when we acknowledge all of the hard work, confidence, heart and soul that went on behind the scenes just to make it to that moment – something he achieved entirely on his own, without my involvement at all.

Davis' vision, when fully executed, will spark all of our imaginations on how we can easily and effortlessly positively impact those suffering from poverty nearest to us. I can't wait to see it fully realized.

Activating the Imagination in Others

This week, the focus is on how we can partner up, team up and positively impact our family, our community and our world. When we think of imagination, extend that mantra beyond sparking your own vision into the divine. Yes, that is the most important, first step. However, we stand next to a lot of people throughout the course of the day, so we want to make sure that we are inspiring them, rather than being the shadows or dark clouds blocking their light.

When Davis was in middle school, he was in a gifted mathematics class. Different kids learn differently and have different strengths. Davis' strength was spatial visioning. He *sees* things in pictures – something he inherited from his dad, who is also very gifted in art. Math was easy for Davis because he was visualizing the solution as a picture – not because he did the linear formulas and came up with the right answer.

Most teachers applauded Davis' natural academic ability, particularly in math, but not his pedantic 6th grade teacher. Even though Davis got all of the answers on tests right, she would mark every answer wrong if he didn't show all of the formulas he used to come up with that answer. Consequently, the student with the highest aptitude and achievement was the only one receiving an F in her class. This teacher and these F's were killing Davis' spirit, making him doubt his own natural talents and making him hate school – exactly the opposite of what school should be doing.

Fortunately, the national testing exam was coming up soon. I told Davis that if he scored highly on the exam, I would take those results to the principal, have his grade changed, move him out of the class and ensure that he never had to worry about this particular teacher again. Davis scored in the 94th percentile. I kept my word. I don't know if telling the teacher face-to-face that she was destroying Davis' spirit had any effect on her heart. But having the principal as a witness to a teacher giving F's to an A student – one that made the school look good on a *national* level – ensured that what happened to him wasn't going to happen in the future to other students. Hopefully everyone involved learned more about respecting the various and different ways that students learn.

As parents, it's not enough to set a good example in the home. We must also be advocates for our children in the outside world. Yes, there are times when the Peace Zone is going to be used a lot and your child is making bad choices. I encouraged Davis to write down the formulas on his tests, to avoid the teacher's nasty grades. It's a good way to check your work and ensure that you've really got the right result, in addition to being what his teacher wanted him to do. But visualizing the right answer takes time, too, so there simply weren't ample minutes to do both well.

There are many times over the course of their lives, when your child's grievances are the most important thing going on – more important than earning a living. I used to say that the moments I invested in my son was money that I wouldn't have to spend on therapy. If you are not present or plugged in enough with your kids, then you'll miss the opportunity to keep the spark of imagination alive.

As a junior in high school, when I was living with a foster family in Phoenix, I wrote a poem for the history/language arts class. I researched the historical moments I wanted to include and counted out the beats to the iambic pentameter with a metronome to get everything right. I guess I did a great job because the teacher gave me a D- *for plagiarism.*

No one was there to stand up for me. I knew that my foster mother, with her newborn baby, wasn't going to have the time to even listen to my problem. I had never been comfortable discussing anything with the foster father. The only thing that kept this bad grade when I'd worked soooo hard – from killing my spirits was the backhanded compliment. It was good enough to have been penned by a professional.

Imagine, if instead of insulting me and attacking me for plagiarism, I had been applauded for my talent and dedication! I might have actually graduated from high school! I might have published my first book before the age of 40!

Stay Plugged into Other's Lives

One of the ways that I stayed plugged in was to be active in Davis' soccer, and to drive him and his friends to other outside activities (like paintball and surfing). It was through soccer that Davis got his first taste of helping a family that was struggling with poverty.

In the early days of soccer, we used to call it Swarm Ball. The kids never stayed in their positions. Instead, they were like bees swarming wherever the ball went. When the ice-cream truck came, the bees flew over to the truck. One child used to just sit and pick flowers the whole time, while the game raged around him.

One day, when the swarm was buzzing by the ice-cream truck, I saw a seven-year-old on the sidelines practicing his bicycle kick. I went over to say hi to his mother. She was shy and eventually opened up to say that she couldn't afford to pay for the team, so she just let him come to the park to practice on his own.

The league had a scholarship system in place, so all it took was a few calls to start the process. One of the best coaches, Roberto, who was a personal friend, helped with the application process and put Jose on his team, along with Davis. I'm not sure how much any of the kids knew about the scholarship, or our role in getting Jose in the league, but Jose went on to become quite a star. And, what I do know is that everything Davis experienced growing up, from serving Thanksgiving dinners to the homeless with his father, to buying Christmas gifts for abused children, to helping Jose get on the soccer team, are part of his field of imagination – which is currently hyper-focused on poverty alleviation.

Whose imagination are you seeding right now? A friend of mine told me something that I'll never forget. "Sometimes you're the only Bible anyone will ever read."

Children don't really listen to you as much as you think they do. But they watch and learn from your every move. And if you're not around, then they are getting their imagination from video games and television.

I doubt that Davis would have ended up at a conference where he was brainstorming on how to launch his poverty alleviation social business, and featured on-air in a Q&A segment with President Clinton and Stephen Colbert, if the fertile fields of his imagination were being watered predominantly by sitcoms and war games. (There was too much exposure to War Craft, even with all of the projects we were involved in! I can't imagine how bad the addiction would have been without soccer, school and surfing.)

Activating Your Imagination

After eighteen days, you have walked a few miles up the road to prosperity and abundance. You can't just read and envision and pray for prosperity and abundance. A better life is created, not just dreamed of. As you've read in these pages, I've adventured all over the world to find solutions. 21 days in a foreign land, where nothing is routine, will definitely get your creative juices flowing. But there are other ways to activate your imagination.

If you are still stuck on the darker side of the continuum of emotions – deficient of love, deficient of creation, of honor, of pleasure, stuck more in pain, guilt, remorse, in hatred and resentments – then that is where *the practice* is important. You may get to the end of this series and need to do it all over again to reinforce the habits and take them deeper, or to give yourself ample time to do all of the action plans.

Playing the Fire Ritual *again* might release your angst and activate your imagination to create the solutions. Are you thinking of solutions that are too outlandish to write down? I've been there! The act of writing them down anyway is important, even when they seem far out of reach. So many things that we enjoy today were once wild and crazy dreams. If you think about it, you can make quite a list – from men walking on the moon to videoconferencing on your smart phone with someone who is in Europe. Most people watching the *Star Trek* television series in the 1960s assumed the kind of communication we enjoy today would always be only science fiction.

Meditation

Answers can come to us when we are quiet. Our active brain relies quite heavily on repetition. Our unconscious brain has stored so much information that we might not access if we're just going through the motions. Meditation allows us to sit quietly and rummage through the attic of interesting revelations and occurrences that we've noticed passively, which might be quite relevant. Meditation, or if you prefer to call it prayer, invites in answers and miracles from angels in our lives.

It's important to quiet the answers that circle around and around in your head. They have participated in the problem. Step into heaven in your thoughts. How does that change your perspective? What insights lie waiting for you to pick them up, like treasures in a video game, to help you on your path?

When you meditate today, ask yourself, "What treasures lie in my path today?" That way you are present and searching for them. Ask yourself, "What can I learn, who can I partner with and how can I mature, so that this problem is put behind me?" These questions activate your own imagination…

Forgive yourself for making mistakes. If you'd known more, you would have made a different choice. You do now, and you will make more-informed decisions in the coming days. Don't focus so much on the loss or the debt behind you that you are unable to imagine the gains and the riches that lie in the path ahead.

If you're afraid of repeating the past, that's what you create because that is all that you can see. When you imagine a better outcome, then you'll work to make it real. The more details you add to the optimal outcome, the faster and better it comes true because you know what you are creating. You can buy a ticket to fly to Peru and climb Machu Picchu. You can't buy a ticket to just *go on a vacation*. You have to get specific before you can go anywhere.

We create what we fear and we create what we know, until we change the possibilities by envisioning and enacting something different. I developed this 21-day series to provide a framework for you to create, envision and enact wealth, health, prosperity, peace and abundance. The origin of money is gratitude. The seeds of prosperity are adding value. When you are richer, healthier and happier, you are better able to enrich your family and your community. When you are educated and informed, you are more capable of creating value and receiving the gains of that in your active work and your passive income. When you're ready to take these teachings to the next level, then it's time to add enlightened partners.

As I've said repeatedly in these pages, when your partners are the opposition, you end up with a plan that benefits them – at your own expense. Don't allow the debt collectors to decide where and how you spend your income, or salesmen to determine what you can and can't afford to buy. You need smart, savvy, ethical partners to co-create a better tomorrow. Always be creating solutions instead of stewing in the problems. Create your world so that you don't have to blame others for destroying your life.

Imagine and Create Your Team

You cannot do it all by yourself. You need people who are *for* you and *with* you. That's why it's so important to find *your people*. They can make your business bigger than it can possibly be if you are trying to do everything alone on your own.

Imagine how many years and plans and money and manpower it took to build the Golden Gate Bridge. The Civil Rights Movement. Imagine how hard it is for a child bride to imagine a world where she can go to high school instead of having children, or for a child soldier to imagine a world where he holds a stethoscope, instead of a gun. The majority of people might be secretly hoping for that world. It becomes real when they come together and share their collective dream with the world. Oftentimes it only takes a few brave souls to step forward and speak what others are praying for.

Are others the answer to your dream, or are you the answer to their prayer? With all of the challenges we face, there are ample opportunities for you to step up and find people who are in complete alignment with your vision and want to help you shine.

Dream Big

Larry Page, the co-founder and current CEO of Google, told the 2009 graduates of the University of Michigan, "It is often easier to make progress on mega-ambitious dreams. I know that sounds completely nuts. But, since no one else is crazy enough to do it, you have little competition."

Dream big for *our world*, but also dream big for *your world*. Below are 10 tips and reminders to help you.

Rich People Don't Put Money in Jars.
Here are 12 Ways That the Wealthy Think Differently Than Most People.

Lottery winners, athletes and other instant millionaires, who haven't adopted the strategies of the wealthy, often find themselves broke within a few years of their windfall. Meanwhile, many European royals and American aristocrats preserve their estates through the centuries. What do the wealthy know that you don't?

1. **Rich People Don't Put Their Money in Jars.**
2. **Rich People Think About Capital Preservation *Before* Paying Bills.**

3. **Rich People Think About Compounding Gains; Poor People Think About Paying Off Debt.**
4. **Passive Income, Capital Preservation and Financial Husbandry Are Paramount.**
5. **Take Advantage of Free Money.**
6. **Compound Gains at 10%.**
7. **Stop Making Everyone Else Rich.**
8. **Self-Insure.**
9. **You're the CEO; Your CFP Works For You.**
10. **Throwing Money at Problems is the Wrong Answer.**
11. **Tax Strategies.**
12. **Write One Big Check and Sit on the Board.**

And here are the two cents on the details...

1. Rich People Don't Put Their Money in Jars. Rich people deposit their money into as many tax-protected and financial-predator-proof protected accounts as possible. Why? To reduce their tax burden. To compound their gains at a lower (or free) tax rate. To prevent their own hands from dipping into the jar. And to ensure that if anyone in the family has a lawsuit, the estate is protected from any judgment. (In the U.S., your retirement plans are protected from everyone and everything. That's how O.J. Simpson played golf and lived in a beautiful home in Florida, even when he owed $33 million to the Goldman family and hadn't paid a cent to them.)

2. Rich People Think About Capital Preservation *Before* Paying Bills. Do you worry about your bills incessantly? If you were to add up the amount of time you spend earning passive income, and thinking of ways to increase your gains without taking on too much risk, would it dwarf the amount of time that you spend worrying about bills and the economy? Does fear give you paralysis by over-analysis – keeping you from doing anything to improve your situation? Do you look for solutions to your challenges (including high-interest debt), educate yourself on how to improve your earning potential and get smart about protecting your assets?

3. Rich People Think About Compounding Gains; Poor People Think About Paying Off Debt. I can't tell you how many times I've heard the phrase, "I'm going to start saving just as soon as I pay off all of my debt." This only adds up when you *don't understand* the power of compounding, the tax incentives of retirement accounts and the massive savings potential of energy efficiency upgrades. Rich people do the math. So should you.

4. Passive Income, Capital Preservation and Financial Husbandry Are Paramount. Wealthy people lease their real estate instead of selling it. They preserve their capital instead of "reaching for yield." They don't lend money to people who have no hope of paying it back. And, they base their annual budget on the returns they make on their investments, rather than depleting their retirement accounts and trusts to party with strangers, live above their means and rack up expensive credit card debt.

5. Take Advantage of Free Money. When you can borrow in the low single digits, as people can today, that is almost free money. Instead of paying off your home or all of your student loans early, start focusing on reducing the interest to 4% or lower and compounding your investment gains at 10% or higher. The power of compounding is why you need to save and invest **now**, even if you have debt, and why you should think about ROI *before paying everything off*. Remember. If you deposit 10% of your income into a tax-protected retirement account, and that earns a 10% annualized gain, you'll have more money than you earn within seven years, and your money will make more than you do within 25 years.

6. Compound Gains at 10%. Rich people think about earning 10% interest annually, over time, employing the best strategies of the day to achieve that. Gamblers make Hail Mary investments praying for astronomical returns to save the day, which more often result in massive losses. (The more desperate you are, the more susceptible you are to financial predators.) Over the last five years, between 2009 and 2014, NASDAQ has tripled, going from 1372 to 4397.93. That is a gain of 38% every year, and is double the returns of the Dow Jones Industrial Average!

Performance of the NASDAQ Composite Index
March 2009 to June 26, 2014

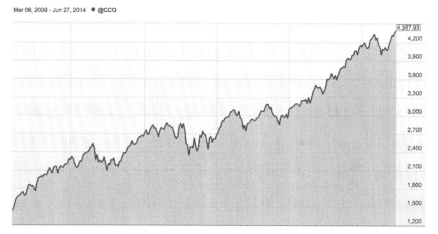

Source: Money.MSN.com. Used with permission from Microsoft.

7. Stop Making Everyone Else Rich. Most people buy a car, get a job, get a home, get insurance, turn up the air conditioning, and run out of money before the end of the month. You might think that rich people just have it easier because they have more money. However, the truth is that anyone can live a richer life if they start thinking more strategically. Healthy people can cut their health insurance in half with a Health Savings Account and a high deductible health insurance plan. Commuters can slash their gasoline bills by riding a bike, buying a hybrid or an electric car, moving closer to work or telecommuting some days. Everyone can save (up to 90%) on her energy bills with a few smart, low cost conservation tricks. (I consulted with a NASA electrical engineer to offer the energy reduction tips outlined in *The ABCs of Money*.)

8. Self-Insure. Are your life insurance payments killing your budget? Is your annuity really as safe as you have been led to believe? Most of us, outside of the few unlucky who will die early, can build up a far more secure future by having a solid investment plan, an informed will and tax-protected retirement accounts than we can by making the insurance companies rich.

9. You're the CEO; Your CFP Works For You. Rich people hire specialists and hold them accountable. Do you consider your CFP and CPA your friends? Or are you the CEO of your life, hiring financial experts to *work for you*? Do your CPA and CFP provide you with a rationale for their investing strategy and quarterly reports on their returns?

10. Throwing Money at Problems is the Wrong Answer. Rather than thinking money can solve all of the problems of friends and family, legacy wealth understands that writing a check is rarely the right answer. In *The Queen of Versailles*, Jackie Siegel gives thousands of dollars to a friend to try and save her home from foreclosure. The bank happily took the money and then just foreclosed on the home a few months later. So, who was Jackie really helping? Her friend, or the bank? If Jackie really wanted to help, she would have helped her friend design a better life plan, rather than giving her a few months extension on something that was bound to fail.

11. Tax Strategies. By now you have heard that Warren Buffett and Mitt Romney pay less in taxes (on a percentage basis) than their secretaries. How? Long-term capital gains are taxed at 20%, or lower in some cases, including no capital gains in qualified retirement accounts. So, if you're earning every penny you make, and getting taxed above 20%, then you are definitely working too hard. It's time to learn how to make money while you sleep.

12. Write One Big Check and Sit on the Board. Don't write a lot of small checks to various charities in an attempt to be fair and equitable. Pick one thing that you want to improve in this world. Write one big check. Sit on the board. And put a little of your own sweat into the endeavor. You'll get a lot more in return.

Now that you have a peek into how others create and retain their wealth, start imagining some of the ways that you can learn more to do the same for yourself. Imagine first, and then make it real.

Daily Task & Action Plan:
1. Meditate for 30 minutes today. Ask yourself, "What treasures lie in my path today?" That way you are present and searching for them. Ask yourself, "What can I learn, who can I partner with and how can I mature, so that this problem is put behind me?"
2. Meditate on the solutions. Envision the solutions. Enact the solutions.
3. Write down five successful people whom you'd like to learn from. Find out how you can. Do they have a blog? An annual letter to shareholders? Have they recently spoken at a conference or given the commencement address at a university? Have they written an autobiography or endorsed a biography?

Learning New Skills

I like to activate my imagination to solve problems before I go to sleep, by asking the questions that I have outlined above in the Daily Action Plan. I keep a journal and a recorder beside my bed. If I dream up a brilliant idea, then I just reach for the voice memo and record it (or write it in my journal). If you keep the lights out and record the idea when you first wake up with it, it's pretty easy to go back to sleep. Most of the time, the ideas are great! Don't think that you have to do a formal, sitting meditation to access the most creative, unconscious areas of your brain. I write my best speeches while I sleep. If you open up the door of possibilities on what works best for you, you'll find something that works.

Additional Resources

You can connect with Sir Richard Branson easily on Google+. You can read Warren Buffett's letters to shareholders, and other messages from him, on BerkshireHathaway.com. Kay Koplovitz, the founder of USA Networks, the first female CEO of a television network and a current board member at Time Inc., has a blog on her website at Koplovitz.com. Annual conferences like the Clinton Global Initiative, the World Economic Forum and the Milken Global Conference feature almost every statesman, politician, economist, business leader and disrupter that you'd want to learn more from. Many of their panels are available for public view online.

Day 19: Sanctuary Home
Today's Mantra:
Sanctuary Home

Home is where you wake up each morning, where you renew your spirit each evening and where you take in your sustenance at meal times. Creating a sanctuary home is the most important thing that you can do for yourself. It has nothing to do with how big your home is or how many people (or animals) you share your home with. It has everything to do with how you feel when you are there.

Every Soul Has Her Own Geography

We've already discussed how every soul has her own geography. Where you are *physically* plays a role in whether or not you feel renewed or depleted. When, at the age of twelve, I moved to California, I felt like a dying, wilted plant that had finally been watered – just a few days before giving up the ghost. The ocean air still renews me. Even if I had the same job, the same income and the same Sacred Union, in the desert I tend to feel depleted and despondent, while the ocean vivifies me.

This hasn't changed over time. However, after decades of living in Santa Monica, California, I'm now ready for a new adventure. It has more to do with the feeling of wanting to give back to the world, and that my services are needed in many different places. So, my soul's geography today is different than it was in the past. But when I need renewal, I know it's time to get back to the beach.

While traveling through Colorado recently, I met a Romanian man who felt blessed to be able to move to Switzerland for work in the technology industry. While there, he discovered that an advanced degree at a prestigious Zurich university offered a passport to the world. So, he invested his savings into a four-year degree, which he anticipated would be his ticket to America. That is how he wound up working for a marquise technology company in Boulder. Outside of work, his passion is tango. Boulder has a large community with virtuoso instructors, as does Denver, which is only half an hour away. So, he's living the dream at work and at play. Honestly, hearing the way he talks about Zurich, I do believe he'll be living back there someday.

If you are honest with yourself, would you rather be living somewhere else? Is there a topography that suits you best? What changes and choices do you need to make to get there?

What is a Sanctuary Home?

Homes might be comfortable, expensive even, and still not be a sanctuary. Sanctuary Homes are a place where you:

- Gather inspiration,
- Feel that anything is possible,
- Wake up in the morning feeling rejuvenated,
- Promote health, and,
- Are full of love.

Do Sacred Unions Automatically Create Sanctuary Homes?

It's not as simple as just picking the right partner, although that is a great step in the right direction. There are many, many good partners who come to me asking for help. This is not because they are not loving and spiritual. It is because the circumstance of their lives is depleting them. Other areas of your life can be draining you, and, if you bring that home, which is easy to do, the home will stink to. Remember in week one where we discussed how if you are brushing up against poison ivy every day, you have to remove the weed, rather than just put ointment on the rash and pretend the poison ivy isn't there. A positive attitude and a deep spiritual practice are not enough if the daily life truly sucks.

So, how can you set up the foundation where that love that you have for your family flourishes more, where you wake up inspired and want to be the best soul mate for your partner and the best parent to your kids? The best way is to ask yourself if everyone feels renewed, inspired, loved, safe and healthy.

Start listing the areas that need to be improved. Are your expenses so high that even a parking ticket can bring you to tears? The solution is adopting a more sustainable budget that allows wiggle room for unpleasant surprises. Yes, you'll have to get creative and make brave choices. Today's world is expensive and hard. Most of the reasons that people are stressed out can be traced back to money.

The Peace Zone is a great addition to any home – an area of the house that is dedicated to self-reflection and has inspirational quotes on the walls and books on the shelves. Family playrooms, or the local park, can be a way to renew and unwind with your loved ones. Try evening walks and talks after dinner.

Sanctuary home isn't just the *dwelling*. The space you occupy can be cramped, while the joy and optimism that you have about life can be infinite. I know families who live in cottages at Venice Beach, California, who consider the oceanfront to be their giant backyard – even though they share that public space with millions of people during the summer.

Many religious organizations encourage a weekly family night – something I loved doing with my son. Every Monday night we turned off the electronic devices and did different things together. Sometimes it was something he wanted to do, and other nights it was my choice. We invited friends for dinner and board games, or played miniature golf, or painted, or played music or went to movies together. I love that old time tradition of back porch banjo picking. A friend of mine is pretty mean on the spoons. What fun it is for her daughter to see that side of her!

Family Night and driving the kids to various games and events were my way to stay plugged into the conversations, concerns and celebrations going on in my son's life – particularly during that stage when teens withdraw from their parents. (When you're the chauffeur it's almost like the teens forget you are in close proximity; they speak freely, which is very enlightening to the parent who would otherwise be pretty clueless.) Staying connected is a big part of creating a sanctuary home and thriving in a close living environment, in a real world full of many challenges and frustrations. Now that my son is off on his own, I appreciate the investment of time in those family nights and weekend soccer games even more.

Praising your loved ones is effective, too. Remember to sort for things that your kids and your companion are doing right and to thank them out loud for it. My sister says, "I love you, handsome man!" to her husband daily. It is routine, but it never sounds like a platitude. She's always sincere. Her daughters have picked up the habit and greet her, saying, "Hello, pretty Momma!"

Over the years, the bathroom might have been unfinished for too long, and the backyard wasn't as manicured as they would have liked. However, in a town where a lot of the kids settle for work at the local copper mine, one daughter is now a doctor and the other has become a prominent business leader at the local college. When you believe in someone's potential, they are more likely to see greater possibilities for themselves. They shine when you remind them of just how bright they are.

There are an awful lot of challenges in the world, so think of sanctuary as a journey, more than an arrival. Don't judge yourself and feel that you've failed to create the perfect home. It doesn't exist. Just when you think you've come close, there will be other improvements to make. You'll come upon great ideas, like I did with the Dalai Lama's Peace Zone, too late to use for your own kids – but just in time for their generation to use for themselves.

Remember that kids watch you far more than they listen to you. They pick up so many of your habits and mannerisms, and they grow up thinking that your home life is *normal.*

Does Therapy Work?

When the issue is money, it's hard to find a therapy that works better than financial literacy, education and a better life plan. So many *couple* problems are, at their core, *money* problems. Many relationship problems can be solved with the Thrive Budget.

With almost $12 trillion in consumer debt, far too many Americans are living above their means. If you're overspending on everything, particularly the big-ticket items, it's hard to enjoy life. You'll feel buried alive in bills and struggling to survive – whether you are living in a McMansion or a hermit's hovel. Now, many people don't consider their unsustainable budget to be overspending, even if they are filling in the gaps with credit cards or shaving all of the fun out of their spending. Many think that if they earned more, or when they become more successful, they'll be able to fix everything. While I encourage everyone to pursue their dreams, you'll get there much faster if you have a sustainable plan to transport you out of the status quo, which is where most of us are stuck, and into a budget that is fueled up to drive you to Avalon.

We've talked about the ways to adopt a more sustainable plan. Vacations and adventure are a lot more fun than transportation and utilities. Who wouldn't want to spend $50 on dancing rather than on a tank of gas?

A poorly designed budget creates a lot of tension in the home. Putting money in jars means that you are not benefiting from the Mitt Romney 14% tax plan and protecting your assets from financial predators – including the most common one – you dipping your hand in the jar. Cutting out café lattes is not as effective as trimming back on the amount of gasoline, electricity and even lawn irrigation water that you guzzle. A sustainable plan and money while you sleep gains will improve the mood in your home – even more than a new coat of paint (although that might help, too).

31 Ways to Green Your Home (and *our* Planet Home) and Reduce Your Energy Costs

Ironically, it was almost Earth Day in 2010 when the Deepwater Horizon exploded in the Gulf of Mexico, killing 11 men and spewing at least 4.9 million *barrels* of oil into the Gulf. (The exact day was April 20, 2010). The Bike Power Community has been celebrating Earth Day (April 22nd) as Bike Power Day ever since. There is a national Bike to Work Day on May 15th, as well.

There are no rules. The Bike Power organizers just encourage everyone to garage the car and bike power our lives for a day – or a week, if you can. There is so much to learn from, and be inspired by, when you take a break from oil. The day moves slower. Ideas spark. Meaningful and lasting change takes root.

31 Suggestions to Make Earth Day Every Day

1. **Gift a bike** to your local Goodwill or children's advocacy group, so that those in most need can pedal their way to school, work, health and greater fiscal health, too.
2. **Ride a bike** to work and for your chores. Plan now to make this happen all day (or all weekend) long.
3. If you can't ride a bike or walk on Earth Day, **choose mass transit or carpool**, instead of driving, or telecommute one day to work.
4. **Videoconference**, instead of flying, to a meeting.
5. Use **canvas bags** instead of plastic.
6. **Eat local, organic** and low on the food chain. Drink local beer, wine and spirits. (This means cutting back on chocolate and coffee for Americans and Canadians. Acck!)
7. **Plant a tree.**
8. **Pay bills online.**
9. **Reduce, reuse and recycle.**
10. **Compost.**
11. Replace your light bulbs and CFLs with **LED lighting**.
12. Test drive an **electric car**.

13. Send these tips to **your local newspaper** and ask them to publicize Bike Power on Earth Day.

14. Send these tips to **10 friends** and ask them to forward them to 10 friends.

15. **Put a timer on your water heater**, so that you're not heating water while you're at work.

16. **Turn off the heating or air conditioning** while you're at work, so that you're not gassing an empty home.

17. **Organize an Earth Day event** at a **local school**; help parents peddle their kids to school.

18. **Stop investing in old school, dirty energy** in your 401K, IRA, annuity and pension. 19. Invest in a **clean energy exchange traded fund**.

20. Use **wind, solar and geothermal energy** to power your home, office and electric car.

21. **Insulate your home** to avoid energy leaks. Check out PassiveHouse.US for tips.

22. Reduce your reliance on **petroleum products, such as plastic bags and bottles**.

23. **Wear cotton instead of polyester**.

24. Organize a monthly **bike ride** in your town or city.

25. Put your computer and cell phone chargers on a power strip, and **power down** when you are not charging these devices. (Leaving it plugged in is like leaving the lights on all the time – a big energy drain.)

26. Take a virtual tour of **the first platinum LEED-rated home in the U.S.** online at LivingHomes.net.

27. Join or start a **Bicycle Advocacy Group** to make your community more bike-friendly and to raise awareness of the benefits of bikes through advocacy, programs, education and outreach.

28. Get green tips in the **Energy Savers Guide** at EnergySavers. gov/tips.

29. Learn more about **energy efficiency retrofits** and Passive House building at PassiveHouse.US.

30. **Buy and use less of everything!**
31. Check out the **physical and fiscal health benefits** enjoyed by the citizens of bike-friendly cities, like Amsterdam – either online or by traveling there for a vacation.

If you would like to save up to 90% on your electric bill, be sure to read "How to Save Money on Your Electric Bill Forever," from *The ABCs of Money*. Every dollar you don't give to the gas pump and utility company can add up to $7,500 in annual savings for many Americans. $7,500!

These shifts can create more room in the budget for fun – something that makes every home and every life more beautiful.

The Toxic Home

Many people stay in an abusive relationship/home, thinking that they can't afford to leave. That certainly was the case for me as a child – until I finally ran away from home at the age of 12. That desperate act woke all of my relatives up. My aunt offered to take me into her home, and in so doing saved my life. (Thank you, Aunt Sue, Uncle Jerry, Wayne, Karen, Craig and Sean!)

The sad thing is that a lot of relatives and friends don't get involved until something desperate has happened – and sometimes that's too late. Think of Nicole Brown and the pictures she had placed in storage of her with a black eye, which were found *after* her murder.

The truth is, you can't afford to stay. Your family and friends want the best for you and will be enormously helpful *if you step up and ask for their support*. Not everyone will be. Some of your friends will not want to get involved, and others will feel that when a couple has problems, it's both people who are creating chaos in the home. Don't worry about them. Turn to the ones who are willing to help.

Abusers don't take out ads. In fact, they are often the most fun person in the room. When a bully threatens, mocks, steals from or hurts someone, it is *never* the victim's fault, even though the abuser will always try to rationalize her actions with that claim. We all make

choices on how we act and react to situations. The only time violence is really justified is self-defense or to protect someone we love.
If you're constantly on the lookout in your home, then it's time to
get the abuser out of the house *to protect yourself and those you love* –
and avoid the tragedy that is just waiting to happen.

If someone harms you and then says that if you behaved differently,
they wouldn't, that's abuse. Or, conversely, if you are constantly berating someone, even if it is a defiant teen or a cheating spouse, that's
abuse – and further, it's not going to produce the desired outcome.
No one's behavior should "*make*" you hit her or hurt her, emotionally,
financially, verbally or physically. If you want to inspire, encourage or
enforce a shift in behavior, then peace negotiations, not war tactics,
are appropriate – particularly if the goal is a sanctuary home.

I've talked a lot about taking ownership of your life. When
you find yourself being treated unfairly, then it's time to step up
and make a change. No amount of walking on egg shells, or being
accommodating, or watching your words, or not spilling the milk
will ever prevent the other person from blowing their fuse, if that's
what they do. You owe it to yourself, and to your children, to get the
abuse out of the home. Otherwise, your kids will receive the terrible
message that bullying is okay, and you're setting yourself up for a
hellish experience during their teen years.

Breaking the Cycle of Poverty (and Abuse)

When I started mentoring schoolgirls in Kenya, I became
informed about the harsh issues they face, most of which are rooted
on poverty. In the poorest countries in the world, 1/3 of girls have
babies before they are 18. (Teen pregnancy and poverty are a big
challenge in the U.S. and other developed world nations, as well.)
In the developing world, many teen girls are getting pregnant right
after puberty because they are married off to older men, as the 3rd
or 4th wife, for the gift of a cow or other compensation to the
family –instead of getting a high school or college education.
According to the World Health Organization, two million girls
under the age of 15 give birth every year.

One young Kenyan woman convinced her family not to *marry her off*, and to allow her to attend college in the United States instead. She did this by excelling in elementary school and by attracting the support of a mentor from the U.S., whom she'd met through an American nonprofit organization that was helping her high school. Vivian promised her family that she could eventually earn her own keep *and* be more helpful to them, after an initial investment of time in an education. Vivian is well on her way to this. During her time at college, Vivian had the honor of interviewing Bono onstage during the 2014 ONE Power Summit. With her degree, her rolodex, her mentor and her connections, the future looks very bright for this ambitious young woman. Vivian's chance at a sanctuary home is only possible because strangers cared enough to reach across the world to help her achieve her dreams.

I've mentioned the impressive rise of Asian Americans, who invested in the education of their children to rise from the bottom to the top income earners in the U.S. With a goal like that, even cramped quarters can be a sanctuary home. Don't underestimate the power of having your family united toward a goal. And don't shortchange yourself or your kids by focusing too much on Keeping Up With the Joneses, and buying all of the latest fashion and toys. There are a lot of national resources and opportunities for people to improve their lot in life through education – particularly in the developed world.

I wish you a sacred union and sanctuary home, where prosperity and abundance flourish. If you wish the same for yourself, then you have already started the process of attaining it.

Daily Task & Action Plan
1. Pull out a map. Where in the world would you really like to live? Why not take a vacation there? Put that on the list of possibilities for your long-term fun budget.
2. Write down three things that you love about your home and three things that you need to improve to make it more of a sanctuary. Commit to making those three changes. Give

yourself a timeline and hold yourself accountable to getting them done.

3. Make today a day of telling everyone in your family how much you love them and why.

Learning New Skills

There is no doubt that uplifting yourself will make you a better partner. Would you be happier if you were exercising more? Singing more? Dancing more? Meditating more? Going to church more? Reading more?

Knowing the various stages of child development will help make your child's natural mood swings more understandable. The more you know, the more you can be in front of, instead of crushed by, the challenges that your child faces and the changes that occur as your child matures.

Additional Resources

If you're looking for ways to reduce your utility bill, try tips from PassiveHouse.US and Energy.gov, as well as the chapter on reducing your energy bill that is in *The ABCs of Money*.

Day 20: Co-Create

Today's Mantra: Co-Create with Other Masters of the Light

"Give me six hours to chop down a tree and I will spend the first four sharpening the axe," Abraham Lincoln.

Let's say that you want to build your dream house. You've decided that a Passive Home is right for you because your energy bills might be reduced by up to 90%. You want to super-insulate it. You know how many rooms that you want. You know how many bathrooms and how much square footage. You know what you can afford and where you want to build your home.

These are all decisions that you have to make *before* building your house. If you let someone else make these decisions for you, you can end up with a home that is too expensive for you to live in. You could lose it to the bank before you even step foot across the threshold. You could end up with a home in the wrong area, and have the extra expense of paying for private school, or of maintaining an active security system. You could end up with too much square footage, making it a pain to clean, or with plumbing leaks and drafts that take your utility expenses through the roof. By understanding what it is that you want, and interviewing the contractors who are going to build it for you, you are more likely to get the house that you envision and something that you can actually afford.

Take those four hours to sharpen the axe before attempting to chop down any tree.

This is something that we must learn to apply to all aspects of our lives. Sometimes we are working so hard in our "day job," that we cut corners on important decisions (like our home and nest egg) that end up making us miserable – when it would have been far easier to invest more time and focus up front. Not a lot. Just a little… Because information, knowledge and wisdom are cumulative. Once we get information and base our lives in wisdom and form great fiscal/physical habits, then that becomes *the way life is*. Small adjustments can have substantial positive affects because they are building upon this strong foundation.

I've stressed repeatedly in this book that almost everything we buy is based on commission-based sales. In almost every area that you can imagine, someone is going to benefit by selling you something bigger and more expensive than you came in to buy. Your home. Your car. Your insurance plan. A get-rich-quick scheme. If you build your own house, the contractor is going to make more money and work longer if he can convince you to build a bigger one. So, finding great partners requires understanding this, and doing the due diligence required to find those individuals who are in it *for you* and not just for themselves.

If you aren't factoring in all of your expenses – including the unexpected ones like parking tickets – *and* all of your purchases – including retail therapy – into your Thrive Budget, then you'll be making up the difference on expensive, high-interest credit card debt in no time. When you take charge and have a vision for everything, you start on the path to prosperity and abundance, instead of falling into the chains of debt consciousness, which is so prevalent in today's world. According to a report by the Urban Institute in August of 2014, 35% of adults with a credit file – 77 million Americans – have debt that is in collections, more than 180 days past due. In essence, one out of every three of your friends is partnered with a debt collector, instead of a great financial team. Taking charge of your own budget and investments – *before* you get into trouble *and after*, too – is the only way that you'll ever thrive in today's Debt World.

Choose Your Financial Partners Based Upon Expertise

When you choose your partners carefully, and do your own research into the things you want to buy, then you free yourself from the commercial system where we erroneously rely upon salesmen as our fountain of wisdom. Walk onto the lot, or take a tour of homes, or browse the options at the brokerage, or peruse the insurance plans, *after* you have already researched and know what model, characteristics and price range are right for you. It's better to ask an experienced car mechanic which car she recommends and why than to rely on the dealer or an advertisement for this information. It's better to determine whether or not you can afford the house you are interested in, by seeing how all of the expenses – including maintenance, property taxes, mortgage payments and upkeep – factor into a Thrive Budget.

The Monster under the Bed.

Remember as a child being afraid of the monster under the bed? If you were like me, it took a few times of peeking under the box springs, flashlight in hand, to debunk that fear. And that is exactly the way it is with so many of our worries. Once we pull the covers back and shine a light, wisdom sets in, and everything shifts. The fear is gone forever. There is no more stress. What is left is confidence, and sometimes, a little chuckle on how silly and misinformed you were, and how much easier everything is now.

The bigger the consequences, the bigger the terror... and the more monumental and lasting the shift, once wisdom steps in. (I keep thinking of the reluctance of people in the Dark Ages to accept that the Sun, not the Earth, was the center of our world.) I've had that happen more than a few times, but I'll relate two to you.

Recurring Ear Infections and Chronic Hearing Loss

My son's pediatrician always jokes that he does his job too well. He only saw my son during well child checkups! This wasn't always the case, however.

The pediatrician I was using only one year prior to finding Dr. Jay Gordon lost her job when she prescribed year-round antibiotics to treat my son's recurring ear infections. I can't tell you how much worry and how many tears I shed every time Davis got an ear infection, was prescribed antibiotics, which failed, prompting another more resistant strain of bacteria to take hold. This happened non-stop for six months when Davis was a toddler. My anxiety was high and the stakes were enormous. Davis' immune system and hearing were both at risk. I was worn out from lack of sleep – staying up all night to monitor his fevers – which were dangerously high. The medical bills were crushing.

Clearly we needed a new plan. Thankfully, after asking every mother I knew, searching in every corner for a possible solution, and after countless tears of frustration and desperation, I found Dr. Jay Gordon.

Dr. Jay's pro-immune system, anti-allergy approach cured the problem in three short months, and promoted health so well that my son rarely got sick again! Dr. Jay identified and eliminated the allergen – milk! – and added in probiotics, Essential Fatty Acids, nutrients and alternative sources of calcium.

The doctor who wanted to treat recurring ear infections with antibiotics was literally *causing* the problem in the first place – by scaring me into pouring 24 ounces of milk into my half-Asian son *daily*. Most Asians, such as my son, are allergic to cow's milk. The allergic reaction was mucous, which created the perfect environment for bacteria – and ear infections. Once we eliminated the allergic reaction, and boosted Davis' immune system, the ear infections disappeared.

Almost Losing My Home

In the second example, the cure was wisdom, too; however, the supplements were financial literacy, self-empowerment and right action.

When my husband and I divorced, I inherited a home that was underwater, with monthly bills that were more than my salary as a substitute teacher. The books I read encouraged me to cut out café lattes to make ends meet. I had already cut out every ounce of fun, and my son and I were still drowning. Things were so dire that I was about to lose my home!

It was in that pivotal moment that I stopped listening to the conventional wisdom, and started charting my own course. I got a higher paying job. I looked deeper into real estate trends, and held on long enough (just two short years) to sell my condo for a profit. (The condo was unaffordable and in the wrong neighborhood for middle school.) I cut my expenses by moving in with another single mom. I learned how to invest, and almost tripled my money within 18 months. (This required *a lot of research* because if I had done what the "money manager" told me to do, I would have lost 75% or more in the Dot Com Recession.) I created the Thrive Budget system – 50% to Thrive and 50% to Survive – which works infinitely better than cutting out café lattes.

Before I knew it, all of my friends asked me to teach them what I know. With the encouragement, support and assistance of a few friends in my Mom Network, I founded the Women's Investment Network, LLC, with a mission to make stocks as sexy as shoes. Since women are 30% more likely to end up in poverty than men, and only 4.6% of Fortune 500 CEOs are women, financial literacy remains my mission and my passion, in addition to being my business. About 40% of my subscribers are men. I welcome everyone with open arms. Financial literacy is a partner that all Americans need.

You can see how valuable my charitable giving has been to my success. Without it, I wouldn't have received the support of the Mom Network to launch WIN LLC in the first place. These were moms that I had raised money with for the local public elementary school. Charity is definitely the best networking, and is a great place to find conscientious, gifted partners for your personal board of advisors.

Wisdom is the Cure

Both of these crises scared me to the core of my being. I couldn't see a solution. I knew the conventional wisdom was wrong. But I didn't have the skillset, tools, vision or information to see a better way. I spent too much time tearing my hair out, but, thankfully, just enough time searching for a better way. I found better partners and mentors, and, in the case of investing and personal finance, I lived my way into the solution and then became the expert myself.

Sometimes you need someone else's flashlight to illuminate the darkness. Dr. Jay Gordon was that for Davis' health. I am that light for the fiscal health of my readers and subscribers. We both promote daily fiscal/physical habits– a holistic approach, so that health becomes *who you are* and *the way life is.* You definitely are what you eat, think and do! Imagine how much easier everything becomes when those things are healthy for you.

Once you learn there's no monster under your bed, you're no longer afraid of the dark. Wisdom is the cure.

12 million people entered the foreclosure process between 2007 and 2013. If these homeowners knew that the average returns of real estate are less than 5%, would they have purchased their homes at an all-time high? Wisdom is the cure: knowing the average annual returns of real estate, stocks, bonds, gold and more.

Total consumer indebtedness is almost \$12 trillion (source: New York Federal Reserve Bank). No wonder everyone feels that they are struggling to survive! The Thrive Budget is a far better plan than being Buried Alive in Bills and living on credit cards to make ends meet. Wisdom is the cure.

75% of diseases are preventable, according to the Center for Disease Control. Nutrition, exercise, avoiding smoke (even second hand) and limiting your alcohol intake are the cure. Health is wealth!

Only 4.6% of Fortune 500 CEOs are female. Meanwhile, our sisters in India are twice as likely to be CEO, using one effective tool – The Mom (and Grandparent) Network. Families in India are more likely to be multi-generational. When the mother has a C-level job, often it is the grandparents who are caring for the children and home, and cooking meals. This support makes it far easier for the executive parent to focus on her job with the assurance that the children are being well provided for. In the evenings, rather than toiling over a stove, the CEO mom comes home to a cooked meal and can sit down and enjoy it!

Consider the Grandparent, the Mom, the Sibling, the Colleague and the Mentor Network when you are considering who to partner up with on your path to greater abundance and prosperity.

Women are 30% more likely to live in poverty than men; women of color are three times more likely than white men. At the same time, for the first time in U.S. history, women under 30 are graduating in greater numbers from college and graduate school and making more money than their male counterparts. Will this trend shift the poverty imbalance in the other direction?

Start on your own path of replacing fear of money, with prosperity wisdom. It will integrate your spiritual practice into your daily life, while at the same time making your material world easier and more enjoyable.

If you know anyone who is:

- Drowning in credit card debt
- Property rich and cash poor
- Struggling to make ends meet
- Needs to get their nest egg safe
- Interested in investing in safe, income-producing assets,
- Being hounded by debt collectors,
- Worried about the Bond Exodus, or
- Wants to reduce the amount they spend on energy and gasoline

Wisdom is the cure.

Salesmen are *Not* Light Houses of Truth

You can absolutely find financial partners who are there for your benefit and will be important team players for you. And you are more likely to achieve that desirable goal if you have enough knowledge and discernment to interview them for the job, than if you rely upon a referral, or if you just hire a friend or family member. FINRA.org warns that 70% of investment scam victims relied primarily upon advice that they received from a relative or a friend. That was true of Madoff's victims, and is the downfall of quite a lot of the nouveau riche – like sports stars, entertainers and lottery winners.

Last year, a business colleague came to me with a big problem. "My insurance payments are killing me!" she confided. About two years previously, she had purchased a million dollar life insurance plan from a relative to help her kids pay taxes on her estate when she passed away. The trouble was because she was advanced in age, as was her husband who was also in declining health, the plan premiums were $40,000 a year. As a result, she was at a point where she would have to pull equity out of her home to pay for the insurance. Rightfully, this had her worried. "Is there a better option," she asked, "or should we stick with this plan?"

Oh, the things we do to avoid taxes, when the better strategy would be to set up a trust or LLC, write a will, start the process of transferring the estate under the gift tax level annually, earn gains and have relatively no taxes due on the estate by the time she passed on! The truth is, based on her having trouble making the payments during relatively good times, odds were that the only one getting a million in the future would be the insurance company – not her kids. Why? Because when the day comes that she can't make the payment, her policy will lapse and she will lose the coverage that she was already struggling to pay. Yes, she might have *some* of the premiums available to her, but that would be far less than she was sold into or counting on, and on terms that are less beneficial, since she would be in a default situation. Also, by tapping into her home equity, she had already begun pouring her estate down the insurance drain!

People are living so much longer, making these annuities and life insurance plans far more risky by nature than they *appear* to be. By the time you retire, you will be living on a fixed income, which is typically a fraction of what your earned income was prior to retirement. Retirement puts the squeeze on an already tight budget. Add in the escalating health care costs that accompany old age, and the fact that seniors are more likely to be scammed on by financial predators, and you have a very real possibility that the life insurance premium can't be paid. Most people spend more money on health care in the last six months of living than they have earned their entire life. Many seniors *want* to keep their life insurance going, but simply can't afford it.

In other words, rather than increasing her net worth and compounding gains, which is what investments can and should do, her estate was at great risk of losing value the longer that she lived. If she died suddenly and soon, then her kids would win, and inherit that million dollars (when they would rather have her still alive). However, if she stuck around another twenty years, there was little chance that she could keep the payments up to keep the million dollar pay-out alive, and *no chance* that her kids could have done this on her (or their) behalf either.

Annuities and life insurance have become more and more popular lately, for many reasons. Retirees and people nearing retirement have vivid memories of the Great Recession. Even with the stock market at all-time highs again, they just don't trust it. With interest rates at all-time lows, bonds and savings accounts offer no income. So, life insurance companies can offer a "guaranteed" single-digit interest rate (under 9%) that looks attractive by comparison – until you read the fine print, understand the surrender fees and costs, realize the risk of default, and do the math on other options.

Most people don't know that insurance companies are not FDIC-insured. Life insurance policies are not backstopped by the national government, like bank deposits are. If the insurance company goes under, your life insurance or annuity could be worth a lot less than you were promised. When you purchase life insurance or an annuity, you are placing your full faith in one, single company that might not be worthy of that. States have a guaranty fund to help in insolvencies, but most states have a benefit cap of $300,000 – putting the value of your million-dollar plan at one-third of what you've been promised, in the worst-case scenario.

On the other hand, if you were just saving that $40,000 a year, within 20 years you'd have $800,000, *even if you didn't earn a dime of return on investment.* Since stocks and bonds – both – earned 10% annualized over the last 30-year period, chances are you'd be worth a million within *thirteen* years – *without* the insurance policy.

By the eighth year of disciplined, tax-protected investing with 10% annualized returns, your money will be depositing more into the account annually than you are.

10% Annualized Return on $40,000 Deposit

Year	Deposit	10% Gain	Total
1	$40,000	$4,000	$44,000
2	$40,000	$8,400	$92,400
3	$40,000	$13,240	$145,640
4	$40,000	$18,564	$204,204
5	$40,000	$24,420	$268,624.40
6	$40,000	$30,862	$339,486.84
7	$40,000	$37,949	$417,435.52
8	**$40,000**	**$45,744**	**$503,179.08**
9	$40,000	$54,312	$597,496.98
10	$40,000	$63,745	$701,246.68
11	$40,000	$74,125	$815,371.35
12	$40,000	$85,537	$94,908.49
13	**$40,000**	**$98,091**	**$1,078,999.33**

In a scenario where you live another 20 years, your kids could have almost $2.5 million – plenty for them to keep *and* pay taxes on – and 2.5 times as much as the million-dollar life insurance plan.

And there are more than a few ways whereby you can will your stock and your estate to your kids, so that by the time you pass away they are the owners and there is no death tax due.

10% Annualized Return on $40,000 Deposit
Years 13-20

13	$40,000	$98,091	$1,078,999.33
14	$40,000	$111,900	$1,238,099.27
15	$40,000	$127,090	$1,397.989.19
16	$40,000	$143,799	$1,581,788.11
17	$40,000	$162,179	$1,783,966.93
18	$40,000	$178,797	$1,966,763.62
19	$40,000	$200,676	$2,207,439.98
20	$40,000	$224,744	$2,472,183.98

As with almost everything in your life, if you cast your view 15-20 years in the future, imagine what life will be like then and make your decisions from that perspective, you'll develop a more sustainable and rewarding plan. The scenarios that salesmen offer you are ABC – always be closing – not *The ABCs of Money*. Good financial partners, like good doctors, will put you on a plan that works great now and twenty years from now.

Thinking 15-20 Years Over the Horizon

Here are a few examples of how thinking 15-20 years ahead will affect the decisions you make right now.

If I'm 50 and I'm thinking of buying a house, then I want to consider where I want to be living when I'm 65 or 70. If I'm working in an expensive city, such as San Francisco, then I might buy a place in Florida or Arizona and rent it out. The 20-year plan would be that it will be paid off when I'm ready to retire (if I've selected a 15-year, fixed-rate mortgage). I can receive a little extra income in the meantime. And both of those states are more affordable to live in for folks on a fixed income, with real estate prices that are still priced lower than the bubble real estate pricing of 2006.

If I'm 27, married and buying my first house, then I might pay a little more for a neighborhood with a good middle and high school, and use some of my education budget to help afford any additional cost. My rationale would be that I wouldn't have to pay for private school for my kids.

If I were looking to become CEO, I'd think of how I could live close to my parents – or conversely buy a home with a guesthouse out back for them to live in.

Many high net worth individuals, like Warren Buffett and J. Paul Getty before him, set up foundations for their kids to run. This type of legacy planning is a great way to preserve family assets, pay less in taxes, enjoy gains, ensure that the money is overseen by a board of advisors who can limit the shenanigans of the kids, and *do good* in the bargain.

Attracting Dream Come True Partners

I wasn't rich when I chaired the Silent Auction at my son's elementary school – raising money for the Booster Club to hire music and art teachers, to put computers in the library and to maintain a grassy field for the kids to play on. I'm just an ordinary person who wanted my son to have a great experience at school. And I selfishly thought that if I put chairman on my resume, I'd be able to climb the career ladder faster. (It worked!) What I didn't realize is that the partners in that charitable endeavor would become my first partners in the WIN LLC business endeavor, too.

Malala Yousafzai wasn't rich when she gambled with her life to promote the right of young women to get an education. She's now partnered with Vital Voices, a worldwide nonprofit organization, to promote educational opportunities for women and girls in the developing world.

Nelson Mandela wasn't rich when he ran for President of South Africa. He'd just emerged from 28 years in prison. The year that he was elected as President was the first year that he was ever allowed to vote.

Remember just how valuable time and talent can be – often far more valuable than just writing a check.

Stars Shine

Once you step up and become the dream come true *you*, you're going to be amazed at the dream come true partners you attract. When I first launched the Women's Investment Network, LLC back in 2002, one of the first people I met, through a series of unexpected events, was Kay Koplovitz. We had a brief meeting, at the end of which I posed an important question. "Why did you take this meeting?" I asked.

"I always trust my gut instinct," Kay said. "When I was younger, I used to question it. Then, years later, I'd discover that what I knew in the first few minutes of meeting someone was always right."

If you are experienced and smart, like Kay is, then your gut instinct is actually complicated pattern recognition. There are a lot of successful people who are going to see you for exactly who you are. And, when you stumble on their path, if you're doing something that impresses them, they can be very beneficial to you. As Thomas Edison said, "Good fortune happens when opportunity meets preparation."

Melanee Meets Warren Buffett and Bill Gates

I first met Melanee when she won a seat at my Investor Educational Retreat in a raffle at her church. Within a few years, she had attended two of my retreats and had met Bill Gates – something she discovered that she wanted to do by playing the Billionaire Game on the beach.

How did she manifest this amazing feat? Much more easily than you think. She decided that learning to invest was important, since she was retired. She values getting the best information, so, in addition to learning my systems, she wanted to learn from the Oracle of Omaha – Warren Buffett. During the commitments section of the Billionaire Game, the group helped her to brainstorm the simple idea that she could attend the Berkshire Hathaway annual meetings if she owned the stock, and hear Buffett's wisdom live, in person. (See: even partners in a *game* can be beneficial!)

Voila! The following May, Melanee flew off to attend the annual Berkshire Hathaway meeting. The year after, she found herself at a bridge table with Bill Gates during the annual Berkshire Hathaway meeting. "Now I'll have to learn bridge!" she told me, amazed and elated at her good fortune.

Do Bill Gates and Warren Buffett follow Melanee on Twitter? No, but they are definitely on her team, and are sources from whom she draws her investing strategies. When she has questions about the markets, she knows where to get great answers. And when she plays the Billionaire Game, she knows the value of making commitments to herself.

Make Today the Best Day of the Rest of Your Life

No matter where you are in life or what you've been through, now is the best time to start fresh. The sky truly can be the limit. As J.K. Rowling said in her 2008 commencement address at Harvard University, "You will never truly know yourself or the strength of your relationships until you are tested by adversity. Rock bottom became the solid foundation upon which I rebuilt my life."

Joanne Rowling was living on government assistance, trying to provide for her daughter as a single mother. She dreamed up a new life, and a new world of *Harry Potter*, and is now a multi-millionaire. She didn't get there alone. Someone had to believe in her book to get the process started. In fact, twelve publishers turned her down before Bloomsbury agreed to publish. It is reported that an 8-year-old girl, Alice Newbury, the daughter of the chairman, was the champion of the book. It was Rowling's publisher's idea to use J.K. instead of Joanne to appeal to boys – a large audience of the *Harry Potter* series. That was a smart move that paid off.

Co-Creating a Better World

When you think about making the *world* better, chances are organizations leap first to mind. If you think the world's problems are best solved through our elected officials, then you might want to get involved in local politics – whether it is running for office, collecting funds and signatures or making biking safer. You might want to promote clean energy, or poverty alleviation or organic farming. Sharing a few memes on social media is not as effective as getting directly involved. But, who has the time?

So, what is really preventing you from writing a check, or spending your Saturday on the front lines of change or making sure that you are not invested in the companies that you are protesting? For most of us, it is feeling *spent* already – overworked, underpaid, indebted and exhausted… This might make turning on a mindless comedy, popping the top of a cold beer, taking a nap, or retail therapy tempting – particularly if the television or radio is on in the background, enticing us in this direction. There just aren't as many ads to *do good* as there are to spend spend spend, or as many TV shows encouraging you to volunteer at your child's school as there are shows about forensic DNA analysis of crime scenes.

And yet, if you do spend your spare time and money on *doing good*, even when you are exhausted, you'll find that everything starts shifting in your life and, eventually, you'll have more of everything that you desire – including energy. By vivifying your brain cells, you'll think of things unimagined. By working with others, you'll form valuable bonds. By numbing your brain cells with alcohol, the blue blur of TV or purchasing more things, you're just doing the laps – like a hamster on a wheel.

Start by doing something close to home. If your child is in Kindergarten, volunteer to help in the garden weekly, or to help the teacher incubate some butterflies or chicks in the classroom. If you can't do it once a week, try once a month – or even once a year. Get involved in the Booster Club to make sure that there is funding for P.E., music and arts teachers, computers, instruments and play structures. Mentor someone. Ride a bike and form partnerships with others who want to make it a safer way to get around.

Why Spiritual People Need To Focus More on Money

You can't be generous if your relationship with money is tenuous.

That's why so many spiritual, kind-hearted people can be so tight with their giving – or be involved in careers and business practices that are not good for humanity *at all*. There were plenty of churchgoing real estate and mortgage brokers who were selling homes to people who couldn't afford them at the height of the real estate bubble – just so that they could pay their own mortgages. At church, I often see people drop nothing, or just a dollar or two, when the basket it passed, when you know that they are spending $25 or more freely at a movie theater. Studies have found that only 4% of Americans tithe, and that 25% of Christians give away no money at all.

Many people *want* to give, but they feel like they have nothing to spare. If your expenses are too high, it doesn't matter whether you are middle class, high class or just above the poverty line. You'll feel too constrained to play and be charitable. (Think again about the laundress who donated a quarter of a million dollars to charity.)

In a state of abundance, you give from the overflow, which is what charity is all about. A well that has run dry offers no water for anyone. So, how do you start the flow of prosperity when you already feel dried up? Money habits are more like muscles than arid land. The more you practice, the stronger the muscle. Giving *and* receiving are necessary to the *flow* of prosperity. You must *get into the flow* to *start* the flow, just as you must start lifting weights to see muscle tone.

Time and talent can be even more valuable than money. So, if you still feel too strapped for cash to donate to your favorite cause, then start by donating your time and talent.

As you build up your muscle of confidence that you *can* have more than enough time, talent and money to give, then you have to get money smart, so that you can set up your life to support this, with the Thrive Budget and an effective passive income strategy. As long as you fear money, you'll find it hard to give to charity with an open heart – if you have the courage to give anything at all.

Scrooge

It is easy to think others are Scrooge, neglecting to point the finger at ourselves when we are stingy with our money. Because no one ever *feels* stingy.

If you're rich and you don't give 10% of your income to charity, it's probably because you're already paying a very high tax rate, and everyone around you is always asking for money. So, even if you're not very generous – in terms of donating 10% of your income to charity – you still feel taken advantage of. If you're middle class or below, then you feel like wages have stalled, the cost of living is out of reach, and you're someone who is *in need* of a better shake of the profits. So both rich and poor people can feel taken advantage of. Anyone who feels broke, or worries about going broke, will cling to their money too tightly. It has very little to do with being rich or poor, or how ethical or spiritual you are.

Add Colors to Your Rainbow

You're going to need great partners to achieve any success in life. And once you become a dedicated, well-rounded, optimistic, passionate, informed individual who is doing what you are here on this planet to do – you'll attract them. Once you feel confident in your ability to earn active and passive income, and provide for your family, you'll enjoy giving from the overflow, and reaping the benefits of, charity…

Relax and dream up a great life. Live it and you'll attract those great partners.

Daily Task & Action Plan:
1. Think 10 years into the future about what you want to be doing in your career, and 20 years out on where you want

to be living. Journal about this. Start envisioning how you'll get there.

2. J.K. Rowling was inspired to write the *Harry Potter* story after a four-hour delay on a train. I've often said that 21 days off the grid – out of your normal life and routine – will spark your creativity and inspire you. Whether it is one day, or one weekend, or 21 days, mark off time on your calendar to go someplace new, with a journal and a pen in your hand *alone*. Don't go there to write. Go there to experience and live. Carry the writing devices because as you are living, you will be inspired and will want to jot things down.

3. Write down five people you want to meet with – one who excels in investing, another in charity, another in education, one for adventure and one to help you brainstorm on how to get your basic needs under 50% of your income. Set up the meetings today. Meet with them this week.

Learning New Skills

If you're having trouble connecting with people you want to be surrounded by, start first by volunteering for their pet projects, or, like Melanee did, find a way to be in the audience listening to their wisdom. This doesn't have to be physically, although it is far better if it is. You can find the blogs, speeches and communication of a lot of the world's leaders online. Have you thought of investing the time and money to go to a conference or concert to hear them in person? That is going to put you in close contact with a lot of other people who value wisdom – who might be very helpful to you personally.

Additional Resources

Imagine having:

- An ethical, competent CPA who reduces your taxes and sets up a great estate plan

- A sharp CFP who protects your assets and compounds your gains
- A sustainable budget that you don't have to think about
- Money while you sleep in your passive income and investments
- Adventures and fun every step of the way

This life is yours for the taking – if you focus on putting veteran players on your team and effective systems in place. Who do you have to reach out to in order to find your perfect partners?

It's really hard to see beyond where you are. If you're working hard for a living, and who isn't these days, it's hard to envision a time when you are retired. You just want to close your eyes and relax at the end of a hard day. But if you don't have the vision to imagine tomorrow now, then, when you are ready to retire, you'll be broke. It's all on you these days. If you assign your estate over to someone else without looking into their real intentions, commissions, motivation and expertise, and without regular checkups on their progress toward your goals, then you could be in real trouble.

If you start your IRA with your first job, then, provided that you employ an investing strategy that works well in today's Debt World, you should have millions by the time you retire. If you get a great team in place, then you can start leveraging the power of partnerships to compound your gains and enjoy a much richer life.

Great partners and sound strategies are the additional resources you need. Focus on this and get them in place. The sooner you do, the sooner your life transforms.

Day 21: The Best *You*
Today's Mantra:
Be the Best *You*

Last night I was watching *The Fisher King* – a great movie starring Robin Williams, Jeff Bridges and Mercedes Ruehl. This was just a few weeks after the sad suicide of Robin Williams. It's so hard to imagine a man who lit up the screen as he did and inspired such love in our hearts, feeling so despondent that he took himself from his own family. But it also tells us about the inner demons that can darken the light and shadow truth.

Being *the best you* is certainly easier if you have been programmed to think this way from the start. I'm very grateful that my mother and my father and many of my relatives empowered me early on with the belief that I was the "skinny, smart girl." This is why it is so important to have a sacred union and sanctuary as the foundation of your home – for you and for your kids. That is also why the optimism exercises outlined in the first chapters of *The Gratitude Game* are so important to practice and embody.

In *The Fisher King,* the lead character, who goes mad after experiencing his wife shot and killed in front of him, is dogged by visions of a red knight/dragon demon, who always shows up to destroy his most beautiful moments. It reminded me of a recurring dream that I had as a young woman. A Grim Reaper, riding on his black steed, managed to find me in my dreams on a far too regular basis. I'm not sure whether he was going to rape or kill me, or drag me into the depths of hell. As he neared, I always had that terrible jolt of terror shock me back into reality – wide-awake, dripping in sweat. This happened again and again, over and over, year after year, just as it did for Robin Williams' character in *The Fisher King*.

I've been brutally honest in these pages about some of the horrors I experienced as a child (and the admission that many people experience far worse – particularly in the developing world). One of the most damaging experiences I've ever lived through had to do with an encounter with a bishop, who abused his authority. At the age of 12, before I'd even known my first *kiss*, I was raped. The bishop at my church learned of this and disfellowshipped me for *adultery*. He told me that adultery was next to murder in the eyes of the Lord and that, technically, he should be excommunicating me. Excommunication was reserved for only the most evil people on the planet, who were condemned forever to hell. Disfellowship meant that I must appear in church every Sunday to pray for forgiveness and refuse the Sacrament in front of the entire congregation because I was too unclean to take it. I humiliated myself in this way a few Sundays, nodding reverently when the church members craned their necks to glare superciliously at me, as I passed the bread and the water without partaking. Then I grew numb. Then I didn't care. And then I became self-destructive.

As a result of this judgment that was cast upon me, and the fears that judgment instilled in me – from visions of hell to a belief that I was an evil, rotten person who was probably capable of murder – I conjured up demons to torture me in my dreams and in my life circumstances, as well. When you believe something about yourself, you can create that hell over and over and over again – until you break through the lies and the darkness, and catch a glimpse of other possibilities. (On the other hand, if you believe that you are capable of greatness, then you can create that over and over again! A much better habit…)

Through therapy, love and a complete reworking of my conscious and subconscious beliefs, day by day, I began to understand that children are never responsible for the terrible things that adults do to them.

As I healed, I learned to fly – in my dreams. The Grim Reaper would show up uninvited, come galloping toward me and then, rather than run – I faced him and stared him down. As he raced faster toward me, I began running right back at him, and just when we were about to collide, and I worried I might smash into smithereens, I would soar above his head.

In the beginning of this series of recurring dreams, I didn't know how to land. So, I'd wake up with a jolt of adrenalin after falling into the branches of a tree – thankfully alive. Eventually, I learned to land as gracefully as if a parachute were gliding me down, allowing me to hit the ground running. As I envisioned life on the other side of the galloping Grim Reaper, I created it. Soon, the Grim Reaper disappeared, and I've never seen him since.

There is always a way to conquer our demons – whether they are imaginary, a vice, an abuser, a debt collector, a warmonger or a disease. You can learn to fly over the fiery red knight/dragon, who is galloping toward you. We can be inspired by Nelson Mandela, by Christopher Reeves, by Malala Yousafzai, by Stephen Hawking, by Oprah Winfrey and by many others who have overcome so much to achieve so much.

Eliminating Hypocrisy

As we start fine-tuning our light, we realize that there is always more to improve. The more you know, the more you realize that there is so much more to know.

How many times do we protest against "evil" in our world, without realizing our role in the matter? How many of us are up in arms about fracking, without realizing that domestic natural gas has made us less reliant upon foreign petroleum and coal? (That doesn't mean that I'm pro-fracking, or think that we should have natural gas as our primary source of energy forever. Please keep reading.) Are we keeping our computers and phone chargers plugged in 24/7 and our lights and air conditioning running when we're out of the house, expecting electricity to magically show up cheap, without fracking? Would you prefer that we use coal? Are you willing to reduce your energy consumption, so that we don't need fracking in the first place? Renewable energy makes up only 13% of the U.S. grid. So if you are an energy vampire, almost 90% of what you are sucking up is coal (39%), natural gas/fracking (27%), and nuclear (19%).

Being *the best you* also means being the change you wish to see.

Did we curse BP during the oil spill even as we commuted to work, without ever once noticing that BP and other oil companies simply service *our* oil and gasoline addiction?

In becoming the *best me*, I must examine everything that I complain about more deeply to see where my fingers are in the pie. Almost everything in our daily lives is a reflection of our habits, conveniences, desires and creations. It is either servicing us or we are profiting from it – even if we don't realize that. The power we have to change the world is truly profound. The minute we choose to stop using a product or stop investing in a company, it goes extinct, or it is forced to make something new. How many typewriting corporations do you see in the world today? Smith Corona was once the king of typewriters. Now the company sells barcodes. Imagine forcing Phillip Morris out of cigarettes and into incense. Aging nuclear power plants are decommissioning. What will replace them? What will those sites become? Should they be wind farms? Can you imagine some renewable energy source taking their place?

Often we justify the status quo, thinking that we can't make the choice to change because:

- We need to drive to work, or
- We have to feed our family or pay rent, or
- It will cost money we can't afford, or
- It's just too much trouble to figure out what the best solution is, or
- It's *them* causing the problem, or
- Fill in the blank excuse.

The truth is that self-reflection can spark a blaze of inspiration that creates dramatic, wonderful, lasting, positive shifts in our lives and in our world. This is always less expensive than the amount of time we spend worrying, and the amount of money we spend cleaning up the messes of an unsustainable way of life. (The BP Oil Spill leaps to mind again, as does Fukushima.)

If you admit that you'd like to stop using so much gasoline, you might be inspired to ride a bike to work or downsize and move closer, so that the commute is less. Those choices could put thousands of extra dollars in your budget every year – affording you a fantastic annual vacation. Or maybe you decide to see if your dream come true company is hiring in another city, while you're at it with this re-visioning process. That focus might land you a raise and a promotion.

If you come at the process with the attitude that a miracle might lie on the other side (just as I did when facing the Grim Reaper), then your drudgery can become fun and spark new, as yet unimagined possibilities. You'll be amazed what life-transforming new lands become available to you when you explore.

Why not be as brave as Columbus in searching for your own New World? Why not live this day as if it is the one you'll be most remembered for? Angels and partners will show up to assist you on your journey.

From Commander in Chief to Chief Commitment Officer.

He was the first person in his family to go to college.

He went on to become the 3rd-youngest President of the United States, at age 46.

The story of William Jefferson Clinton is one that is uniquely American – ripe with education, opportunity and upward mobility that is still rather unique among the nations of the world.

When he was in office, his personal life and a very vocal and persistent opposition challenged President Clinton at every turn and clouded over his achievements. No matter how you felt then, history now recognizes Clinton as the President who led the U.S. to the longest economic expansion in American history, including the creation of more than 22 million jobs. One of my hardcore right wing friends now admits that, "We just didn't know what a good President he was at the time."

What I find even more inspiring, however, is President Clinton's latest endeavor – the Clinton Global Initiative. He certainly could be just resting on his laurels, while earning a few million a year on book sales and speaking engagements. Instead, he created CGI to be a nonpartisan global gathering place for Presidents, CEOs, NGOs and activists who are committed to solving the world's most pressing problems. Honestly, at the age of 68 when most people are retired, it looks like Bill Clinton is busier than ever.

Creating Partnerships of Purpose

As President Clinton is fond of saying, "Talent and ability are evenly distributed across the human race, but opportunity is not."

The main difference of the CGI model from normal economic and business conferences is that members cannot just talk about solutions. They have to collaborate, brainstorm, form partnerships and *create* meaningful change. The octane of optimism at CGI is, simply, astonishing. It makes the droning lectures of most conferences seem rather last century – where participants get fired up for a day, and then return to their silos and routine, carrying very few of the ideas forward.

At the Closing Plenary of CGI America, on June 25, 2014, Tony Hsieh, the CEO of Zappos.com and the author of *Delivering Happiness*, described his Downtown Vegas project – how he is transforming a blighted and abandoned area into a mecca of "inspiration, entrepreneurial energy, creativity, innovation, upward mobility, discovery, and all that good stuff." Tony and his friends have committed $350 million to his Downtown Project, where entrepreneurs can incubate their small businesses, tech companies have access to startup capital, and $50 million is set aside for the arts, music and education. According to Tony, "If we can do it there, then hopefully that will inspire other communities and cities."

Whether you join Tony in his dream, or have your own for your friends and community, remember that our nation's most valuable businesses were launched out of garages.

One of the unique approaches that Tony is taking is to value ROC over ROI. What is ROC? Return on Community; Return on Collisions. Tony told the CGI America audience that he "uses the word collisions a lot," in terms of thinking, "How do we get people in the community to have serendipitous encounters with each other as often as possible?"

Hmmm. Could a serendipitous encounter be just what you need to jumpstart the *best you*? (Maybe a trip to Downtown Vegas is in your future...)

To promote interaction between Zappos' employees and people in the community, Tony removed the bridge that runs directly from the parking lot into the office building. This forces employees to walk past the parks, cafes and musicians in the neighborhood before winding their way into the office. Some of the outside community might even find their way into the Zappos' campus pub – at least during the tours that Zappos offers.

How often do you invite serendipity into your own life? If you were to do something today on a whim, where would you go and what would you do?

At CGI America, there were NGOs, CEOs and policymakers working on the challenges of Detroit and West Virginia, where jobs have been lost and industries are struggling – due to the decline of American auto manufacturing in Detroit and coal mining in Appalachia. Colorado, the host state of CGI America, faced a similar challenge of how to migrate away from coal mining, and into cleaner fuels and energy, without losing jobs. The state made a commitment to one of the most aggressive renewable standards in the nation – to reach 30% clean energy in the urban grid by 2020. Coal jobs are being replaced with wind, solar and hydrothermal jobs. According to a Vestas Wind Energy spokesperson, Vestas currently employs 1500 people in Colorado, and is hiring more.

A few decades ago, the city of Denver made a commitment to maintain one of the most elaborate multi-use trail systems in the U.S. The trails make commuting by bicycle safe and enjoyable, and surely contribute to the state's boasting rights of having the leanest population in America, at 21% obesity, compared to a national average of 35%. To reach a larger audience about the benefits of biking to work, Denver hosts an annual Bike to Work Day, which Colorado Governor Hickenlooper and Denver Mayor Michael B. Hancock rode in on June 25, 2014. (There is a separate annual Bike to Work Day in the U.S. – in mid-May each year.)

Simple solutions can indeed have amazing results. When you think about promoting health, prosperity and abundance for yourself and your neighbors, what comes to mind? What does your neighborhood need to become a sanctuary for the citizens who live there? If it feels too daunting to transform the entire city, can you take your ideas to the local high school and start there? Can you sing and read to children at a local day care center? Or hold premature babies in the hospital?

There is something that you are uniquely positioned to do in this world. When each one of us does what we're good at, that adds up to a lot of bases getting covered, and infinite opportunities for each one of us to shine.

One of my favorite success stories is about a ragtag group of high school students from a ghetto community in Phoenix, Arizona, who challenged the nation's brightest engineering college students from MIT in an underwater robot-building contest. These students had only creative thinking and cheap materials to compete against the nation's top academics, who were funded with a much bigger budget. *Underwater Dreams* documents the contest, retraces the journey and reveals the surprising results.

At the screening of the documentary on June 24, 2014, Chelsea Clinton commented, "Resilience is possibly the best predictor of success." When you view the *Underwater Dreams* documentary, it's easy to see that mentors (Fredi and Allan), partnerships (the team was great at distributing tasks), creativity and solving problems on the fly were key, too.

In *Underwater Dreams*, the team used tampons to soak up water that could have sunk their robot. What affordable, creative solutions will you employ to keep your dreams from remaining underwater?

Becoming the best you is often a daunting journey. Once you get past your inner demons, there are plenty of other real-world obstacles to face. So, if resilience is your best friend, and wisdom is your guide, which mentors and partners will you enlist? How will you course-correct when you hit a wall?

Our thoughts and our actions are far more powerful than we know. We are always manifesting something. Even when we think that we are passive and doing nothing, there is something going on as a result of our inactivity – because *we are letting it happen*. The most obvious example of this is where our retirement money is invested. Most people have no clue that our collective power is in the trillions, and that we hold the key to the future in our retirement plans.

Are we creating a cleaner, greener planet or are we depleting our resources at an alarming rate? Are we empowering our friends and loved ones, or draining them? Are we embodying and consciously creating peace, beauty and prosperity… prosperity born of abundance, rather than greed? Are we adding value or taking from someone else to increase our own comfort?

How you do the smallest thing is indicative of how you do *everything*. Be careful making exceptions. It's hard to reach your destination if you keep making detours.

Be the Answer to Someone's Prayer

When you see somebody who needs your help, support that person in whatever way that you can – even if it doesn't have an apparent ROI for you immediately. You are hoping that someone will do that for you, so you should set the example by first embodying that for someone else. So often we are praying for a miracle, without ever realizing that we could be the answer to *someone else's prayer*.

Success doesn't happen by accident or by luck. Kay Koplovitz had to wait patiently *for years* for satellites to be approved for television before she could broadcast the famous "Thrilla in Manila" on her fledgling USA Network. She used that time to become an experienced television executive. Being the best *you* requires commitment, innovation, hard work, partnerships, confidence and never giving up.

Be very, very careful of whining and complaining. If you are crying in the forest, the wolf will be the first to find you. Scam artists knowingly target easy prey. The easiest to take in are the lonely. That means you need to be on the watch for the elderly in your life. They are the ones who actually believe that someone in Nigeria trusts them enough to enlist their help to get money out of the country. Youth are also easy targets – particularly with regard to credit card and student loan debt. (Junior colleges cut the cost of a university degree in half. How many college students are thinking about this?)

Make It Easy for Your Angels to Help You

There are a lot of people – natural allies – who would really love to help you. Often they just don't know how. Time for all of us is extremely limited and valuable. The easier you make things for people, and the more you look for a win-win that includes what's in it for them, the more you'll see them saying "Yes" to you.

During my $1 for 1 Day sale, I told everyone that I was giving 30 books to 30 friends for the same price that I could normally only give 2 books. That's a pretty compelling BOGO – Buy One Get Fifteen.

Preface everything with a "Thank you." Thank you for reaching out. Thank you in advance for your time and consideration. Thank you for thinking of me. Their participation in your life is a blessing – something to be grateful for.

Think Like a Winner

Think score gains, not stop losses.

Winners focus on scoring *and* on defending their territory. Offense and defense are both necessary – particularly in today's world where everyone is trying so desperately to get rich on your dime, and have practiced and time-proven sales lines to lure you in. Remember, however, that defending yourself is different than fear.

Keep your eye on the goal and outmaneuver anyone who tries to trip you up.

Fear can only be replaced with confidence when you have a good plan in place. There's no short cut. Trying to exude confidence before you have the strength and ability to win is not effective. However, once you are healthy, strong, informed and disciplined, you're in a position to win friends, partners and gains.

You and Your Realm

Your retirement dollars are invested in the corporations that define our existence. As a consumer, a voter and an investor, we create our world. Creators think of money as freedom and responsibility. Creators take charge and solve problems with their resources – knowing that, most of the time, talent and creative solutions are more effective than writing a check. Creators celebrate, collaborate and enjoy their money. Creators are generous with their time, talents and currency because they know the power of leveraging and that the night sky is lit up by a thousand stars. Your light doesn't diminish mine.

As I get older and what I'm capable of in this lifetime changes, my achievements live only by handing them down. As parents, the investments we make in our children – in making them loving, empowered and capable – enable us to have more comfort when we become dependent upon them to provide for and protect us in our retirement years.

As my neighbors and I become more invested in our world, the streets I walk and drive are greener and safer. As our citizens get healthier, we can spend more on education (investing in our future), and less on hospitals and urgent care facilities (just trying to stay alive). "*Money*" is so much more than just which income bracket you occupy. Taking ownership of our lives is so much more fulfilling than just having more dough in the bank account (although having enough dough is a great start to eliminating that feeling of desperation that dogs so many debt-ridden consumers in the U.S.).

When a community comes together to create the best computers or music, like Silicon Valley and Nashville, they challenge one another to achieve greater heights, attract the best and the brightest in their industry from around the world, and prosperity flourishes. When yesterday's products fall out of favor, like coal has across the U.S., those communities that invest in cleaner fuel – like wind power in Colorado – can transition in time to avoid crippling unemployment. Rather than suffering under devastating losses in real estate values, the citizens enjoy prosperity and better air quality. If Tony Hsieh is successful in a Downtown Vegas renaissance that is rich in successful entrepreneurs and thriving businesses, then he'll reap the rewards of buying in on the cheap – when no one believed in that area.

Abundance and prosperity follow those who create value and things that others desire or desperately need. Drink in the wisdom, the therapy, the systems, the meditation, the forgiveness, the gratitude, the love and the information that you need to create the *best you and add the most value.*

There is no end to the problems that can be solved when we move trillions out of the old industries of oil, gas and cigarettes, and invest it in clean energy, goods and services that contribute to a healthy, sustainable world. Imagine a world where the Middle East is no longer rich and powerful on our oil addiction. Where organic food is the norm. Where biking is safe. Where we reduce our energy consumption by 90%, without a change in lifestyle – through efficiency upgrades, LED lighting and passive solar. These are all realities that are already in existence in some places in the world. We don't have to dream them up. We just have to care enough to learn about them and make the necessary adjustments to adopt them.

Envision yourself as a creator of your life, a co-creator of your home, a co-creator of your city and community and even planet Earth. The planet has never needed you more.

Let's co-create something worthy of being remembered.

Daily Task & Action Plan:
1. Write at least 3 paragraphs today about how you becoming the *best you* is going to change your home, your community,

your city and our world. Write down your wildest dreams. The act of putting it down on paper and reaching higher and farther than you dared before will make something possible that would never have been in your vision.

2. Ask yourself today constantly, "What am I creating with this action? What am I creating with this inaction?" Focus on acting with intention – focused on a goal.

3. Preface everything with "Thank you" today.

4. My name means literally Birth of Peace. What does yours mean? Who is the *best you*? What are you going to get done this year?

Learning New Skills

Let creativity and optimism fuel your life. Meditate and ask good questions. In your meditation, when you are envisioning what you desire, ask for miracles, for angels to show up in your life bearing gifts and wisdom. Pray for the clarity of vision to recognize allies and receive the gifts that they bring to you. Notice when you might be the answer to someone else's prayer.

Additional Resources

Listen to the song "The Man in the Mirror," made popular by Michael Jackson.

CONCLUSION: THRIVE
TODAY'S MANTRA: THRIVE.

It's so much easier than struggling to survive, being buried alive in bills, being chased by the debt collector and making everyone else rich.

These 21 days were designed to make prosperity and abundance your daily habit. Here's how it works.

The minute that you:

- Set up your Thrive Budget,
- Reduce your expenses to 50% of your income,
- Compound your gains in tax-protected retirement accounts,
- Diversify, rebalance and capture your gains annually in your liquid investments,
- Find *your people,*
- Become *the best you,* and
- Realize the power of your investments to reshape our world,

Life will be a lot more fun.
You will immediately:

- Have more money for eating out, movies, adventure and vacations,
- Become more charitable,
- Impact your community in positive ways,
- Be inspired to think and problem-solve creatively,
- Earn money while you sleep, and

- Have the funds for education – which unlocks the door to greater earned and passive income, abundance and prosperity.

All of these things increase your ability to live a rich life and to provide for your future.

As we've discussed, getting educated increases your income potential and almost guarantees you a job – with a lot more prospects on who you want to work with and where you want to live. Increasing your personal net worth through tax-protected investments makes you a better candidate for lower interest rates on everything – including the mortgage. Your charity invites in great, like-minded partners. Fun and adventure build confidence and, often, incubate entrepreneurial ideas. You'll also smile more, making you more attractive. You'll be healthier and spend a lot less on doctors, hospitals and pharmaceuticals.

Charity and most retirement accounts (including the Health Savings Account) are tax deductible – meaning that you are taking from Uncle Sam, instead of finding more room in your budget. Education expenses might be tax deductible if they're in your field of expertise. Even if education is not tax deductible, it is still highly correlated with income – both active and passive.

Financial literacy means that you know the average returns of real estate, stocks, bonds, gold and more. You diversify and rebalance annually. In the new millennium this is key. There have already been two recessions that have dropped people's assets by more than half in under a dozen years. It's a lot easier to capture your gains annually, and compound your gains upon that solid foundation. (If not, then you're crawling back to even every seven years – the average amount of time between recessions.)

Today we have more freedom than humans have ever known. And we are also still in chains because we allow our financial lives to be ruled by others. When we take control, everything becomes easier. There is less stress. There is greater health. There are more celebrations. We're kinder to our family, friends and colleagues.

In other words, the Thrive Budget and Easy-as-a-Pie-Chart investing are the tickets to financial freedom and to creating heaven on Earth.

Be blessed. Get smart.

The success that you enjoy is directly in proportion to the diligence and energy that you put into creating your success. Gold medals aren't won on a whim or a prayer. They require training and a very rigorous workout commitment. Our outcome is equal to our exertion.

If you have been trapped in debt consciousness, or feeling like you are struggling to survive and buried alive in bills. If you are one of the 35% of adult Americans who are being pursued by a debt collector. If you lost your home. If you are unemployed. Getting to prosperity and abundance will not happen overnight. It will take longer than 21 days. The farther away from *thriving* that you start, the more religiously and diligently you'll have to increase your wisdom and application of these precepts in order to transform your life.

Others are here to help – if you seek them out and make it easy for them to support you. (A college student crowd-funded her education…)

So:

Love. Laugh. Breath more deeply. Give thanks. Count your blessings. Forgive. Send a $21 gift to someone who *owes you.* Have faith, not blind faith, that as you acquire the tools and skills and wisdom, you'll build the money house of your dreams. Avoid drama. Create peace. Envision, enact and embody solutions. Double your fun budget. Say "Yes." Put your heart into your work and your play, and know that extra, added value is the root of abundance. Exercise. Shine. Radiate from the source of your inner beauty; let your soul shine through your eyes.

Be a Master of the Light in your sacred union and sanctuary home, and in so doing inspire all of your closest partners – from your sacred beloved, to your children and business partners – to become stars, too. Imagine what a more beautiful community looks like. Create it by being the best you, and then by partnering up to co-create it with *your people*.

Invest in the products, goods and services that make our world a more beautiful place. Yes, you can get rich and enrich by putting your money where your heart is.

Additional Resources

Check out *The Gratitude Game* audio book for a bonus feature of my song "Peace."

Join NataliePace.com now to jump-start your new wealth game plan. Simply go to NataliePace.com. Click on Join Now for 30 Days Free. Use the promo code: **GratitudeGame**. And you will receive:

90 days free subscription to my monthly teleconferences and ezine.

Ongoing financial education, information and forensic, investigative news.

Wealth and business tips from A-list thought leaders.

Mid-month market and economic outlook update.

Peace
I saw a war-torn child in a war-torn world
But it feels just like the tides will turn
Like a raging sea rolling over me
It might be real, or be a dream.
Cause a war-torn child can always find a
Way to freedom, a way to shine.

When reason beats out of time
And killing is seen as saving lives
No cure seems sure
No change seems right
But love must be the place to start
Strangers make the kindest friends
Give a helping heart, give a loving hand.

Make peace on Earth.
Like a raging sea rolling over me
I'm going to find the truth or die trying
A war-torn child can always find
A way to freedom. A way to shine.

It might be, it might be a dream.
Of peace on Earth.

Fools are making history.
There's murder in the name of peace.
Slow this dance, I'm begging you.
Who was that man on the evening news.
Does he leave behind a family?
With eyes of stone, with hearts of steel?

Make peace on Earth.
Like a raging sea rolling over me
I'm going to find the truth or die trying
A war-torn child can always find
A way to freedom. A way to shine.

Acknowledgements:

Bill Gladstone: Thank you for taking this project under your wing. You have been the best agent anyone could ever ask for: visionary, supportive, enthusiastic, experienced, wise and connected.

Thanks to everyone at Waterfront Digital Publishing for getting *The Gratitude Game* published at the speed of light, including Kenneth Kales, Margot Hutchison, Johanna Maaghul, Kimberly Brabec and Maureen Mahoney.

Trista Ann Martin: You are a joy to work with and a dream come true copy editor.

A true list of acknowledgements would include everyone I've ever interacted with. My adversaries have helped me grow even more than my friends; though, of course, I didn't enjoy them as much and I'm not going to list their names. I also want to acknowledge that if I were to list all of the people who I am *very* grateful for, whom I have enjoyed throughout the years and continue to enjoy today, that would be a book unto itself. I would have to spend countless hours going over every moment in my life, thinking, "Oh, yes! And without her kindness in that moment, or his help here, I'm not even sure I'd still be alive."

My life has been saved over and over and over again by guardian angels. My dreams have been carried on the wings of amazing people, who have inspired me to soar far higher than I would have ever imagined on my own. There are many people whom I haven't mentioned by name in this book who I am grateful to. I know how blessed I am to have each one in my life.

Davis: You will always be my happy place. I'm so impressed with you, and I can't wait to see your dreams come to life. You're going to make us all look like amateurs.

Mom: What a beautiful, wonderful, strong, smart, talented, resilient, loving woman you were! You are the best guardian angel any women could ever hope for, and one of the finest examples of beauty, strength, brains and femininity that I know.

Dad & Mom: Thank you for spoiling me rotten (in those early formative years) and making me believe that anything is possible. I'm sure it wasn't easy raising a hyperactive Tom Boy.

To those in my inner circle, Davis, St. JJM, Dad, GK, Sammie, Denise, Christy: I hold you close in my heart always, even when there are miles between us.

I am very grateful to Uncle Walt, Aunt Joyce, Aunt Rita, Uncle Bernard, Aunt Sue and Uncle Jerry for being there for me through the storms of early life. Thank you, Jonathan, for believing in me during those old school rock dog days and inspiring me to become a better person.

Kay Koplovitz: Thank you for taking that first interview in 2003. You have done much for me personally, but you have done even more for *all* women. When you founded USA Networks, the first cable television network, you saw an opportunity that no one before you had seen, but many after you, including Ted Turner, would embrace. In creating your own role as the first female CEO of a television network, you cracked the glass ceiling with a stylish stiletto heel – embracing your femininity, vision, intelligence, effervescence and beauty. Since that time, you have been a mentor to many businesswomen, including me, while providing a springboard to capital from which other female CEOs have launched their own IPOs. I encourage all *Bold Women With Big Ideas* to check out Springboard Enterprises at SB.co.

Harriet Mouchly-Weiss at Strategy XXI has been in charge of branding for our team since the beginning. What a wonderful partner you are, and a huge inspiration to me daily. Patrick Fraoili is an outstanding business attorney. I can't wait to see what the next chapter of partnership with you brings.

Ambassador Melanne Verveer: Thank you for your tireless commitment to advance the rights and opportunities for women worldwide. Your wisdom and advocacy helps me to sleep better at night, knowing that women who are often silenced have a spokesperson.

RIP: Dr. Gary Becker. The world is far more beautiful with your important contributions to economics, sociology and humanity. I am personally indebted to you for believing in the value and importance of this work early on.

Thank you, Dr. Marc Miles, Ben Horowitz, Justice Sandra Day O'Connor, Sir Richard Branson, H.R.H. Prince Charles, Kay Koplovitz, President Clinton, Joe Moglia, Queen Noor, and others for contributing to the WIN mission of adding a splash of green to Wall Street and transforming lives on Main Street. I am honored to feature your wisdom, guidance and commitment to finding solutions for the world's most pressing problems in my blog and ezine.

Thank you, Paula Wolak and Bleu Mortensen, for hosting me during the last mad dash of writing of this book, and for recording the audio book and songs.

I want to thank all of the members and subscribers of the Women's Investment Network, LLC and the Green is Good Investment Club. A special thanks to all of my retreat volunteers, who are the highlight of my year. You inspire me, and give me the fuel to keep up this important work. Thank you, Mateo Brown, for setting up the volunteers, so many years ago.

Bryan Zee (audio engineer extraordinaire) and Marie Commiskey (Avalon Photography) are talented artists who do great work. Thank you for providing audio and visual enhancements to this mission and this book.

Thank you so much, Diane, Carol, Rita, Carmel, Marie, Kevin and Linda for your hospitality.

It might seem odd to thank a hotel chain, but I want to thank the Ritz-Carlton. I've enjoyed accommodations all around the world at the Ritz-Carlton, from Tucson and Denver, to London and Ireland. Everywhere I go, they make me feel like royalty. The Ritz-Carlton team is the marquise standard of hospitality. All of the ladies and gentlemen I've had the opportunity of meeting embody the Currency of the Smile.

Natalie Wynne Pace is the bestselling author of The ABCs of Money and Put Your Money Where Your Heart Is (aka You Vs. Wall Street, in paperback). She is the founder and CEO of the Women's Investment Network, LLC (a global financial news, information and education site), with a mission of adding a splash of green to Wall Street and transforming lives on Main Street™. Follow her on Twitter.com/NataliePace and Facebook.com/NatalieWynnePace. For more information please visit NataliePace.com.

Made in United States
Orlando, FL
23 April 2022

17117072R00200